Wade Fly F

Mosquito Lagoon and

North Indian River Lagoon

(Florida)

From Canaveral National Seashore and

Merritt Island National Wildlife Refuge

By Luc Desjarlais

To my wife Claire, the most patient and forgiving of all fishing widows.

This book is available in Kindle eBook and in full-color paperback from Amazon.com.

Graphic concept of front and back covers by Eleza Mendoza.
Inside cover photo: Station Island viewed from Parking Lot 5 of Canaveral National Seashore on a glorious December sunset.
Back cover photo: ancient pilings and modern radar at Live Oak on North Indian River Lagoon.
Fish illustrations and sketches by Duane Raver, U.S. Fish and Wildlife Service, NOAA, and University of Washington Library, all public domain.
Wildlife photos by John C. Gamble.
All other photos by author unless otherwise noted.
All maps by author; background aerial photos from Digital Globe by Google earth.

ISBN 978-2-924439-02-9 (ePub)
ISBN 978-2-924439-03-6 (paperback)

Legal deposit – Bibliothèque et Archives nationales du Québec, 2016.
Legal deposit – Library and Archives Canada, 2016.

Desjarlais, Luc
    Wade Fly Fishing Mosquito Lagoon and North Indian River Lagoon (Florida) from Canaveral National Seashore and Merritt Island National Wildlife Refuge / Luc Desjarlais — First edition.
    Includes index.
    Key Words: Fly fishing; Mosquito Lagoon, Florida; Indian River Lagoon, Florida; Guidebook.

CONTENTS

FOREWORD

This book is about wade fly-fishing Mosquito Lagoon and North Indian River Lagoon, Florida, on foot, from Canaveral National Seashore and Merritt Island National Wildlife Refuge.

Let us have a second look at this long sentence.

Wade – Yes, we will actually be wading, as opposed to fishing from a boat, and you will see that it is not as hard as it looks. Of course you can use this book as a guide and fish from a boat, sometimes, in some places. It is not the same experience and at times and in some places the boat is just not the right tool. At other times and in other places a boat will do just fine, the smaller, lighter and shallower the better.

Fly-Fishing – The *hard way*, as some say. Others argue that it is the *only way*. In any case, it is *my way* and the ways of this book. Again, you can use this book as a guide and use light spin-casting gear, sometimes, in some places. I have been outfished regularly by good spin-casters.

On Foot – This is central to this book and is what takes it apart in the fishing literature of East Central Florida: this book focuses on foot access *exclusively*. Again, you may use this book as a guide to reach the fishing areas with a boat. However, you will find that some areas are not easily reached with a boat. On the other hand, a carry-on vessel will easily take you everywhere I am taking you on foot and beyond.

Mosquito Lagoon and North Indian River Lagoon – As all guide books this one focuses on a specific geographical area, and these two lagoons will be our playground. Situated in East Central Florida these two lagoons are a world-class territory for redfish sight fishing. The distance from the northernmost fishing area (Turtle Mound in Mosquito Lagoon) to the southernmost fishing area (Black Point Creek in North Indian River Lagoon) is twenty miles. The territory is big enough to provide some diversity and at the same time small enough for the regular angler to gain a meaningful knowledge of it.

Canaveral National Seashore and Merritt Island National Wildlife Refuge – Part of the security buffer zone of the National Aeronautics and Space Agency (NASA), the Park and Refuge cover most of the two lagoons and provide public and regulated accesses to them *on foot*. This is an important feature and has dictated the focus of this book on Park and Refuge land. Contrary to boat access from the open water—public by default—foot access involves parking and walking on land. Aside from a few public boat ramps there are very few practical accesses to the lagoons other than from the areas of the Park/Refuge open to the public. In addition, here nature is relatively untouched by human development and is keenly preserved. It does not get any better.

You are in the World's Redfish Capital, as claimed by the locals. Although the fish are abundant in the two lagoons, it is like any other fishery: the fish are generally concentrated in a few spots and you must know your way around them. My purpose is to get you up to speed quickly. In this book I will give you my accumulation of several years of winter-time experience in pursuing Red Drum, Spotted Seatrout, Black Drum, Snook, and Tarpon by wading the two lagoons with a fly rod. A disproportionately large section of this book focuses on the access to Mosquito Lagoon from Parking Lot 5 of Canaveral National Seashore off New Smyrna Beach. This is where I began to wade fly-fish the lagoons several years ago. Although I have since explored thoroughly the

Red Drum. Image by Duane Raver / U.S. Fish and Wildlife Service.

A tailing redfish: always an exciting moment in the lagoon.

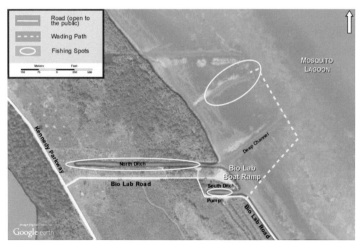

Example of a large-scale detailed map: Bio Lab Boat Ramp area on Mosquito Lagoon.

much larger territory covered in this book the section of Mosquito Lagoon accessible from Parking Lot 5 of Canaveral National Seashore remains the best for wading.

Mosquito Lagoon and the Indian River Lagoon system in general are renowned fishing destinations and are featured in books, articles, videos and TV shows. Quality guiding services are widely available. And fly-fishing is gaining in popularity. Why another guide book?

Firstly, most of the existing material involves fishing from a boat. Not everybody has a boat. And of those who do, not everybody wants to put a boat in these lagoons, especially in the low waters of the winter. Not much literature exists on foot access to the lagoons, and this is one gap that this book is filling.

Secondly, hunting the fish of the lagoons while wading is a different experience than fishing from a boat. Indeed, those paranoid redfish that are being pounded almost daily in some areas of the lagoons are increasingly wary of boats. Hunting these fish on foot and *undetected* is a very different experience. It must be learned and this book will do this.

Finally, in keeping with the ways of each book of the series, this guide book focuses on very precise fishing spots. Boaters can cover lots of water. Waders do not have this privilege. Once they have reached a general fishing area waders are committed to it. Moreover, while boaters will try to see fish in the distance from the top of an elevated platform waders have to detect or guess the presence of fish. Fishing these precise spots where fish are likely to be holding is the only way for the wader to improve the odds. Contrary to most others this guide book shows the precise location of these fishing spots on large-scale, detailed maps.

Here is an example.

I am sure you would eventually have discovered all these foot accesses, all these general fishing areas, all these precise fishing spots, and the ways to hunt these fish wading.

How about cutting down your learning curve by 15 years?

PART I

INTRODUCTION TO THE LAGOONS

AND TO THE FISHES

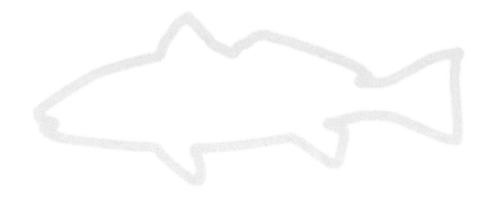

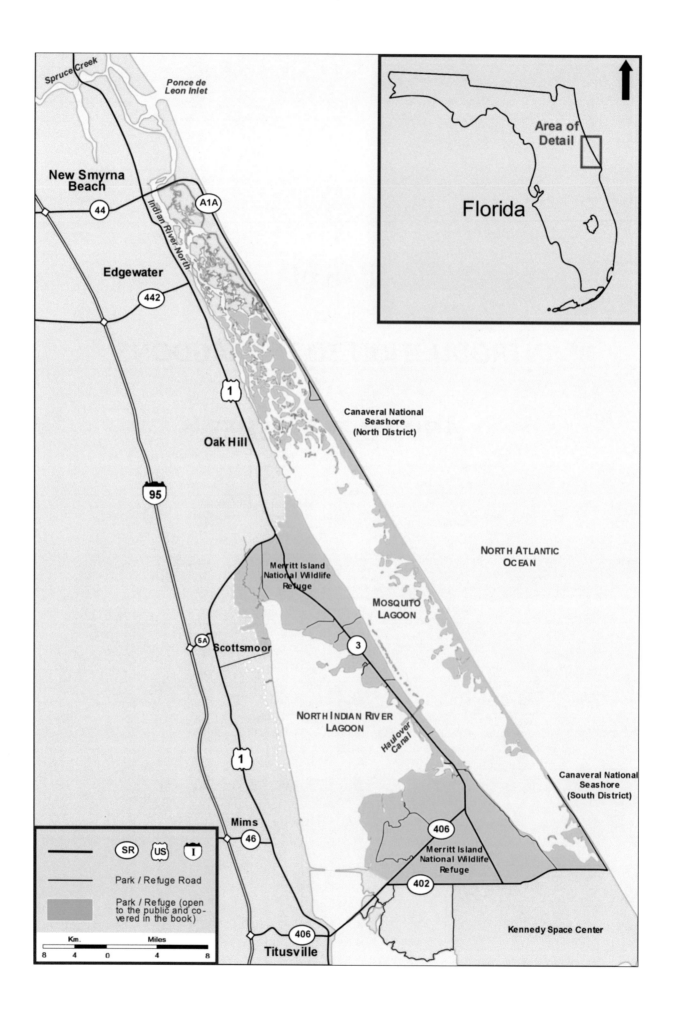

THE LAGOONS

Mosquito Lagoon and North Indian River Lagoon are the two northernmost lagoons of the Indian River Lagoon (IRL) system. The IRL system is part of the longest barrier island complex in the United States, occupying more than 30% of the coast in East Central Florida. It is a huge body of brackish (mixture of salt and fresh, but in this case mostly salt) shallow water that runs approximately 156 miles from Ponce de Leon Inlet (north of New Smyrna Beach) to Jupiter Inlet near West Palm Beach. Most of the northern stretch of the IRL system, from Ponce de Leon Inlet to Sebastian Inlet, is insulated from the North Atlantic Ocean since the two inlets are an enormous 90 miles apart.

What Is a Lagoon?

A lagoon is a shallow body of water separated from a larger body of water—here the North Atlantic Ocean—by barrier islands (in the case of coastal lagoons). Mosquito Lagoon is a particularly good example of a coastal lagoon.[1]

Coastal lagoons occur on mixed sand and gravel coastlines and their classification sometimes overlaps with estuaries. Also overlapping in the vocabulary are the words "river" and "lagoon". In fact lagoons are not rivers, and if they do have current it is mostly tidal. The connection with the ocean is by inlets, natural or man-made, that make the lagoons saltwater bodies. Fresh water is brought into the mix from direct rainfalls, seepage from the water table, drainage of the land near shore, and the inflow of rivers and creeks draining the mainland; therefore, the salinity of the water will vary with the input of fresh water, the speed of flushing at the inlets, and the rate of evaporation, which can be significant because lagoons are shallow.

In the Indian River Lagoon system water salinity often exceeds that of the ocean during the summer. This is because the large surface of shallow water accelerates evaporation and because there is normally little fresh water coming into the lagoon. Indeed, while the inlet bringing the salt water are very far apart the sources of fresh water are equally very modest. The St. Johns River is the drainage of the east coast along the northern part of the Indian River Lagoon system and it takes the fresh water north and away from the lagoons. Spruce Creek is the significant coastal tributary north of Mosquito Lagoon and it drains directly into the North Atlantic Ocean through Ponce de Leon Inlet, therefore adding no fresh water to the lagoons. Turnbull Creek, entering the northern end of North Indian River Lagoon is the only real freshwater stream in the territory covered in this book and it has a very modest watershed.

Also because they are shallow lagoons tend to have water temperatures that mimic the air temperature. This is a significant characteristic of the two lagoons covered in this book. The lagoons being situated at the limit of the frost zone the water temperature can drop to alarming levels in the winter. Also specific to the two lagoons covered in this book, the water level is not (or so little) influenced by tide. The water level in the lagoons does not change much with the constant action of the waves and the regular ups and downs of the tide. To the contrary it is very

---

[1] Sources for this section: National Park Service; Smithsonian Institute, Harbor Branch Oceanographic Institution; and personal research.

well defined; therefore, the seasonal changes become obvious. And those seasonal changes in the water level are magnified by the large shallow areas that become exposed during long periods of low water.

Lagoons have a high productivity and biodiversity. Lagoons and their estuaries are among the most productive ecosystems in the world: 72% of commercial and 74% of sport fishes and invertebrates of Florida spend part or all their lives in or near an estuarine system. The Indian River Lagoon (and especially the northern part, covered in this book) is one of the richest ecosystems in the world. Being at the limit of the frost zone it provides a unique combination of temperate and subtropical plant and animal species. There are more than 2,100 different species of plants, 2,200 species of animals, including 700 species of fish and 330 species of birds. Because the north and south inlets are so far apart fish tend to stay inside the lagoons to spawn and grow big instead of running off to the ocean. This has not always been the case and it may not be permanent. Indeed, very old maps show an inlet between Cape Canaveral and Mosquito Inlet (now Ponce de Leon). Several inlets have appeared and disappeared since the discovery of Florida. There are records of five inlets that have been created between Bethune Beach (south end of New Smyrna Beach) and Cape Canaveral over the last five hundred years, all of them filled back by successive storms. The most recent was at Turtle Mound. And merely a few hundred years ago a freak storm opened a shallow inlet through the barrier island approximately half-a-mile south of Parking Lot 5 of Canaveral National Seashore. This inlet has long disappeared. The next hurricane may very well punch a new inlet in the very narrow dune.

Indeed, the level of the oceans is rising due to the warming of the water and the melting of the land glaciers. According to NOAA (National Oceanic and Atmospheric Administration) the sea level has risen 2.75 inches since 1992. By definition the barrier islands are the ones that take the brunt of the rise in the water level. You can still wait until next month to wade fly-fish the lagoons. I would not. Why spend a day without fishing? But when you pass this book to your children there may be changes to the landscape. This is nothing new, as we will see next.

Geology and Natural History

Florida is generally associated with water. And so it should be, given the length of its beaches and constellation of lakes. But there is more. Indeed, for much of its ancient existence Florida was under water. Much of the underlying rock base of limestone comes from this long submerged period. As boring as millions of years under water can be there was some interesting action.[2]

Unknown until recently it is now believed that Florida was part of the African continent until the tectonic plates of Africa and America collided. When the tectonic plates separated Florida remained stuck to Georgia and became part of the American continent.

While this makes for interesting conversation the major influence in shaping Florida, and more precisely the coastal lagoons, were the fluctuations in water levels. These are recent in geological time. Indeed, the end of the Pliocene and most of the Quaternary Periods[3] were marked by successive cooling and warming of the earth's climate. At least four glaciations and

---

[2] Sources: Lane, E. ed. 1994. *Florida's Geological History and Geological Resources*. Special Publication No. 35. Department of Environmental Protection, Florida Geological Survey. Tallahassee, FL; National Park Service; and personal research.

[3] The Quaternary Period is the last 1.8 million years of geological history. Of this period, we are mostly interested in the Pleistocene Epoch, from 1.8 million years to 10,000 years ago, when the ice ages took place. The Pliocene is the period preceding the Quaternary.

deglaciations took place between 1.8 million years and 10,000 years ago. During the cool periods large parts of North America were covered with glaciers that stored water. While Florida remained free of ice the water level in the sea receded to approximately 300 feet below its current level. Florida was much larger than it is today, covering all the Florida Plateau. This 250- to 400-mile wide plateau includes a significant section of the continental shelf, extends some 100 miles into the Gulf, and is very much visible on many maps and on Google earth. During the warm periods the melting of the glaciers caused the level of the oceans to rise to approximately 150 feet above current level. Most of Florida was under water during these periods.

It is these fluctuations in water levels, and more specifically the receding periods, that shaped the coastal lagoons as we see them today. Erosion by waves and current formed the flat terraces on today's mainland during the periods of high water. During the periods of receding sea levels dune ridges were formed: first the Atlantic Coastal Ridge that is the west shore of the lagoons; later the barrier islands along the North Atlantic Ocean.

You will note that the action of the waves and currents formed a solid and regular *west* shoreline on both Mosquito Lagoon and North Indian River Lagoon, very comparable to the ocean shoreline. On the other hand, the *east* shorelines (before the mosquito impoundments) of both lagoons are all jagged and carved up with channels, basins, islands, and flats. The irregular geomorphology of the east shore of both lagoons is where fishing is generally the best and where the best wade fly-fishing opportunities generally are.

Inasmuch as the past changes in the climate shaped our lagoons the current warming of the climate and rising water level will most likely change the lagoons again.

While it is always interesting to know the origin of the water that we are wading, there are practical applications of geology to fishing. As mentioned above most of the favorable geomorphology is along the east shore of each lagoon, shaped during the last period of receding water. This is mostly where you will find those shallow flats where sight fishing can be so exciting. Given the fluctuating water levels of the lagoons it is a natural for fish to seek the deepest water in any area; not all the fish and not all the time, but at least some fish some of the time. And where will this slightly deeper water be in these vast and flat expanses? This is where geology and natural history help.

Picture the place during ancient periods of lower sea level. The last episode is only ten thousand years ago. The lagoons were smaller and shallower. Parts of today's lagoons were flowing creeks, some seasonal, or even small rivers. The paths of these ancient streams exist today at the mouth in the lagoons in the form of slightly, sometimes so slightly, deeper water; they also exist in some very recognizable channels. Two good examples are: Max Hoeck Back Creek, whose streambed you can follow into the south end of Mosquito Lagoon (page 145); and Turnbull Creek, whose streambed you can follow into the north end of North Indian River Lagoon (page 179).

Another use of geology is understanding what you are stepping on when wading the lagoons, not a trivial preoccupation you will agree, what with these urban legends of people getting stuck in the

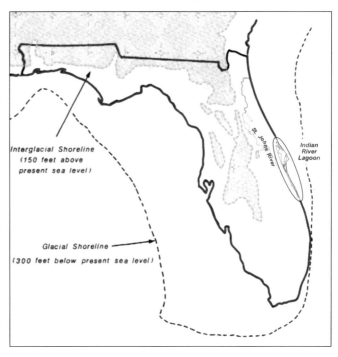

This map shows the Florida Peninsula during periods of low and high water levels of the Pleistocene Epoch of the Quaternary Period. Map base from Florida's Geological History and Geological Resources, State of Florida.

mud, sinking in sediments accumulated over millions of years, etc. The truth is our lagoons are relatively young. The last deglaciation (water rising *back* into the lagoons) took place a mere 10,000 years ago and the last five feet of water, by definition our wading territory, came in between 3,500 and 2,000 years ago—yesterday in geological time; therefore, the accumulation of sediments is modest in most areas.

Moreover, a large part of the bottom of the lagoons—and this is particularly the case for the middle section of Mosquito Lagoon—is made of white, sandy sediments of quartz and shell fragments that do not catch particle-reactive contaminants and therefore remain clean and hard: perfect wading grounds. Of course there are certain areas, deeper or sheltered, with fine-grain organic mud called *muck* that can be from half-an-inch to six feet deep, or more. These areas are black, usually right along the shore, and you will learn to avoid them. You will, if not the first, at least certainly the *second* time… Trust me.

Heritage

The first humans came to the North American continent from the Siberian land bridge 12,000 years ago. They crossed the continent and settled in Florida at a time when the sea was approximately 160 feet below current level and therefore when Florida was much larger than we know it today. Humans most likely occupied areas flooded today. When the last glaciers had retreated and the oceans had risen to near-current level Paleo-Indians were the first to inhabit the Indian River Lagoon area. The first aboriginal sites were on today's Cape Canaveral approximately 4,000 years ago. Two thousand years ago there were two distinct tribes: the Ais, named by Ponce de Leon upon first contact in 1513, lived south of *Haul Over*, and the Timucuans, who let a very distinctive sign of their presence in the form of shell mounds, lived north of *Haul Over*. Seasonally, groups of Indians settled along the lagoons to gather clams, oysters, and fish. The same sites were revisited year after year and large mounds of discarded shells were created. The white settlers later destroyed most of these mounds, using them as a cheap source of material to build roads. The best known and preserved of these mounds is Turtle Mound, located near the entrance of the North District (off New Smyrna Beach) of Canaveral National Seashore.[4]

The Eclectic docked on the Indian River, *circa 1900, at the old village of Allenhurst. Photo State Archives of Florida,* Florida Memory.

Most likely the earliest permanent occupation by Europeans of the land in the area, Elliott Plantation was built in the late 1760s and covered approximately 2,500 acres straddling a large part of the high grounds between the two lagoons in the northern part of today's Merritt Island National Wildlife Refuge. According to National Park Service, today's ruins "contain the remains of a complete sugar works factory … two overseers' homes and two slave villages, … This is one of the most significant and well-preserved African-American landscapes known, and is unique in its

[4] Sources (entire Heritage section): Brevard County Historical Commission; U.S. Fish and Wildlife Service; Indian River Anthropological Society; National Park Service; and personal research.

quality of preservation." It is believed to be the southernmost and earliest British-Colonial-period sugar plantation in North America. Ross Hammock, part of Elliott Plantation and still shown on topographical maps today, could also be the site of a Confederate Salt Work at a later date; however, this remains to be confirmed.

Permanent settlement around Mosquito Lagoon and Indian River Lagoon only began after the Civil War. Early settlers of the area were growing oranges and fishing. Among others, the community of Eldora became a prosperous point for shipping the crop and moving people by boat. The location of the village, on the *East* shore of Mosquito Lagoon—and therefore removed from the north-south main road on the west bank—could be a little surprising at a time when no bridge existed. The key is in the original waterway. Today's Intracoastal runs straight and along the west bank of Mosquito Lagoon. The old channel was there up to Oak Hill. However, south of Oak Hill the natural channel (of what was called Hillsboro River) turns easterly and continues to the east shore of the lagoon a short distance north of Turtle Mound. The old channel was about four feet deep and it was the marine highway of the time. Sections have been dug further since and it is extensively used today by boats as a running lane. The relocation of the waterway along the west shore was a blow to the budding community of Eldora. As it happened elsewhere at this latitude bad frosts killed the citrus-growing business. Hard economic times and the hurricanes dealt the final blows to Eldora so that it all but disappeared. Later, fishing and hunting camps were established around Eldora and some operated until the takeover by NASA.

Indian River Lagoon is connected to Mosquito Lagoon by Haulover Canal. Before construction of the first connecting canal the two bodies of water were separate.[5] The narrow strip of land that separates the two bodies of water has history that runs deep. The shortest connecting point was called *Haul Over* and it was used to move goods from one lagoon to the other as early as during the First Seminole War. Because of its strategic importance during the Seminole Wars Fort Ann was built in 1837 on the Indian River side of the *Haul Over* site. At times 800 to 1,000 troops were stationed on the narrow spit of land to carry supplies. The first Haulover Canal was constructed in 1854, reportedly by slaves under a U.S. Government contract. It was shallow and designed to accommodate the small boats of the army. After the end of the war in 1858 the canal was not maintained by the army and was of limited use in low water.

While the construction of the first Haulover Canal in 1854 favored the establishment of the groves and a nascent transportation trade, construction of the new Haulover Canal in 1887 and of the Intracoastal Waterway allowed for a significant expansion and diversification of the area's economy. Sportfishing became a significant source of economic activities and the remnants of old subdivisions can be seen today in the former Allenhurst area, now Haulover Canal Recreation Area. The new canal also had a significant impact on the ecosystems of the two lagoons, allowing for tides and fish to move between the two lagoons.

Shiloh is a significant historical area with several burial mounds associated with ancient Indian villages. One village site includes a midden and two burial mounds believed to date to 800-900 A.D. Other artifacts in this area date back 2,000 years. The village of Shiloh was the northernmost settlement on Merritt Island. Established in the seventeenth

Eldora State House. Image from Canaveral National Seashore.

---

[5] Scientists believe that the two lagoons and Banana River may have been connected in ancient times.

century during the post-Civil War period it became a trade center for citrus in the 1880s. It had 35 residents in 1886.

In 1872, an African-American community was formed from the shores of Mosquito Lagoon (where the post office was situated as part of a boat house) and the trail that linked the mainland road (Kings Highway) and Haulover Canal, between Shiloh and today's new Haulover Canal. Initially called Laughing Waters and Haulover, it later changed its named to Clifton. It was the site of the first African-American school of the area.

Established in 1843 south of Haulover Canal, Dummett Grove became the largest in the state and is the origin of the famous Indian River fruits.

For a number of reasons, killing frosts and economic depression among others, the area south of New Smyrna (today New Smyrna *Beach*) to Titusville was slow to develop in the early part of the twentieth century. But it would have followed the residential development boom of Florida brought about by the development of the railroads and later of the Interstate system and the increasing wealth of a fast-growing nation. It did not happen because somebody wanted the United States to go to space, quick. (See next.)

You will find short historical vignettes in text boxes in the relevant sections of this book as we pass the location of historical places on our way to the wading accesses to the lagoons.

Geomorphology and Accesses

Three lagoons make up the northern end of the Indian River Lagoon (IRL) system: Mosquito Lagoon, Indian River Lagoon (both north and south of Titusville), and Banana River. These lagoons are the three largest bodies of water of the IRL system. Their grouping at the north end of the IRL system is from the building up of Cape Canaveral over geological time by the strong northerly current of the North Atlantic Ocean.

Mosquito Lagoon is the northernmost. It ends in the north with the Indian River (also called Indian River North) in New Smyrna Beach and Ponce de Leon Inlet. Indian River Lagoon is the second northernmost and is the one that is the most removed from the ocean at this location. North of Titusville it is a big bowl and this is the part included in this book. South of Titusville it is typically long and narrowing as one progresses south to Cocoa. Stuck between Indian River Lagoon and Cape Canaveral lies the third lagoon called Banana River, although it is not a river but a genuine lagoon. It is bordered on the west by Merritt Island, not technically an island but a peninsula. Access to the northern part of this third lagoon is restricted as it lies between Kennedy

What's in a Name

North Indian River Lagoon is the name that I use for that part of the Indian River Lagoon (IRL) that lies north of State Road 406 and the railroad in Titusville. This big bowl of water is well defined geographically but has surprisingly no official name. The authority for names should be the St. Johns River Water Management District (SJRWMD) and it refers to this end of the IRL as "the northern portion of the Indian River Lagoon". Not to be confounded with *Northern* Indian River Lagoon *system*, which includes Mosquito Lagoon, Banana River and *the northern portion of the Indian River Lagoon* proper, and which extends south past Titusville. In some reports the same SJRWMD uses "N-NIRL" for the *North* section of the *Northern* Indian River Lagoon. And you will find *Upper* Indian River Lagoon in some publications of U.S. Geological Survey. Not very practical.

Many locals call it *North* Indian River Lagoon, and so do I. The reader will understand that sometimes erring in simplicity is a lesser sin than complicating for precision.

Space Center and Cape Canaveral Air Force Station. It is a no-motor zone. Banana River is excluded from this book. South of these three large bodies of water the IRL extends south for several miles to Jupiter Inlet in a narrow ribbon that is closer to a river, thus the name, although it is technically a lagoon. There are several inlets and a few rivers draining the mainland in this long stretch that becomes densely urbanized as one progresses south.

The territory covered in this book is the northernmost part of the IRL system, between New Smyrna Beach to the north and Titusville to the south. Since a large section of the northern part of the IRL system is within the security buffer zone of Kennedy Space Center much of the area is Refuge or Park land, either Merritt Island National Wildlife Refuge (the Refuge) or Canaveral National Seashore (the Park), and is therefore preserved. The territory in green on the map is covered in this book as *land* access—this is a guide book on *wade* fly-fishing. Of course, the area is regulated and some regulations or their enforcement may change from time to time, but generally access to both lagoons is open to the public.

Mosquito Lagoon

Mosquito Lagoon is the northernmost of the three lagoons of the Indian River Lagoon system. The

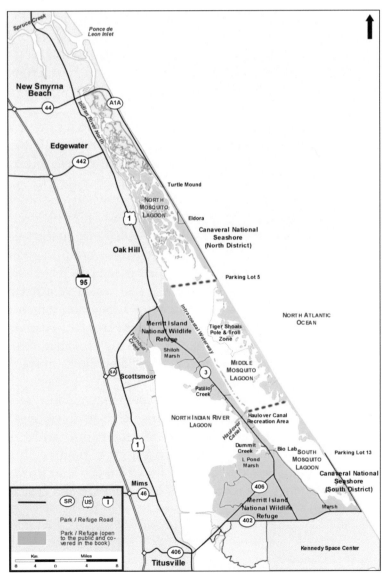

northeast and northwest banks of Mosquito Lagoon are occupied by New Smyrna Beach, Edgewater, and Oak Hill. The northern end of Mosquito lagoon may be considered as being Indian River North and the Intracoastal Waterway, with a large adjoining marsh.

Generally defined as lying north of George's Bar, Middle Island and Parking Lot 5 of Canaveral National Seashore, *North* Mosquito Lagoon is a maze of islands, shallow channels, tidal ponds, and flooded marsh where you will get lost, even with a good map. Navigation is restricted to the Intracoastal Waterway and to a few channels for any boat other than the flats boats piloted by experienced people. This is the only section of the territory covered in this book that has a tide causing significant current and changes in the water level. The shores are mostly private. *North* Mosquito Lagoon is not covered in this book except for the small part situated in the Park. Indeed, limited wading access is possible from Turtle Mound to Parking Lot 3 of Canaveral National Seashore. The County Boat Ramp is located just inside the admission gate of the Park and is the main boat access to *North* and *Middle* Mosquito Lagoon.

Middle Mosquito Lagoon is generally defined as being south of Parking

Lot 5 of Canaveral National Seashore and north of Haulover Canal. This is mostly open water, the equivalent of a big lake and the deepest of the three sections of Mosquito Lagoon. Most of the deep water, actually less than 10 feet, is on the west (mainland) side of the lagoon. So is the Intracoastal Waterway, whose dredging to a minimum depth of 12 feet has created spoil islands that dot the otherwise regular west shore. The east side of *Middle* Mosquito Lagoon is partly occupied by Tiger Shoals, the best known of the numerous shallow flats that have made the reputation of Mosquito Lagoon. Tiger Shoals is off limits to motoring (Pole and Troll Zone). There is no noticeable tide in *Middle* Mosquito Lagoon other than in the Intracoastal Waterway, where there is little in terms of tide-related changes in the water level. But there is a significant tide-related current in and around Haulover Canal.

South Mosquito Lagoon (south of Haulover Canal) is shallow and ends in a large salt marsh where the shoreline would be almost undistinguishable if it were not for the diking of the mosquito impoundments.

Middle and *South* Mosquito Lagoon are entirely within the limits of NASA security buffer zone and under the control of Canaveral National Seashore and Merritt Island National Wildlife Refuge / U.S. Fish and Wildlife Service. Most of this territory is open to the public and entirely covered in this book. Because most of the lagoon is so shallow the seasonal fluctuations in the water level have a dramatic impact on the seascape. Navigating the middle and south sections of Mosquito Lagoon by boat can be hazardous if you venture out of the deep sections and main channels. Unless you are experienced and have the right boat it should be left to the guides.

The main foot access to the east shore of Mosquito Lagoon is from Parking Lot 5 of the North District of Canaveral National Seashore (the Park). Access may be facilitated by a truck road, also called Klondike Beach Trail, which runs the full length of the barrier island between the North and the South Districts of the Park. Regulations of foot access to this truck road from Parking Lot 5 are relatively recent and subject to change. As of this writing the truck road was open to the public for a distance of six miles to the south; you were not allowed to walk over the dune to the beach; you needed a Background permit available at the admission gate at a cost of $2.00; and a maximum of 25 persons per day were allowed. Considering the state of the road it is unlikely that this last regulation would have to be enforced. As of this writing the road was simply chained at the ramp; there were no signs anywhere restricting access; and the web site of the Park did not mention it. Access and regulations of this truck road may change in the future. This book therefore shows the accesses with and without using the truck road.

The entire east shore of Mosquito Lagoon along the barrier island has no fresh water—other than some very limited ground seepage—and is generally free of alligators except for the very south end. Everywhere else, watch your back.

The southeast shore of Mosquito Lagoon is accessible from the paved beach road of the South District of the Park. It is the southern carbon copy of the North District, without the Eldora Loop, and with most parking areas dedicated to the beach and just a few accesses to the lagoon. The truck road is not open to the public from the South District and this book assumes that it will remain closed.

The west shore and south end of Mosquito Lagoon are under the control of Merritt Island National Wildlife Refuge (the Refuge). Two boat ramps provide only limited wading accesses to the west shore of Mosquito Lagoon north of Haulover Canal. Haulover Canal Recreation Area is a major access point and has a large improved boat ramp that gives access to both lagoons. The southwest shore is accessible from Bio Lab Road, one of the last dike roads that remain open to driving. The south end of Mosquito Lagoon is accessible on foot from an old dike road.

Adjacent to and south of Mosquito Lagoon is Indian River Lagoon. The narrow strip of land that separates both lagoons is open at Haulover Canal. *North* Indian River Lagoon is my definition of that part of the lagoon that lies north of State Road 406 and the railroad in Titusville and on Merritt Island. Scottsmoor, Mims, and Titusville occupy most of the western shore of North Indian River Lagoon. This is mostly private and not covered in this book. Equally not covered in this book is the small area of the Refuge *south* of State Road 406 and the railroad, not technically part of *North* Indian River Lagoon. This section, shown in a different shade of green on the maps, is easily accessible by dike roads that were still open to motor vehicles as of this writing. The entire east shore of North Indian River Lagoon is public land under the control of Merritt Island National Wildlife Refuge (the Refuge).

The geomorphology of the east shore of North Indian River Lagoon is similar to the one of the east shore of Mosquito Lagoon, with salt marshes at the north and south ends, also diked for mosquito impoundments, shallow flats, a jagged shoreline (where there is no dike), a few islands and channels, etc. Contrary to the east shore of Mosquito Lagoon, which is the barrier island and has never been inhabited south of Eldora in modern times, the east shore of North Indian River Lagoon bears the footprint of earlier settlements and pre-NASA development. Dike roads associated with the mosquito impoundments used to provide an easy car access to most of the east shore of North Indian River Lagoon. The dike roads are now closed to motor vehicles but are open to foot and bicycle traffic. L Pond Road gives foot access to the southernmost fishing spots covered in this book. The southeast end of North Indian River Lagoon is also accessible on foot from Sendler Education Center (Dummit Creek) and Haulover Canal Recreation Area. The entire east and northeast shore of North Indian River Lagoon is accessible on foot by the old dike road Shiloh Marsh Road, with a few access points still open to motor vehicles, including the well-known Patillo Creek area. At the northern end of the lagoon you can access Turnbull Creek from an unimproved boat ramp and parking areas off US 1. You can also access the mouth of Turnbull Creek and the north end of North Indian River Lagoon by a Refuge road open to motor vehicles.

The Park and the Refuge

In the late fifties, when National Aeronautical Space Agency (NASA) chose Cape Canaveral as its launch site, a very large area was set aside for security purposes and as a buffer for Kennedy Space Center.[6] This large buffer zone was initially given to U.S. Fish and Wildlife Service. In 1963 Merritt Island National Wildlife Refuge (the Refuge) was established. The 140,000-acre Refuge is owned by NASA. Given the size of the acreage and its popularity as a recreational and commercial fishery among the growing population in the surrounding area, part of the land was given to U.S. National Park Service in 1975 and it, along with additional land in the North District, became Canaveral National Seashore (the Park). The North District (also called Apollo Beach) is off New Smyrna Beach and the South District (also called Playalinda Beach) is off Titusville and Merritt Island. The North and South Districts are separated by 12 miles of untouched beach, a very narrow barrier island and a single 12-foot-high dune, very much as the Indians left it. In all, the 24 miles of beach are the longest undeveloped stretch of beach in Florida's East Coast. The Park is subject

---

[6] Kennedy Space Center is at the southern end of the territory covered in this book and is a must for visitors of East Central Florida as well as for residents.

to a daily fee and strict regulations as to hours, usage, and accesses. The Visitors Information Center is near the entrance of the North District on Route A1A off New Smyrna Beach. The Refuge is open to the public, mostly free, and less regulated. The Visitors Information Center is on Merritt Island on Max Brewer Memorial Parkway (State Road 402) approximately four miles east of Titusville.

The Challenges of the Lagoons

Barrier islands are the firsts to take the hits from hurricanes. With the rising water level and the increasing severity of the weather-related events the barrier island will be breached again, eventually. Mosquito Lagoon will be affected. While such an event remains uncertain and the consequences unknown, there are more immediate threats to the lagoons.[7]

Lagoons are vulnerable by definition. While the barrier island is the buffer of the mainland for storms the lagoons are the buffer between the fresh water—and everything else flowing from the mainland—and the ocean. The Indian River Lagoon system carries all the pollution of the mainland and, in a certain measure, processes it before it reaches the ocean through the inlet. In the original setup before human settlement the process most likely worked well, but there may have been the occasional hiccup as well. Human settlement significantly altered the environment on the mainland and on the inhabited part of the barrier island with canals, drainage, storm water, wastewater, septic tanks, fertilizers. Humans also altered the lagoons themselves with causeways, bridges, seawalls, mosquito impoundments, dredging of channels and waterways, among others. The lagoon's way of naturally processing pollution may have become less effective but it is also being overwhelmed.

In 1990 the State Legislature passed the Indian River Lagoon Protection Act, which resulted in a huge reduction in wastewater, significant improvements in storm-water treatment, and the removal of septic tanks (unfortunately never completed). For a time, the Indian River Lagoon system seemed to cope. Then, a few years ago, things began to skid again. In 2011 there was an outbreak of blue-green algae. From 2012 to this writing there were outbreaks of a brown algae (*Aureoumbra lagunensis*). Algal blooms as well as turbidity block sun light for months and have a series of adverse ecosystem impacts including reduction of zooplankton populations, losses of seagrass, losses of shellfish, and slower growth of certain larvae. Manatee and dolphin mortality has increased as their populations have increased. A study by NOAA (National Oceanic and Atmospheric Administration) in 2013 suggests that dolphins had perished due to starvation. Given the increase in the population of manatee a similar cause of death for them is possible. Fish kills can also occur with these blooms due to depleted oxygen levels. Sport-fish populations could suffer if this trend continues, and this is serious business. While decades of ditching, draining, and pollution are most likely to blame nature itself may have contributed to the problem in the form of a general rise in the water temperature of two (and potentially four) degrees F as well as a series of recent climate events. Several years of below-normal rainfalls increased water salinity from

---

[7] Sources for this section: Dinah Voyles Pulver. 2013. *Trouble Water, The Indian River Lagoon in Peril, a Special Report*. Daytona Beach News-Journal, December 18 to 22;

Yoonja Kang, Florian Koch, Christopher J. Gobler. 2015. *Harmful Algae: The interactive roles of nutrient loading and zooplankton grazing in facilitating the expansion of harmful algal blooms caused by the pelagophyte, Aureoumbra lagunensis, to the Indian River Lagoon, FL, USA*. Stony Brook University, School of Marine and Atmospheric Sciences. Southampton, NY; and

Florida Fish and Wildlife Conservation Commission.

2009 through the early part of 2011 due to the lingering drought. Killer back-to-back freezes in January 2010 and again in December 2010 may have killed plankton and changed the chemistry of the water. The cold snaps seemed to have caused a massive drift algae die-off as well. Drift algae (macro algae) is naturally found in the lagoons and helps the process of removing some of the nutrients from freshwater inflows. This die-off also seemed to coincide with a plankton bloom crash. Heavy rains in March 2011 have increased the influx in fresh water and may have transported pollutants. Finally, the hottest summer on record in 2011 and a top-five-hottest summer in 2015, have likely contributed to the algal blooms.

While nature may have played a role in the recent deterioration in the health of the lagoons there can be little doubts that human footprint is all over the place. Dredging and draining have been going on for 250 years, beginning with the settling of New Smyrna (*Canal* Street…). The volume of fresh water draining into the Indian River Lagoon system at the turn of the century was two and a half times that of one century before while the population of the region grew to seven million.

Massive amounts of money were spent between 1920 and 1970 to prevent flooding of the residential areas during hurricanes by dumping storm runoff directly into the lagoons. At the same time one seemingly obvious solution to the flooding of farms and residential areas in the upper St. Johns River basin was to divert the excess fresh water to the Indian River Lagoon. Equally massive amounts of money have been spent over the last twenty years in reversing these projects, the latest being the re-diversion of C-54 Canal. In the end more fresh water will be retained in the marshes of the upper St. Johns River, to be gradually released in the river, and less fresh water will be diverted into the lagoons.

While the southern end of the Indian River Lagoon system is affected by the massive releases of fresh water from Lake Okeechobee and the large draining basins in the urban areas, the situation of the northern lagoons is more complex. Evidence points to nutrient enrichment such as nitrogen and phosphorus from storm-water runoff, septic tanks, and treated wastewater discharges. The septic tanks of the smaller communities that dot the shore of the northern lagoons are specifically blamed. These communities sit on porous sand that lets wastewater sift into canals that discharge it directly in the lagoons. While the Indian River Lagoon Protection Act of 1990 should have dealt with this it met resistance in some communities. One example is the town council of Oak Hill that adopted a five-year ban on *talking* about sewers…

Our lagoons are very productive but fragile ecosystems. Mosquito Lagoon and North Indian River Lagoon are particularly fragile ecosystems due to the near-absence of tidal currents which flush out the water near inlets but let the water stay a long time in the lagoons. Water movement here is more influenced by freshwater inflow and wind, which makes this area more vulnerable to pollution. These areas act more like a "sink" and the natural processes can remove the pollutants or trigger algal blooms, depending on the extent of the pollution.

For the best part of the twentieth century man has ignored this fragility and used the lagoons as an economic tool. In fact, it started well before the last century, with the dredging of channels in the flats and the digging of canals inland for the shipping of oranges. Existing channels were dredged and new channels dug in North Mosquito Lagoon to facilitate navigation. The first, but mostly the second, Haulover Canal were major changes to the ecosystem, reuniting two bodies of water that were previously separated. The dredging of the Intracoastal Waterway into the bed of the lagoons and the associated creation of the spoil islands were also major changes to the ecosystem. The waterway carries the tide from Ponce de Leon Inlet well past Haulover Canal into North Indian River Lagoon. Very large barges navigate this channel.

From the early settlers to the modern subdivisions man had to fight two curve balls from nature: floods and mosquitoes. (Where did you think the name came from?) In both cases the solution was digging. Drainage and diversion canals allowed fresh water to be dumped into the lagoons, sometimes away from the natural drainage of the St. Johns River and of Lake Okeechobee, thus altering the natural chemistry of the water and carrying pollutants and nutrients to the lagoons.

Mosquito control was crucial to the habitability of the area. If you have ever been in a hatch at sunset you understand. The two species of saltmarsh mosquitoes breed under certain drying and flooding conditions, typically in the high marsh dominated by Black Mangrove and *Salicornia* spp. in this area. Dry up or flood the marshes and mosquitoes do not breed. The advent of the power shovel made possible the construction of dikes around the vast marshes of the lagoons, mostly along the east and south shores of both lagoons. The material required to build the dikes came from the marsh itself from the digging of a continuous ditch inside the dike. Gated culverts allow lagoon water to flood the marshes during times of high water levels and keep the marsh flooded when the water levels recede. Sometimes pumps were added to maintain the level inside the marsh. Done. No more (or much less) breeding of the nasty bug. And in premium the dike becomes a road that you can drive to your favorite fishing spot; or to hunt for the flocks of ducks that found paradise in this new, controlled environment; or to observe the wildlife, including the *other* wildlife. Proliferating alligators could not find a better environment of newly created ponds retaining some much needed fresh water. A work of art, really. Until the perverse side effects began to gain traction.

Indeed, marshes function as buffers and filters of the lagoons, functions they no longer perform when diked. Quite the contrary, water captive inside the dikes no longer mixes with the currents in the lagoons and becomes stagnant, low in oxygen, and warms up to lethal temperatures in the summer. Fish trapped inside the dikes die. The Park, the Refuge, the Water Management District, and the County have begun to remove some of the dikes and to restore the landscape to its original state or as close to it as possible. Biologists say that the productivity of these newly restored areas of the lagoons increases by several folds. Where the dike is still in place the maintenance of the dike roads is increasingly expensive in the face of tight budgets and increasingly violent storms. Consequently, the Refuge has closed most of the dike roads to motor traffic. But they remain open to foot and bicycle traffic. All in all, not a bad outcome for wade fly-fishers who can walk, by definition.

While it is easy to point fingers to some obvious man-made causes of the deterioration in the quality of the water of the lagoons it must be remembered that many of the factors at play may not yet be well understood. For example, the recent study by Y. Kang (see footnote 7 on page 10) states that higher levels of a different form of nitrogen (ammonium and urea), higher than normal salinities, and low grazing by zooplankton (presumably reduced by the freezes of 2010) contributed to the brown algae (*Aureoumbra lagunensis*) bloom in the Indian River Lagoon system. While natural causes of the outbreaks, such as hypersalinity of the lagoons water, may have natural causes, the Kang report points to the septic tanks, again: "The large expansion of domiciles with on-site septic systems in the watershed . . . largely provide the enhanced level of nitrogen loading required to support high biomass harmful algal bloom such as brown tides in a manner not plausible before this expansion." In the footsteps of the recent study of the St. Johns River (as a potential source of drinking water for Central Florida), the St. Johns River Water Management District has commissioned a 3.7-million-dollar three-year study whose full report due in 2017 will be based on the best available science. I suggest you do not wait for the release of this study and do your own, using a long stick, a floating line, and your favorite fly… and gently release your conclusion to be caught another day.

THE FISHES OF THE LAGOONS

Mosquito Lagoon and North Indian River Lagoon owe their reputation to redfish, particularly to sight fishing for redfish on the shallow flats. People come from far away and hire guides to do this. Close seconds come Spotted Seatrout and Black Drum, which are found in the same general environment. While the approach and fishing technique are a little different it is common for anglers targeting Red Drum to catch a big Spotted Seatrout or a Black Drum. Catching one legal-size fish of each of these three species in a day in the lagoons is considered the *local* equivalent to a grand slam. (IGFA rule for a grand slam on the East Central Coast of Florida is one redfish, one Spotted Seatrout, and one Tarpon. You will not likely see, let alone catch, an adult Tarpon wading the flats of the lagoons.)

I include Tarpon and Snook in the group of five species of game fish that you can target wade fly-fishing the lagoons, but only in specific locations. For Tarpon this is juvenile fish only; migrating adults will indeed show up in the lagoons in the summer, but generally not in the wading territory. Snook is a fish that you will find in all sizes, including adults, in the general areas where juvenile Tarpon live.

Red Drum

Red Drum (Sciaenops ocellatus). *Image by Duane Raver / U.S. Fish and Wildlife Service.*

Commonly called redfish, red, channel or spottail bass—and strangely rarely called by its real name by the locals—Red Drum is the prey of choice in the Indian River Lagoon system and the focus of this guide book. It is a member of the *Sciaenidae* family. The name "drum" is from the drum-like noise members of this family make when they compress air with special muscles rubbing against an inflated air bladder. Red Drum are an inshore species until they attain roughly 30 inches and 4 years. Then, they should migrate to join the ocean nearshore population for spawning, which on the Atlantic coast occurs from August to December, peaking in September and October. Red Drum spawn in inlets, passes, within estuaries, or in nearshore shelf waters. Most Red Drum from the northern Indian River Lagoon system spawn within the estuary probably due to the long distance between inlets and a significant number use North Indian River Lagoon for spawning. [8] Therefore, very big and very small reds can be found in the territory covered in this book. Longevity is routinely 20 years or more; maximum age in Florida is around 40 years old. There have been reports of Red Drum up to 60 years old in North Carolina and the maximum documented size is 63 inches. The Florida record weighed 52 pounds, 5 ounces.

There is no closed season. The daily bag limit is one fish[9] and it must fit within the slot: minimum length (to tip of pinched tail) of 18 inches and maximum length of 27 inches. You will often hear the expression "slot size" and it refers to fish between 18 and 27 inches. Most mature reds that you will catch on the flats in the lagoons are between 22 and 26 inches (3 to 7 pounds). Larger reds, to approximately 12 pounds, are also caught by waders and there seems to be an increase in the number of large fish. Maybe we are simply getting better at this. Nevertheless, most catches of larger reds are done from boats around Haulover Canal where spin casters target reds that are presumably moving to spawning grounds. Smaller reds behave like, and often school with, the small Spotted Seatrout and we do not count them as "a catch".

The head of a redfish comprises a large part of its body, with a relatively small mouth under the snout. You can immediately tell that they are bottom feeders (not that it makes much of a difference in nine inches of water…) and that they will *tend* to eat large quantities of small things (instead of a few large preys). Of course, all fish are opportunistic and reds are no exception. Their diet in the lagoons consists of shrimp, crab and the occasional small fish. Since I cannot think of much else that they could eat, I would summarize it for fly-fishing as being *anything that moves…*

Reds will routinely hold in the deep holes and you will find them there, opportunity feeding

Doug Brady wears a large smile and holds a nice red from Mosquito Lagoon in December 2004.

on your blind casts. However, they tend to favor the shallow flats for lunch. Either individually, in small groups or as entire schools depending on the season, reds will roam the flats. Threats to fish come mostly from the sky. Reds in inches of water are extremely nervous: they do not know that they are now big enough not to be prey to birds. There is only one way to approach them in shallow water and this is by keeping low. I mean it, really. At times, you will not make it simply walking on your knees: you may have to crawl…

Relaxed reds move at a slow to moderate speed. However, when they bite they will often charge the prey and turn sharply after swallowing it. This is when we break on the hook set. Using the best possible tippet, with some elasticity, will help reduce the breaks, but you will break occasionally when you will see the fish taking the fly. The combination of your hook set with the simultaneous turning of the fish is simply beyond the strength of any normal tippet.

Reds *tail*, and when they do our heartbeat accelerates. We call it *tailing* when a fish burrows in

[8] Sources: Eric Reyier, Ph.D. 2012-2013. InoMedic Health Applications Environmental Services (NASA medical and environmental contractor at Kennedy Space Center), verbal communications; Florida Fish and Wildlife Conservation Commission.

[9] Starting in 2012 the limit was increased to two fish in the North East and North West regulation zones: this is north of the Volusia-Flagler county line. In the territory covered in this book the daily limit remains one fish.

the grass or mud at an angle that can almost reach vertical. When the water depth is less than the length of the fish, the tail sticks out of the water and can be seen wagging from a good distance. Reds have a poor sight to start with—which they make up for with very good hearing—and when tailing, their vision may be limited. They are also concentrating on what is happening just in front of them. You may have to cast a few times to a tailing red before it actually sees the fly. Of course, each cast increases your chances of spooking the fish. Reds do not *tail* all the time. But when they do we fly-fishers just go nuts.

After the hook set reds will take off on a run and often take you into the backing, not unlike bonefish. Very long runs happen but are unusual. Often, at the end of a one-hundred- to two-hundred-foot run, the fish will start circling around you. This is when the line will catch grass (and the waders of your friend if you were foolish enough to fish close, or the anchor rope of your kayak if you were… you get the idea) and the fish will involuntarily pull an ever increasing load of line and grass and will tire quickly. It may make one or two additional shorter runs. Normal fights will last two to five minutes. When the fish finally comes to hand, you can see that it is tired and it will rarely kick back when you pick it up by the gills, or better, slide it into the net.

Some of the most experienced guides will tell you reds in Mosquito Lagoon and North Indian River Lagoon are the spookiest of all spooky fish. Some say the fishing pressure is such that they have *all* been caught before. Consequently, they have become very wary of any unnatural offerings. Indeed, recent studies[10] of the mobility of the fish have revealed a very high capture rate of 41% over three years. Therefore, some red may *remember*, inasmuch as fish can actually remember. I think the fact that they live in very shallow water is a more likely explanation. In any case, they certainly are great sport and force us to use very stealth approaches, ever smaller flies and quieter casts. A red caught sight-fishing with a fly rod on the shallow flats of the lagoons is a trophy. Who is complaining?

The population of reds has risen in the lagoons at the turn of the century, thanks to the net ban and strict bag limit. Past measures undertaken to revive the fishery are considered a success. The most recent stock assessment suggests that the population exceeds the authorities' management goal in all management regions of Florida except the Southeast. Mosquito Lagoon and North Indian River Lagoon are at the northern end of the Southeast management region, which includes high-density urban areas. While most currently available statistics show a positive picture for the Atlantic coast in general, the situation may differ in Mosquito Lagoon and North Indian River Lagoon where increasing recreational fishing pressure and repeated brown algae blooms may stress the population of Red Drum. I believe it is OK to keep one fish for dinner *once in a while*, but certainly not every day. In this fishery, like in most others, catch and release is the right thing to do, now more than ever.

Redfish is white lean meat and is good to eat. Because it is a very sturdy fish, it can be kept alive on a stringer all day and killed only as you come out of the water. The scales are big and the skin relatively tough. Most people fillet them and take the skin off. Filleting reds is not as easy as other fish because of the peculiar rib cage structure just behind the head; these bones are part of the crusher that enables the fish to crack shells before they enter the stomach. A sharp knife (and a knife sharpener) will do the job. The rest of the fish is standard bone structure and is easily filleted. The meat will keep well for a few days; it freezes, but you will lose some flavor and texture. I marinate it in olive oil, balsamic vinegar, spices, and sugar and grill it on the barbeque.

According to the Florida Department of Health, it is safe to consume two meals of Red Drum per week (one meal per month for women of childbearing age and young children). This is the general guideline for all coastal waters. There are no special advisories for Mosquito Lagoon or North Indian River Lagoon. Because they grow relatively quickly during their early years slot-size Red Drum have a relatively low mercury content.

---

[10] Source: Dr. Eric Reyier (see footnote 8 on page 14).

Spotted Seatrout

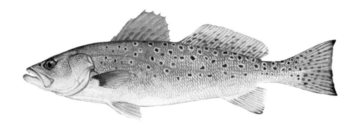

Spotted Seatrout (Cynoscion nebulosus). *Image by Duane Raver / U.S. Fish and Wildlife Service.*

Commonly called trout and speckled trout, the Spotted Seatrout is of the same genus as the Weakfish and has nothing to do, save for some distant similarities in its appearance, with the eponymous freshwater *Salmonidae*. The fish is from the *Sciaenidae* family, surprisingly the same large family of Red and Black drums. Trout live inshore and in nearshore ocean waters over grass and sandy bottoms. They will move into slow-moving or still, deep waters in cold weather. This is the reason why you sometimes find them stacked up in the deeper holes after severe cold fronts. Maximum length is approximately 36 inches. Maximum ages for Florida is eight for females and nine years for males. The Florida record, which is also believed to be the maximum weigh attainable, is 17 pounds, 7 ounces. A fish measuring 34¼ inches was caught in Florida in June 2015, most likely establishing a new world record for length. Despite these impressive numbers the largest fish caught in the Indian River Lagoon system rarely exceed 30 inches and 10 pounds.

Trout spawn inshore from May through August in the Indian River Lagoon system. This is why we catch some very small trout in the lagoons. Adult trout live mainly in estuaries and move only short distances. They feed mainly on shrimp and small fish. The fish is sensitive to cold water and may be killed if trapped in shallow water during cold weather.[11]

Trout used to be off-season in November and December in our territory. Since 2012 there are no longer any closed season. The daily bag limit is four[12] and they must be between 15 and 20 inches long (measured to the tip of the tail), with one fish allowed to exceed 20 inches.

When hooked, trout will not typically do long runs as reds do. Instead, they will fight within close range, flapping and jumping, even charging back and slipping between your legs. To chase trout without a scoop net is a good way to loose trout. Check your tippet often: trout will shred it, not with their frontal conical teeth, but with their small lower teeth.

The author with a sizeable Spotted Seatrout from Marsh Bay Creek (page 152) in 2009.

---

[11] Between January 5 and 15, 2010 air temperature dropped below freezing every night. Top water temperature at the Haulover stream gauge went down to 39°F. As a result, a significant number of big trout were killed in the lagoons. The populations of Snook and juvenile Tarpon were nearly eradicated.

[12] Since 2012 the daily limit is six fish in the Northeast regulation zone: this is north of the Volusia-Flagler county line. In the territory covered in this book, the daily bag limit remains four fish.

Recent stock assessments suggest that the population exceeds the authorities' management goal in all regions. Nevertheless, according to some guides, the population of large trout may be decreasing in the lagoons. This may be related to the increasing fishing pressure. The freeze of January 2010 also had a devastating impact on the stock of larger fish. Unlike reds, trout are slow-growing fish. The big *gator* that you are so proud to have fooled is indeed an old fish and a major contributor to reproduction. Take a quick picture and release it. Food can be as easily provided from a few 18-inchers, at a significantly lower impact on the future fishery. Catch and release is the way to go.

Weakfish (Cynoscion regalis)

Although a fierce predator trout is a delicate fish that will die quickly and will spoil. You may not be able to keep it alive all day on a stringer. Since it will likely be caught early in the morning, you must have a plan if you intend to continue fishing. Either go back to the car and put it on ice, or give the fish all the honor it deserves and release it gently. Trout is lean white meat and delicious when very fresh; it will not keep long and does not freeze well. The scales are very small and the skin delicate. It fillets very easily and will yield an impressive amount of meat for the size of the fish. Try it marinated and grilled on the barbeque. Occasionally, the flesh of trout will harbor a few small white worms. It is safe to cut away the affected area and cook the fish as usual. Even if parasites are present cooking kills them and they are not a risk to public health.[13]

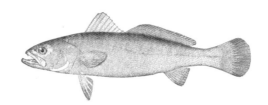

Silver Seatrout (Cynoscion nothus)

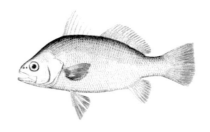

Silver Perch (Bairdiella chrysoura)

Images from NOAA, U.S. Fish and Wildlife Service and University of Washington Library.

According to the Florida Department of Health, it is safe to consume two meals of Spotted Seatrout per week (one meal per month for women of childbearing age and young children). This is the general guideline for all coastal waters. There are no special advisories for the lagoons. Sampling by Florida Fish and Wildlife Conservation Commission (FFWCC) revealed mostly below-threshold levels of mercury in slot-size fish, but increased levels in the larger fish, as one would expect. Aside from the beneficial impact on reproduction this is one more good reason to release the larger trout and keep only the occasional fish in the low twenties for consumption.

Occasionally, you may catch a fish that looks like a Spotted Seatrout but has undefined and smaller spots on the upper flanks. This is most likely a Weakfish (*Cynoscion regalis)* of the same *Sciaenidae* family. They seldom come in a size of more than 12 to 15 inches in the lagoons. You may also hit a fish that looks like a Spotted Seatrout or a Weakfish, but is more silvery, without spots, and with a rounded tail. This is most likely a Silver Seatrout (*Cynoscion nothus*), also of the same *Sciaenidae* family. This fish will rarely exceed 10 inches and will likely be found only in and around the Indian River main and secondary channels. Finally, Silver Perch (*Bairdiella chrysoura)* also of the same *Sciaenidae* family may end up at the business end of your fly line in river-like environments in the main and secondary channels. They are as silver as the name suggests, have a rounder body, no spots, and their fins have a yellowish hue. They are usually in the 8- to 10-inch range and have no front teeth like the other two species described above. The only place where I catch them regularly is at Turtle Mound (page 113). All these fish are good to eat and there are no specific regulations for them in our area.

[13] Florida Fish and Wildlife Conservation Commission – Fish and Wildlife Research Institute.

Black Drum

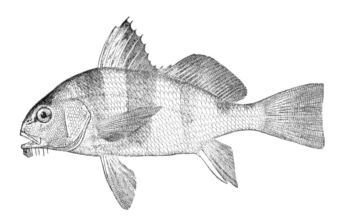

Black Drum (Pogonias cromis). *Image from University of Washington Library.*

Fly-fishing was invented in Heaven, as we all know. Man took to it and, after lots of practice and on a particularly lucky day, thought this was an easy way to catch fish. Then, Hell invented the Black Drum…

The fish is from the same *Sciaenidae* family as Red Drum and Spotted Seatrout. Common names are: sea drum, gray drum, striped drum, banded drum, oyster cracker. The locals often call it simply drum. The vertical bars on juvenile Black Drum are somewhat similar to those on sheepshead; these bars disappear when the fish matures. The Black Drum is common to bays and lagoons. However, it also lives in the ocean and is often caught in the surf. The largest member of the drum family, Black Drum will grow to 67 inches and over 100 pounds; the Florida Record is 96 pounds. Black Drum spawn in estuaries and nearshore waters during the winter and early spring months, and like Red Drum, significant spawning activity occurs within the lagoons.

Black Drum feed on oysters, mussels, crab, shrimp, and the occasionally fish. They will grow to approximately 21 inches at age three, which is a typical catch size on the flats of our lagoons, and will routinely live to 35 or more years. Maximum age is estimated to be 58 years on the Atlantic coast. Black Drum is active in a wide range of water temperature, from 54° to 91°F. Sudden drops in the water temperature sends them to deep water and they are found routinely in the Intracoastal Waterway and in the Haulover Canal during the cold spells of the winter. In theory mass mortality should occur during severe drops in the water temperature. The reality of our lagoons suggest that the local population of Black Drum survives these periods since very little change in the catch rate was observed after the deep freezes of 2010.

Blacks are related to reds and share some characteristics: like reds, they "drum" and they *tail*. However, they are not just nipping at stuff on the bottom. They literally bury their face in the mud in pursuit of small crustaceans. Their tail can be easily differentiated from that of the reds: it is translucent, will more likely stick out almost vertically and move very little, like the fish itself. Indeed, a black is a slow moving fish—most of the time. They have a very developed cruncher box in front of the rib cage (pharyngeal teeth), which allows them to crack the shells of oysters. This cruncher is also the organ that makes them grunt. Indeed, you will clearly hear them grunting when you land them. You may even hear them grunting in the water as well.

All head, with a very small mouth, blacks eat small things, exclusively at the bottom. Therefore, small weighed flies in the crab patterns are appropriate for them. This said, I routinely catch blacks on the *orange* McVay's Gotcha, a shrimp pattern pictured on page 74, and this becomes my default fly, in sizes four and six, the moment I suspect that I have Black Drum around. While small blacks will eat more aggressively, not unlike small reds, larger blacks will not typically chase their food. When blind casting in the deeper water, let the fly fall all the way to the bottom and let it stay for a while. A slow retrieve in very small strips along the bottom will entice the bite, sometimes… When you see a Black Drum tailing in shallow water, most of the time the fish will have its head buried deep in the mud and will see little around it. It is often better to wait for the fish to straighten. You must then put the fly right in front of its mouth and make it escape in the cloud of mud, but slowly, as a critter that has been disturbed by the burrowing. In theory, the fish will eat it, sometimes… I often snag blacks. Is it curiosity or simply the fact that they would not move out of the way? I will hunt them any way I can get them.

There is no closed season. The daily bag limit is five fish and they must be bigger than 14 inches (measured to the tip of the pinched tail) and smaller than 24 inches, but you can keep one fish longer than 24 inches. I cannot think of any reason why anybody would keep *five* Black Drum when one mid-sized fish kept *occasionally* is plenty. The fish is a trophy and will survive the picture with the hero and the release of the sensible fly-fisher to be caught another day. The latest stock assessment by the Atlantic States Marine Fisheries Commission suggest that the stock is not experiencing overfishing.

Once hooked a black will not take-off like a red. Instead, it will *depart*. Given the size and weight of many of these fish you will feel connected to a school bus. The black is a two-handed fish. They will take you into the backing anytime they want. However, most of the time they will circle around within 100 feet or less, keep to the bottom and pull steadily until tired.

Relatively young slot-size fish are better eating than larger fish and taste very much like redfish. The meat is lean and white, the flakes are big and the taste is quite delicate, in my opinion. Filleting is much like the red, although a little more difficult since the front part of the rib cage (the cruncher) is more developed. Again, a sharp knife does it. The meat keeps well, like for red. I marinate it and grill it on the barbeque.

According to the Florida Department of Health, it is safe to consume two meals of Black Drum per week (one meal per week for women of childbearing age and young children). This is the general guideline for all coastal waters. There are no special advisories for the lagoons. The diet of Black Drum is largely composed of oysters and crab (instead of fish). Unsurprisingly past samplings by FFWCC revealed low mercury content, especially for those younger slot-size fish. As with all other fish, mercury concentration increases with size.

I consider Black Drum a trophy and I will never tire of pursuing them. Large schools of Black Drum will be found every winter roaming the flats in Tiger Shoals and in the north end of North Indian River Lagoon. Usually, these schools are in slightly deeper water than redfish schools will be and are often inaccessible (or impractical) for the waders. Smaller but accessible groups of fish will often be found in some specific spots in our wading territory: the Black Hole (what else?) off Parking Lot 5 is an obvious one, although it has not been reliable in recent years (see page 97); Glory Hole, also off Parking Lot 5, is more reliable (see page 106); the *Big Bay* in Dummit Creek across Sendler Education Center is also a reliable spot (see page 157); the middle and lower sections of Turnbull Creek are well known spots; however, these blacks tend to be on the smaller side (see pages 183 and following).

The author with a typical Black Drum caught in the Pole and Troll Zone of Mosquito Lagoon. Photo taken by Dalen Mills.

Tarpon

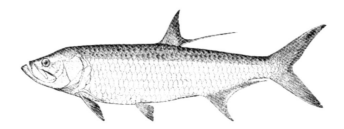

Tarpon (Megalops atlanticus)*. Image from University of Washington Library.*

Tarpon need no introduction to the saltwater fly-fisher. The mythical silver king is the dream of a lifetime for many a fly-fisher and a significant economic asset, drawing fishing tourists from all over the world… to the Florida Keys. Mention Tarpon in Mosquito Lagoon or North Indian River Lagoon and you get a puzzled "yeah, heard of somebody seeing one in the summer a few years ago". Pity. Not only does the fish exist in our lagoons, it can be chased with a fly rod, *on foot*. And it should be. Indeed, while our Tarpon are irreverently referred to as *baby* Tarpon, most are in fact juveniles and, tipping the scale at up to 10 pounds, there is nothing *baby* about them, take my word for it. Before I take you Tarpon fishing, let us have a good look at this peculiar fish that can breathe the same air as you and me.[14]

An old prehistoric relic that has changed little in millions of years, Tarpon populate a wide variety of habitats but are primarily found in coastal waters, bays, estuaries, and mangrove-lined lagoons within tropical, subtropical, and warm-temperate climates. Female Tarpon can grow to over eight feet and reach weights in excess of 280 pounds. The males are generally smaller. Tarpon are slow-growing fish. Females reach sexual maturity at 10 years of age and a length of 50 inches. Tarpon weighing about 100 pounds typically fall between 13 and 16 years of age. Male Tarpon attain lifespans of 43 years, while females may live longer than 50 years. Adult Tarpon are migratory during spring and summer. They move from South Florida and the Keys up the eastern and western Florida Coasts. Some will be found in the lagoons in the summer—George's bar, across from Parking Lot 5, is one of the documented spots—however, adult migratory Tarpon are rarely accessible on foot in our wading areas.

Although a saltwater fish Tarpon can tolerate fresh water. In addition, Tarpon can tolerate oxygen-poor environments due to a modified air bladder that allows them to inhale atmospheric oxygen: this is the famous Tarpon *rolling* behavior. This ability to live in oxygen-poor environments allows small Tarpon to find refuge in habitats that are both food-rich and relatively safe from predatory fish. The only variable that seems to limit their choice of habitat is temperature: rapid decreases in temperature can kill Tarpon. During wide temperature drops juvenile Tarpon must take refuge in warmer waters. In the environment covered in this book, warmer water can only be found in the deepest spots, and this is the key for finding Tarpon in several deep holes, man-made canals and deep ditches connected to the lagoons.

Perhaps the most unique internal feature of Tarpon is the modified air bladder. This air bladder contains spongy alveolar tissue and has a duct leading to the esophagus that Tarpon may

---

[14] Large extracts and some direct quotes from the web site of Florida Museum of Natural History: www.flmnh.ufl.edu (as of this writing); contribution from Jon Mallory (see text box on page 25); and Dr. Eric A. Reyier (see footnote 8 on page 14).

fill directly with air gulped from the surface. This feature allows Tarpon to take oxygen directly from the atmosphere (the *rolling* at the surface) and increases its tolerance of oxygen-poor waters. In fact, studies have shown that Tarpon must have access to atmospheric oxygen in order to survive and that juvenile Tarpon are obligatory air-breathers. Adults living in oxygen-rich waters still roll and gulp air, probably as an imitative pattern based on visual perception of other Tarpon. Juvenile Tarpon give up their presence by surfacing to gulp oxygen: the almost silent rise is easily identified by the prominent dorsal fin extension of Tarpon rolling at the surface. This long spike allows us to differentiate a rolling Tarpon from a rolling Gar, also a prehistoric fish breathing air and living in the same environments. While Gar will generally roll alone Tarpon will often come up to gulp air with other Tarpon. When the fish is inactive the rolling will be spaced out so much that it may look as if Tarpon are no longer in the area. Conversely, when the fish is active it needs more oxygen and will come up frequently. Therefore, when Tarpon are rolling chances are that these fish are active. You may not see them chasing bait, but if they are rolling frequently there is a chance that one may turn on your fly.

Tarpon is primarily an inshore fish but it spawns offshore between May and September. The fish is extremely prolific: large females can lay billions of eggs during their spawning period. This is one reason for the survival of the species, notably in our climate when winter frosts will periodically kill entire populations: the fish fights back with numbers. At the early stage of their life ribbon-like larvae measuring one to one-and-a-half inches are moved at random by the tidal currents into the estuaries and the nearby marshes. Currents and storms will sometimes push some larvae deep inside the lagoons; however, most will remain near the inlet at this early stage. As larvae develop into a small fish baby Tarpon will begin episodic moves inside the lagoons and up the creeks and rivers in search of their juvenile habitat. Periods of high water level and tropical storms are favorable for the dispersion of the babies and their finding adequate habitat where they will eventually grow into juvenile Tarpon. These are our targets. They will stay in the backwaters or within a short distance of them for five to seven years and grow to 20 pounds or more before they become migratory and join their larger relatives offshore.

During this early period of their life Tarpon do not stay put. They will migrate locally from one habitat to another; it is believed that these migrations take place mostly in the summer and in high water. Comes the fall and colder, lower water Tarpon will concentrate in the same deep spots year after year and it is believed that they will not move out of these spots during the winter. Deep waters protect the fish from sudden falls in the water temperature. Indeed, sudden drops in the water temperature can kill Tarpon (see next). Therefore, the fish has a built-in drive to seek these refuges in the winter.

This twenty-two-inch juvenile Tarpon was caught in the north ditch of the Bio Lab Boat Ramp of Mosquito Lagoon.

As mentioned above juvenile Tarpon live in ditches, canals and creeks connected to, or inside our lagoons, in water ranging from brackish to salt. In areas north and south of the territory covered in this book Tarpon also inhabit rivers where they will occasionally be found in fresh water. These fish will rarely exceed 10 pounds, which may seem modest in relation to the 100-pound-plus of adult fish. It will not seem modest at all when you actually hook one while fly-fishing. Indeed, these fish are difficult to find, difficult to entice to hit a fly, and even more difficult to keep once hooked. On top of these dismal odds the *wade* fly-fisher has to deal with the *other* Florida wildlife: juvenile Tarpon invariably live in *Alligator Country*. When it is cold enough for alligators to go to sleep Tarpon become lethargic and are difficult to find, let alone to catch. When the water is warm enough for Tarpon to be active so are alligators. My experience on juvenile Tarpon is for 68°F to be the low end of the range of their optimal water temperature. I have found and caught active Tarpon in colder water, usually when the water temperature was rising. At very low water temperature, entire populations of young juvenile Tarpon can be eradicated in certain habitats of Mid-Florida. This was the case in January 2010 when water temperatures as low as 2°C (36°F) were recorded in some areas of the Indian River Lagoon system. Dead Tarpon lined the banks everywhere in the spots shown on the map next. A further significant cold spell in December 2010 most likely took out any survivor. It took two years for the population of juvenile Tarpon to come back to previous levels.

Juvenile Tarpon prey on baitfish, shrimp and crab, in other words typical fish food. While most fly patterns will work baitfish imitations seem the most effective. Inasmuch as there is religion on adult Tarpon flies, most of the hype about juvenile Tarpon flies is just that, hype. The typical flies shown to Snook and Spotted Seatrout will catch Tarpon as well. They eat the same food in similar environments; in fact, they often live side by side. Many fly-fishers favor the use of top-water, buggy flies that push water, in sizes 2 or bigger. I had some success with them at certain times. However, in most circumstances I find that smaller flies sinking deep and imitating shrimp or baitfish work well. Among the best in the deep canals and ditches are sparsely tied Deep Clouser Minnows, chartreuse/white, natural brown/white, and black/purple being among my favorite colors, in very small sizes like 8 and 10. To increase the chances of a positive hook set I tie these flies on wide-gap, fine-wire, very sharp hooks in sizes six and four. Depending on water depth I will mostly use solid brass eyes that will take the fly down quickly.

Typical Tarpon habitats in the territory covered in this book are the deepest man-made (or man-made-deeper) ditches and canals connected to creeks or directly off the lagoon. In other areas of Central Florida juvenile Tarpon will be found in long ditches and canals where the wade fly-fisher has to cover significant distances to find schools of fish that are on the move. Not in the territory covered in this book. Here there are only a few Tarpon habitats and the fish are always in the same spots. These juvenile Tarpon habitats all share one vital characteristic: the deep water protects Tarpon from the rapid drops in the water temperature that are frequent in the winter.

Following is a short list of the main juvenile Tarpon habitats in the territory covered in this book. The numbers correspond with the map.

1-River Road in Oak Hill. You will find some juvenile Tarpon habitat in a few creeks on the west side of Mosquito Lagoon in the Oak Hill area. One of the few relatively safe and *wadeable* areas is the ditch along River Road just across and north of Goodrich Seafood Restaurant. This is not in the Park/Refuge and therefore not included in this book beyond this mention.

2-Playalinda Beach Road. The road-side ditch harbors juvenile Tarpon at times. While this is mostly a carry-on craft affair you can park in the designated areas and get limited foot access and space for a back cast from the road (detailed map on page 116).

3-Max Hoeck Back Creek. The deep hole on the marsh side at the culvert to Mosquito Lagoon harbors juvenile Tarpon year round and can be effectively fly-fished from the dike (detailed map on page 145).

4-Bio Lab Boat Ramp. You will find juvenile Tarpon, along with Snook most of the times, in the two ditches of the Bio Lab Boat Ramp off Mosquito Lagoon. The north ditch, where you can walk and cast along the bank, is potentially the best wading spot for juvenile Tarpon and Snook in the territory covered in this book (detailed map on page 138). The south ditch harbors baby Tarpon in great numbers but offers a limited fly-fishing opportunity. There are also limited opportunities for juvenile Tarpon in the west-side ditch along Bio Lab Road.

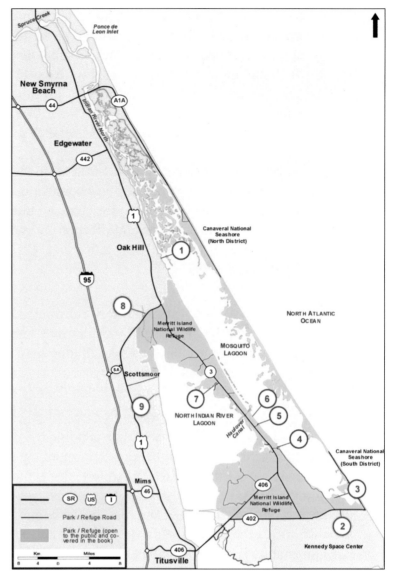

5-Old Haulover Canal. Off Mosquito Lagoon the old canal harbors juvenile Tarpon that can be targeted on foot, although this is not the most practical approach (detailed map on page 135).

6-Second Canal South of Haulover. Also in the same general area off Mosquito Lagoon the second canal south of Haulover harbors juvenile Tarpon that can be targeted on foot, if you follow my directions religiously (detailed map on page 132). Several other smaller canals between the old and the new Haulover Canals on Mosquito Lagoon harbor juvenile Tarpon but are not practical wading spots.

7-Patillo Creek. Off North Indian River Lagoon the main canal of Patillo Creek is one of the largest environments for juvenile Tarpon. The wading opportunities are restricted, but you may hit the fish in the right spot. You may also have a look at the ditch in the marsh across the dike (detailed map on page 169).

8-Turnbull Creek. The ditch along US 1 in the headwaters of Turnbull Creek is one of the best habitats for juvenile Tarpon in the territory covered in this book. While wading access is limited you may be lucky and hit them from the sand point at the junction of the ditch and the creek (detailed map on page 187). However, this is mostly a light boat or carry-on craft affair. I have also seen juvenile Tarpon in the middle section of Turnbull Creek: one spot identified as the *Ghost Chair* in this book sometimes harbor juvenile Tarpon and can be reached on foot (detailed map on page 186).

9-Big Flounder Creek. This is off Scottsmoor Landing Boat Ramp on North Indian River Lagoon and outside official Refuge boundaries as of this writing and therefore not included in this book. You can walk to the creek on the track and fish at the trestle (if allowed) but this is not practical and juvenile Tarpon are typically higher up in the creek. This is mostly a light boat or carry-on craft affair and it is a one-mile paddle from the boat ramp at Scottsmoor.

Since 2013 all Tarpon must be released unharmed. While our local population of juvenile Tarpon may not be threatened by fishing pressure the fish is subject to sudden and pronounced drops in water temperature and takes a long time to attain maturity. Take a picture, measure (to the fork, not tip of pinched tail—sorry, you just lost two inches), weigh, and gently release the fish to be caught another day. Remember that the regulation stipulates that the fish must remain in the water for release (and photo) if it measures more than 40 inches.

Tarpon fishing is very much conditioned by water temperature and light. Juvenile Tarpon are most active in the low light of early morning and evening. Sun light sends the fish down and you may not see them all day. Therefore, this is mostly an early morning and evening affair unless you are lucky enough to hit a thick overcast or better, a light drizzle. Water temperature above 68°F is optimal. This rules out most of the winter in the territory covered in this book. However, there are exceptions to this. When you find active Tarpon in the winter, even if the water temperature is not in the optimal range, go for it. The fish will generally not be as aggressive as in spring or fall, but you should catch one or two if you are patient and change flies often.

Tarpon, being a predator that is on top of its game, may not move on the fly if you allow the fish to have a good look at it. Quick strips and the *escaping-bug move* work well. Tarpon rolling in the middle of the ditch indicate the presence of the fish, but they are not necessarily willing to eat your fly while they come up to the surface to gulp air. A quick strip of the fly at the surface in the general area of activity may yield a hit, most often a *warning* hit, when the fish chases away the intruding bug without really trying to eat it. In this scenario you will get many false bites and most fish hooked will get away after the first jump. While the fish show their presence at the surface they actually live in the deep. One fishing method is to cast a weighed fly into the deep water where Tarpon are rolling and let it fall all the way to the bottom, where the fish are holding. Quick strips to the surface, the escaping bug, will often trigger a hit from the largest fish in the area. You may even try the *reel retrieve* for a fast but regular action that is sometimes the ticket. Again, most hits will be *warning* hits and not many will result in a good hook set and fish to hand. Changing flies from time to time increases your chances of success: Tarpon are relatively intelligent and have very good eyesight. They are likely to turn down a fly that they have already refused once and hit a fly that they see for the first time. For the same reason leaving a group of Tarpon and later coming back to them is often the key to a strike.

Contrary to those Tarpon rolling in the deep spots Tarpon holding close to the bank in relatively shallow water and under cover are fish that are actually eating, or willing to eat, and they are often territorial. These fish will give you a much better bite if you can present the fly right at their doorstep.

The bony mouth of Tarpon requires very sharp hooks. Contrary to their look-alike American Shad, Tarpon do not have much soft tissue at the top of the mouth. In fact, there is precious little for the hook to grab anywhere. The phrase *jumping* a Tarpon was coined for a reason. Often, six to eight hits will yield only one solid hook set.

This baby Tarpon was caught in Turnbull Creek in 2008.

Since Tarpon have minute teeth they are not tippet cutters as Bluefish are. Nevertheless, the rubbing of their sand-paper-like gum against the tippet will damage it. Shock tippet is recommended, but not mandatory. The fish has excellent eyesight and, in theory, should be tippet-shy. In practice, the jury is still out on this. The real problem is that you are likely to hit Snook while fishing for Tarpon. The use of a shock tippet is required whenever Snook are present in the neighborhood, which is often the case if the water is sufficiently oxygenated. (Unlike Tarpon, Snook cannot breathe air to supplement the lack of oxygen in water.) I use 20-pound fluorocarbon, which is the least visible to the fish. Most of the time Tarpon do not seem to mind it; however, Snook occasionally cut off this borderline shock tippet. In addition, there are times when I suspect that Tarpon do discriminate against any shock tippet. In these circumstances I use a smaller regular tippet and hope for the best. Losing a few flies is part of the game; however, going smaller than tippet size 1X is asking for it.

More than any other fish Tarpon have a mind of their own when the time comes to play with fly-fishers. Indeed, the fish is a marvelous killing machine and is clearly on top of the food chain. It will eat on its own terms. Follow all the rules on the choice of flies, presentation, time of day, and weather and you may get… lucky. Indeed, randomness seems to be the most dependable rule.

Jon Mallory and Tarpon Genetic Recapture Program

The author thanks Jon Malory for his contribution to this section of the book and to the art of fly-fishing for juvenile Tarpon. Jon Mallory is a leading member of the Florida Fly Fishing Association. Jon is an experienced fly-fisher who chases juvenile Tarpon on foot in the ditches and small waters of the Melbourne area. Jon Mallory is considered as an authority on the subject and you can read some of Jon's stories at www.examiner.com/article/ditch-tarpon-east-central-florida-advice-from-the-master (as of this writing). Jon was one of the contributors to the Tarpon Genetic Recapture Program of Florida Fish and Wildlife Conservation Commission. Valuable information gathered by contributing anglers were used to estimate Tarpon recapture rates, evaluate movement patterns, determine "homing" tendencies, learn the distribution of the fishery, and provide evidence of Tarpon post-catch long-term survival. The program was recently terminated.

Snook

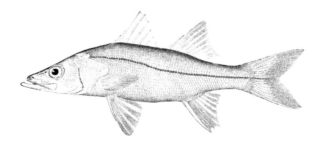

Common Snook (Centropomus undecimalis*). Image from University of Washington Library.*

Sometimes called "Linesider", the Common Snook of the *Centropomidae* family inhabits the inshore brackish waters of South and Central Florida and is one of the most sought-after fish because of its sport and food qualities. In Florida Common Snook can grow to 48 inches. The Florida record is 44 pounds, 3 ounces. Females can live to 21 years and grow to 48 inches while males can live to 15 years and grow to 39 inches. The fish is protandric hermaphrodite, having male sexual organs while young and female organs later in life. Spawning typically occurs in the summer in nearshore ocean waters and near inlets and coastal passes. Juvenile fish move in the protected estuarine areas, often in the same environment as juvenile Tarpon, and can survive in waters relatively low in oxygen and salinity. However, contrary to Tarpon, they cannot breathe air. Juvenile Snook may die when the water temperature drops into the fifties; thus, their preference for juvenile-Tarpon-like environments, which are sheltered from very low temperatures. As they grow they will typically seek more oxygenated and saline waters, but often near the same environment. Adults are found in various environments such as inshore mangrove-lined canals and marshes, estuaries, beaches and nearshore ocean reefs.[15]

Mosquito Lagoon and North Indian River Lagoon are at the northern range of Common Snook and the cold winters will occasionally kill the fish. Like for Tarpon, entire populations of Snook can be eradicated in certain habitats of Mid-Florida. This has been the case in the winter of 2010, when the water temperature stayed below 55°F during a record fourteen days. The good news is that these populations do come back relatively quickly, thanks to the survival of the older fish, the prolific reproduction, and the potential growth rate of juvenile fish.

Snook can be found and wade fly-fished in some creeks, canals and deep ditches in the territory covered in this book, where the fish will find the deep water that protects it against the thermal shocks in the winter. These habitats are often shared with juvenile Tarpon. In the territory covered in this book the spots shown on the Tarpon map on page 23 will generally harbor Snook as well when the water is oxygenated enough. While Tarpon will generally stick to the deeper holes Snook will venture around more in the general environment. Unfortunately, these environments are *Alligator Country* and the problem is the same as for Tarpon: when the water is cold enough for the alligators to be harmless Snook are lethargic and will not bite. When it warms up and Snook become willing to play, the alligators may become dangerous. The north ditch of the Bio Lab Boat Ramp is the best spot where you can walk and cast along the bank in relative safety (see No. 4 on the Tarpon map on page 23 and pages 138 and following).

---

[15] Source: Florida Museum of Natural History, www.flmnh.ufl.edu (as of this writing).

The regulations are understandably stringent for this magnificent game fish, which is also superb table fare. You can only keep one fish per day and you must possess a Snook Permit ($10.00 as of this writing) tagged onto your saltwater license. The season is closed in June, July and August and from December 15 to January 31. Any fish kept must measure at least 28 inches and no more than 32 inches. In other words, most of the time, take a picture… which is the right thing to do in any case for this magnificent but fragile sport fish that is subject to periodical kills at the critical latitude of our lagoons. Should you decide to keep a slot-size fish, consider that the concentration in mercury may be near the threshold deemed safe by the Florida Department of Health.

Adult fish eat small fish, shrimp and crab, in other words typical fish food in our lagoons. They have a preference for surface feeding and often make a typical popping noise when rising on their prey. This noise is a sure sign that there are Snook in the neighborhood. Along with Tarpon and Spotted Seatrout, Snook is a low-light fish. Snook can be fished at night and is the prime target for those fishing in the river under dock lights. If you have the chance of fishing an overcast day you may have active Snook all day. However, on a normal sunny Florida day Snook will be active for one hour in the morning and one hour before dark. When Snook is in the mood to eat you can generally spot it trashing in the baitfish, mostly along the shoreline and under overhanging mangroves. I cast them flies in sizes six to two, mostly baitfish imitations, similar to those flies that I cast to big trout and Tarpon. A Clouser Minnow is one of the best generalist flies in Snook-Tarpon-trout environment. Top-water pushers and poppers are good and white seems the winning color, alone or in combination. However, I had success with several other types of flies when Snook are aggressively feeding. When they are not it is quite another story. Snook at rest will refuse everything shown to them if they have time to think. That is the key. The fish is an instinct killer and it will snap on a fly that suddenly appears in *the* zone and immediately takes off. *The* zone is usually very close to shore, either in mangrove roots or even inches from a steep bank. Using a long leader (you cannot *line* a Snook and expect it to bite), cast either into the mangrove roots or right on the shore and strip as quickly as you can. Do not worry. The fish is faster than your fastest stripping. When the water explodes on your fly set the hook as best as you can (you may have to resort to a rod set) and hope for the best. The fish will try to head back to the mangrove roots while you will try to steer it away. You have less than three seconds to win the tow game. Being gentle and delicate gets you nowhere in this game.

Snook are notorious for cutting tippets. I use a 20-pound fluorocarbon shock tippet and hope for the best. Contrary to popular belief most cuts do not occur from the line rubbing against the gill plates (although these gill plates are razor sharp, will indeed cut leaders, and must be avoided when handling the fish). Most of the time Snook will cut the line with its lower jaw. Hundreds of microscopic teeth act like sandpaper and will go through a normal tippet in seconds when the fish shakes its head—and it will. The moment of greatest danger of tippet cutting is not during the fight, although that happens frequently. Instead, it is when the fish comes to hand and you conveniently pull it to you by the leader or tippet. The tippet is then perfectly placed against the lower jaw and conveniently tight. One or two headshakes and the fish is gone with the fly. If you cannot see the fly when you are bringing the fish close to you, which suggests that the fish has inhaled it and the tippet is rubbing against its lower jaw, use a scoop net to land the fish.

This typical Snook was caught in the north ditch of the Bio Lab Boat Ramp of Mosquito Lagoon.

Incidental Catches

I call them incidental catches in the sense of occasional, but not in the sense of nuisance. You will eventually catch these fish while targeting one of the game fish described in the previous pages. At times and in certain places, you may even decide to make them your prime target. Indeed, save for the occasional fly lost to a Ladyfish or a Bluefish that you did not see coming, these fish deserve their own fishery.

Flounder

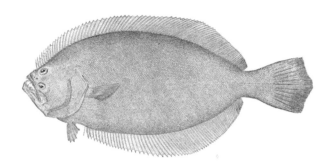

Southern Flounder (Paralichthys lethostigma). *Image from University of Washington Library.*

Flounder on the fly rod? To many this will be new. Not that you may wish to fly across the country just to do this… but while you are already here you might as well know that it exists. The two species that we have in the lagoon are the Southern Flounder and Gulf Flounder of the *Paralichthyidae* family. The Southern Flounder is the one that you will likely catch. (The Gulf Flounder looks similar to the Southern except for three eye-like spots on its back.)

The structure of the fish is peculiar: it swims flat (like a ray) but is built like a normal fish on the top side, except for the misaligned second eye. Indeed, the fish begins its life like a normal (bilateral) one, swimming straight, and one eye on each side. Toward the end of the larval period the fish begins to lie on one side and swim flat against the bottom. This is when the metamorphosis occurs: the skeletal structure of the head changes, the structure of the muscles changes, and the lower-side eye migrates to the upper side of the body.[16]

Dalen Mills with a sizeable Flounder taken in the Trout Hole area off Parking Lot 5. Photo credit Dalen Mills.

Flounder are bottom dwellers living inshore on sandy or mud bottoms, often ranging into tidal creeks. They are occasionally caught on nearshore rocky reefs, such as at the jetty of Ponce de Leon Inlet. They spawn offshore and feed on crustaceans and small fish. Most of my Flounder come from Mosquito Lagoon, which is close to the inlet. They will generally range in size from 12 to 20 inches. The Florida record is 20 pounds, 9 ounces. My biggest Flounder measured 22½ inches and weighed three pounds. I caught it in George's Slough of Mosquito Lagoon off Parking Lot 5 of Canaveral National Seashore in March 2007 on a size-four Kwan.

---

[16] Some material from the Smithsonian Marine Station at Fort Pierce.

I find them in the winter in the white spots on the flats and in the deeper water. One good spot to catch them is in the deeper water that runs along the shore just north of Parking Lot 5. This is hard pack, easy to reach, and easy to wade. They swim at the bottom and will attack a fly fished deep. More often than not they will be among a bunch of small trout that will also attack the fly, so you never know what you will catch. As far as I can tell they do not care which time of day it is and will bite in the wind or in the calm, any time you happen to hit them.

Given the shape of their mouth and the way they attack Flounder are not easy to hook. However, they are aggressive and will come back for more and eventually you will hook them. Flounder fight relatively hard, but do not jump or run. If you cannot figure out what is going on at the business end of your fly line, chances are that it is a Flounder. I suggest you carry a scoop net—these guys do not come with a handle attached—and good pliers to free the hook. Flounder will live on the stringer forever.

There is no closed season for Flounder. The daily bag limit is 10 fish and they must be longer than 12 inches, measured to the tip of the tail. The meat is delicious as everybody knows and keeping one or two fish will not likely impact the population. If you find filleting to be a problem, bake it whole in aluminum foil and you will find the skin and bones easy to remove. According to the Florida Department of Health it is safe to consume two meals of Southern Flounder per week (one meal per week for women of childbearing age and young children). This is the general guideline for all coastal waters. There are no special advisories for the lagoons. Samplings by FFWCC revealed that they are low in mercury.

Ladyfish

Sometimes referred to as the poor-man's Tarpon, Ladyfish (of the *Elopidae* family) are present everywhere in our *wadeable* territory in spring, summer, and fall: they generally leave when the water cools down in November and come back in April. In the winter you will occasionally find them in the deeper water, in typical Snook and Tarpon territory, but generally not on the shallow flats. Considered by some as a trash fish, Ladyfish will give you quite a ride on the fly rod when you catch them in the 15- to 24-inch range. They will take any fly striped quickly. Once hooked the *poor-man's Tarpon* will run, jump, and thrash like few other fish in the lagoons.

Like Tarpon, Ladyfish spawn near shore in the ocean and the transparent larvae are carried by currents into the inlets and nearby estuarine environments. The baby and juvenile phase will last two to three years in the typical backwater spots that are the domain of Snook and baby Tarpon, and for the same reason: to gain some protection against

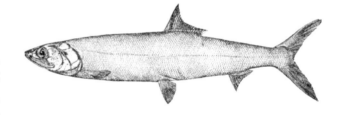

Ladyfish (Elops saurus). *Image from University of Washington Library.*

John C. Gamble with a small Ladyfish in Mosquito Lagoon.

rapid drops in the water temperature. The juveniles are tolerant to a wide range of salinity. Young adults move into the more open waters of the lagoons and eventually leave for their offshore, marine habitats. The fish does not grow big and the Florida record is a modest six pounds, four ounces.

We seldom target Ladyfish. Most catches are incidental while fishing for trout and reds on the flats and for Snook and Tarpon in deep spots. Ladyfish have a very toothy mouth and will readily cut the tippet. Since you will not use a wire tippet on red or trout, you have to accept casualties to the fly box from the occasional encounter with Ladyfish. The fight is worth it. This fish is not considered as being edible and there are no regulations.

Crevalle Jack

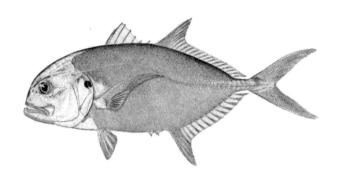

Crevalle Jack (Caranx hippos). *Image from University of Washington Library.*

Among the large family of jacks, Crevalle Jack (of the *Carangidae* family) is the one that you will most likely encounter in the lagoons, and most likely in the northern part of Mosquito Lagoon. Unless you fish along the drop offs far away from shore, you are not likely to find them in the *wadeable* territory of the lagoons but instead in the river-like environments of Eldora and Turtle Mound. You will spot Crevalle Jack when they thrash the baitfish. Cast a fly, preferably a baitfish pattern but any fly will do, in the general direction of the commotion, strip quickly keeping the fly high in the water and hang on! When a Crevalle Jack (of almost any size) hits the fly and takes off you are in for some action.

In the ocean and in the inlets, they are often schooled. In our wading territory you will likely catch fish that are single and often without actually targeting them. I have caught Crevalle Jack during the winter; however, you have more chances to catch them when the water warms up. Indeed, the fish must move to deep water to avoid the quick temperature drops typical of our Mid-Florida winters.

Crevalle Jack typically will attain a weight of 20 to 40 pounds; the state record is 57 pounds. Notwithstanding these impressive numbers, Crevalle Jack caught in the lagoons are generally smaller, in the two-to-three-pound range. Like other forked-tail fishes measurement is at the fork of the tail, thus taking a few inches off your bragging rights.

This fish is not considered as being edible. There are no regulations on Crevalle Jack. Florida Pompano (*Trachinotus carolinus)*, a fish caught mostly in the surf and very good to eat, looks very much like Crevalle Jack. Telling them apart is easy. Slide your finger along the sides of the fish at the base of the tail: if it is smooth, it is a Pompano; if it is spiny, it is a Crevalle Jack.

Small Crevalle Jack caught in Turnbull Creek.

Bluefish

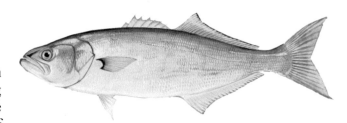

Bluefish (of the *Pomatomidae* family) is a treat on the fly rod. That is unless you are targeting something else and lose one fly per cast on the undesired little pest. Indeed, Bluefish will take off with flies faster than you can tie them. You must use some form of tippet protection when you have Bluefish around. A short length of heavy mono offers some protection. However, metal is better and there are several bite guards on the market that will do an acceptable job. For Bluefish, it is not complicated. Bluefish will attack any fly, with or without metal, as long as it moves fast. Given their diet of small fish Clousers and other streamers are the best flies.

Bluefish (Pomatomus saltatrix)*. Image by Duane Raver / U.S. Fish and Wildlife Service.*

One of the most widely spread fish, Bluefish are known under various names throughout the world and have been harvested to the point of declining stocks in the 1990s. Tougher regulations have caused a rebound of the stocks. Bluefish commonly range in size from seven-inch "snappers" to much larger fish weighing up to 26 pounds. The Florida record is 22 pounds, 2 ounces; however, the average *good* catch is in the 2 to 5 pounds and 10- to 20-pounders are trophies. Life expectancy is approximately nine years; maximum age is 12 years. Bluefish reproduce during spring and summer in the ocean; however, their reproduction cycle is not well known. Bluefish fry are largely at the mercy of the currents and can be transported over long distances. Schools of fish migrate north and south along the coast with the water temperature. The fish will often be of similar sizes, a behavior that is believed to be related to their cannibalistic habits.

This typical Bluefish was caught at Turtle Mound.

In the Indian River Lagoon system Bluefish will be in deep-water, river-like environments. In the wading territory covered in this book I have found Bluefish reliably in only one spot: at Turtle Mound (see page 108), mostly in spring and fall. They are small, up to approximately 12 inches, but feisty enough to give you a whole afternoon of fun. I also strongly recommend the place for practice.

The teeth of this Bluefish will cut your tippet in a snap. Photo by Lars Lutton.

I find Bluefish to have a questionable table value. Others think otherwise. I enjoy Bluefish occasionally after giving the fillets a good trimming to remove the blood and marinating the white meat to remove its bitterness. According to the Florida Department of Health, it is safe to consume one meal of Bluefish per week (one meal per month for women of childbearing age and young children). This is the general guideline for all coastal waters. There are no special advisories for the lagoons. Given that their diet is almost exclusively composed of small fish, Bluefish have a relatively high concentration in mercury. The smaller fish are fine; however, concentration may be above the threshold in the larger fish. The bag limit is 10 fish and they must measure 12 inches to the *fork* of the tail.

FISHING THE LAGOONS

As seen in the previous chapter, several species of fish can be targeted with a fly rod in the lagoons. Some are mostly incidental catches: Flounder, Crevalle Jack, and Ladyfish. You will likely catch these fish while blind casting the deeper spots, targeting reds, trout or blacks. Some are specialized fisheries: Snook and Tarpon. These fish live in just a few places in the parts of the lagoons covered in this book. Just a handful of these spots are safely accessible by foot (which is the essence of this book) and the fishing methods are briefly described in the previous chapter. Three species sit on top of the target list: Red Drum, Spotted Seatrout, and Black Drum. Each one of these three species is worthy of its own book, let alone one chapter of this book. This book is a guide book, not an angling treatise. It is nevertheless the proper role of a guide to give some general indications as to the ways of the fish in the seasons and in the changing environments. Thus the purpose of this chapter. The reader will understand that the art of fly-fishing involves a lifetime of cumulative experience. The minute you feel confident that *you've got it*, the gods of fishing will throw a new curve ball at you.

FROM FRESH TO SALT: CASTING AND STRIPPING

Saltwater fly-fishing does require the capacity to make long and precise casts. There is just no way around it. There is no such thing here as drifting a fly in the run and letting the current do the work for you. This fly must be put precisely in front of the fish, in or against the wind; it must land straight at the end of the leader-tippet and swim (escape) immediately and naturally. Again, there is no current to give action to the fly. Your stripping is the action, the only action.

Before looking at the specifics of each of the three main species targeted let us review the two general methods of fly-fishing the lagoons: sight fishing and blind casting. These two general methods apply to all species, although sight fishing is particularly suited for redfish.

Sight Fishing

Every angler's dream, sight fishing is mostly the domain of the flats. *Boat people* standing on top of elevated poling platforms will do sight fishing in various circumstances. Waders are much more restricted by the shorter vision range. From the short range of a wader a fish that you see is a fish that has already seen you. Nevertheless, sight fishing while wading can be extremely effective. While we cannot see much *in* the water—and will not try to—those fish that we detect we will approach much more efficiently than *boat people*. It all lies in the physics of light, more particularly the reflection of light on the top-water film. Indeed, there is an angle below which a

---

FROM FRESH TO SALT: HIDING FROM FISH

Hiding is not specific to saltwater fishing; however, it is extremely important for the two fish that you will likely target in the lagoons: red and trout. These fish have built into their genes the idea that danger is from the sky. They are absolutely right and those that forget quickly become the next meal for the ospreys. As the fish grows, it does not know that it is no longer bird food. The slightest shade across the flats will send it scurrying for cover. Same for noise. Remember how spooky those wild little brookies are? Red and trout are worse and there is no white-water to hide your presence or cover the noise of your cast.

fish will not see you *above* the water. And there is a distance beyond which a fish will not see you *under* water. Get those two figured out and make a quiet approach and you will get surprisingly close to fish without being detected. In fact, sometimes you will be shocked of being too close to cast.

All this is very good, but you must first see the fish. That is, see them without spooking them. In other words, before they see you. This will mostly happen for redfish *tailing* or *shoreline cruising*, and we will see in the next section what these two terms mean. Catching a redfish tailing on the flats is one great fly-fishing experience. Fish in the right place at the right time and it will happen.

Blind Casting

By definition sight fishing is in shallow water; blind casting is in deep water. Deep as in lagoon terms: generally between 18 inches and three feet. In fact, a "deep" spot can be nothing more than a white (or sand) spot that is inches deeper than the surrounding grass flat. Once such a definition of "deep" is understood, the wise wader will soon figure out that the same physics of light that applies to sight fishing does apply to blind casting. In other words, you may not see this fish in three feet of water because it is not moving, but if you stand up close enough, this fish has seen you. And contrary to sight fishing in shallow water you will not likely see the fish quietly moving out of harm's way. The result will be the same: you will catch nothing. An astounding number of anglers do not understand this. Even experienced wade fly-fishers who should be on top of this basic principle forget about it too often and I am afraid this includes me at times. Therefore, whether you intend to blind cast a deeper holding area or a white spot, stay back and make long casts. And if you must get closer to the spot, lie low.

While sight fishing is generally restricted to Red and Black drums blind casting the deeper holding spots and white spots will catch everything swimming in the lagoons. For trout this is the only way most of the time. Now, "blind" in blind casting must be interpreted. At times, there is such a thing as methodically working an area in the hope that there will be something there. Generally, you will do this when you are confident that the spot holds fish at the time of year and in the conditions that you fish it. This is often the case in the coldest days of the winter, particularly on trout in the thermal refuges. Nevertheless, most of the time blind casting involves some form of targeting. You may not see clearly what you are targeting, but there are signs that a living creature is around: boils, swirls, a shadow, a flash, fleeing bait, etc. These are all signs that something there is not pure H_2O. Cast in the general direction of the movements, any movement. While most of the stuff moving around appears to be mullet, you will be surprised of what swims with or under schools of mullet. Let them decide if they are mullet or not…

Fishing for Redfish

Before starting, allow me to get the record straight concerning the behavior of redfish in relation to its environment. I feel this is required because I hear—and so do you—conflicting tales about their *spookiness*.

I have seen reds that I could not approach from 100 feet. I have seen reds spooked by a small unweighed fly that I had laid on their path long before they ever swam near it. And, yes, I have had many, just too many reds bolt when I *lined* them. And I have had *distant* reds taking off the moment I raised that fly rod to make a cast.

On the other hand, I have caught reds blind casting my brains off, throwing big ugly flies, making all kinds of noise, shouting to my friends (Hey! they are here, come on over!) and generally behaving as quietly as a dump truck.

Are we talking about the same fish? Yes, we are, because reds have a double personality. In deep water, say two feet or more, they sometimes behave like cows. They will attack a big fly without thinking, oblivious to what goes on around them. However, once they get into shallow water, they become another fish altogether. They behave like a deer. Danger is everywhere, especially from the sky, and whenever they see anything that is not what they expected their first reaction is to take off on the double. If a two-inch fly can spook a 10-pound fish, can you imagine its reaction to a 200-pound angler?

Therefore, you must adapt your methods. You can fish for reds in deep water; but you must *hunt* for reds in shallow water.

Tailing Redfish

Every fly-fisher's dream, tailing reds will be found almost exclusively on the flats, in 9 to 18 inches of water and mostly during the early morning feed. Sometimes by 8:00 AM all this action has stopped; however, during the winter months reds will often go back tailing on the flats in the afternoon when the water has warmed up. If there are many fish in an area some tailing will likely be observed throughout the day.

Tailing is when the fish feeds at the bottom in shallow water, either moving slowly with its head down or foraging in the grass and mud for crab and buried crustaceans. Most of the time one tail observed in an area is an indication that other fish are around, although you may not see them; therefore, it is very important to stay down and to approach the targeted fish with great care. You spook one fish in the area and they may transmit their fear to the others, even if they are not closely schooled up.

The only way that I know of approaching tailing fish—any fish in shallow water, for that matter—is to **walk on your knees**. Keeping your profile on the water as low as possible will allow a stealth approach. Given the deflection of light over the top-water film, a fish in shallow water will not see you, if you stay low, *under* its above-water sight angle, and beyond its underwater sight range. You will be amazed how close you can get to a fish. Once well within range, the cast has to be precise, without false casting if possible. If false casting is necessary to extend your line, do it away from the fish, directing only the final cast to it. No overshooting is allowed: it is amazing how spooky these fish are for anything coming from the sky. However, once in the water, the line does not seem to pose a threat to them. Depending on the angle of the fish and water depth, you will clearly see the full tail out or just a triangle (the upper tip). Before you do anything, you must figure out where the head is and this is not easy when you can only see the triangle. Of course, you cannot see the fish under the surface since by now you are crouched or on your knees in the water, keeping the lowest profile that you can. Otherwise, there *was* a tail…

The best cast would be two feet in front and two feet past the fish. If you *line* the fish—that is *overcasting* and having the visible line, instead of the invisible leader and tippet, shown to the fish—there *was* a fish. If the fish does not take because it has not

A tailing Redfish is always an exciting moment.

seen the fly and keeps on tailing because it has not seen the line—and has not seen you—you can cast again, right away. Indeed, at times the fish may not see the fly on the first cast: it either is looking the other way or is too busy with its head buried in the mud. Repeat the process, remaining low and noiseless. If you are convinced that the fish has seen the fly and chosen not to attack it, stop immediately and change your fly. Further casting with the same fly will annoy the fish and it may either leave or ignore your next flies.

Depending upon the nature of the bottom you will let the fly sink to the bottom and strip it slowly or you may have to start stripping right away before it catches grass. Swim the fly in front of the fish, just so that it can see it escaping but not close enough as to spook the fish, and hope. Ideally the fish will charge the fly and nail it in a splash and by then you will be excited to the breaking point… exactly as your tippet. When a big fish turns away at exactly the moment of a hook set that is not properly controlled the tippet breaks. Breaking on a big red after you have done everything right is humiliating. Unfortunately it will happen, as it is still happening to me, after years of trying to restrain my hook set. You must be both skilled and lucky for all of the above to go well. In the best circumstances, when you have done everything right, I estimate the probability of success at 25%. Do not be humiliated if you blow it.

After hooking a fish in this environment try to fight it while remaining low: you may be amazed that there are several others around that you never saw. Often, these fish will stay right there if you stay down. Some will likely "accompany" the fighting fish. This is not sympathy but the hope for a free lunch, either by stealing the bait from your fish, or by picking up the regurgitation of the fighting fish. Allow things to calm down after releasing your fish and all the others will still be around for the next shot. Stand up, make some noise, and you will likely find that the area has become a desert.

Feeding Redfish

Reds do not tail all the time when feeding. They will feed like any other fish, mostly but not exclusively at the bottom pursuing shrimp, crab, and baitfish.

In deep water all this action will escape you. If you happen to actually see fish in deep water it is usually too late: this fish has seen you and is already swimming away. In deep water, blind casting is the only way.

You cannot miss redfish busting baitfish in the lagoons. Photo by John C. Gamble.

In shallow water, fish this size will not go unnoticed when they move around and feed. You will see boils—very mullet-like, unfortunately—scrambles in the small fry and tails when the fish turns. Shoot to the commotion, while staying low, and do quick strips. Overshooting is no more an option in this set-up than in any other. When you lose sight of the fish, shooting in all directions is not an option either. You will eventually *line* the fish, or another one in the area, and this is the end of the fishing session. Instead, stay low and freeze. If you can find a white spot within range, cast the fly and let it rest in it: the line will be fully extended and the fly free of grass and ready when you need it. Now is the time to have a smoke, a drink, or whatever vice you are into and that you can do while remaining immobile. Eventually—most of the time within minutes—your fish will make a move. In this game, the first mover loses…

In normal and high water reds will pursue small baitfish in the bushes along the shoreline. In high water you will often find them well beyond the normal shoreline. This will take place year round, but fall is peak time. These are single reds and generally each fish will do its own thing and work a small area, moving back and forth slowly and stealth, occasionally busting a baitfish in a great deal of splash and commotion. I call them *shoreline bait busters* and you cannot miss them. Catching them is another story. Never attempt to cast from the shore. Instead, move to the open water, take position within casting distance, stay immobile, and wait for the fish to show its presence. Eventually it will crash on something and you will either see it or see signs of its movements. You may try to show it a fly if the water is deep enough. However, most of the time

You cannot miss a redfish swimming in inches of water in the lagoons. Catching it is another matter. Photo by Lars Lutton of the Mid-Coast Flyfishers.

casting to the fish or right in front of it will result in your spooking it. Instead, try to deposit a fly well ahead of the fish on its patrolling path. Wait for the fish to swim near the fly and then strip it, mimicking a baitfish that is moving out of there as it is coming within sight of the red. In ideal circumstances the red will attack your fly as it was attacking the other baitfish. In this situation the choice of fly may become important as the red is looking for a specific type of baitfish. I find that the EP Minnow is a good imitation of these baitfish. However, the standard pattern will sink in the mud when you let it stand while waiting for the fish to swim over and will tend to snag on the multitude of branches and stumps typical of these shorelines. Try tying one that floats by adding a spun deer-hair head. You may also use a popper or a gurgler, but keep them small.

Variations of this are the *shoreline cruisers*. Again this will take place year round, but spring is peak time. These are single reds moving slowly along clean shorelines (as opposed to the bushes for the *bait busters* described above) in four to six inches of water with their dorsal fins and a good part of their backs out of the water. (See picture.) They will typically cover long distances in the same direction and at a constant distance from shore, occasionally busting a fiddler crab. You will spot them easily and you must take a position well ahead of their path. Same as for the *bait busters* described above, never attempt to cast from the shore. Instead, move to the open water, take a position within casting distance of the shore well ahead of the fish, cast your fly right on the shoreline—you may even cast it on dry land—and let it sit. Go down on your knees and wait for the fish. As the fish gets within sight of your fly—this may be no more than one foot in very shallow water—strip it as an escaping crab. The timing of this strip is crucial: too early, the fish will not see it and your chances of casting it again further ahead, undetected, are slim; too late and the fish will be surprised and bolt away and you will not see it again. The choice of fly is easy. These fish are looking for fiddler crab or like critters and the Kwan is a good proposition. Make it small and weedless by adding a weed guard.

Whether you are on *shoreline bait busters* or on *shoreline cruisers* always take into account that in very shallow water the fish has a very short sight range. Moreover, all its senses are alerted and it will spook easily. In this situation showing the fish the proper fly in the proper manner and making it attack may be considered the ultimate hunt.

Schooling Redfish

In the winter, when the water becomes very clear, reds school up: hundreds of fish keep together and roam the flats. When the school settles down for a feed the fish will often spread out nicely. It is no longer a school for us but a large number of fish in an area and we will approach them as tailing or feeding fish.

When the school is on the move or is simply staying in one area with all the fish tight together, a slightly different approach is required. First, seeing the school from our point of view is a challenge: compared with *boat people*, we are clearly at a disadvantage. Unless the fish is right on top of the water, you see them only when it is too late. They have seen you and they are gone.

For us waders the signs of the presence of a school will be either a tail or two, usually for very brief moments, or a small ripple on the water—we call this "nervous" water. Casting in the middle of the school is usually the worst scenario for all the same reasons previously discussed. The problem is that we cannot see where the middle of the school is. Indeed, this *one* fish that is showing tail, while becoming the center of the universe for the fly-fisher in hot pursuit, could be number 12 in line, with the result that your first cast will *line* the first 11 fish… Now, if a single red is a nervous fish, you should see how nervous a school can be. By vibration these fish transmit their fear one to another in a flash. The entire lagoon seems to rise in unison and there goes the fishing session.

Always undershoot a school, extending your cast gradually. Stay low and hope for the best. Worst-case scenario, almost all the time… they spook. Freeze and watch where they are going. Let them rest for a while and try again. Schools are a bounty because you are exposed to so many fish: there is always a dumb one… Schools are also a curse because you can spend the entire day chasing them around without being able to get one good shot.

Redfish in White Spots

After the early morning feed when fish seem to disappear they are in effect going somewhere. They can be low in the grass (forget it), in deeper water that I call holding spots (see next), or they can be in the "white spots". White spots or sand spots are sandy holes within the grass flats. There is no vegetation and the water is a little deeper (by six inches to one foot). Size will vary from five feet in diameter to 100 feet or more. Reds and big trout like staying in white spots. My guess is that they have a good vision of what is going on while they can hide along the grass walls of the spot. They may have their own, different reasons. In any case, white spots are great for the wading fly-fishers. We find them easily and there is no grass to screw up the stripping. Moreover, white spots can be fished in the wind—you chose your angle and make long casts—when they have been the most productive for me.

Stay back from the white spots, for obvious reasons. Cast a sinking fly—I favor crab patterns—and retrieve right up to the edge, where the fish could very well be hiding. Work the white spots systematically. Usually when you catch one red in a white spot there are others around in this white spot and in the other white spots in the same general area. Reds in white spots are much less spooky than on the surrounding flats.

Redfish in Holding Spots

Blind casting on the shallow flats is obviously out of question. On the flats, you always target something, even if it turns out to be mullet. In the holding spots, blind casting is the order of the day. I call holding spot a general area where the fish are feeding or holding in deeper water. Again, deeper in the lagoon's sense: usually more than 18 inches. Finding productive holding spots is a lifetime quest, a game of trial and error. There are likely as many productive holding spots left for me to discover as the ones that I have identified so far.

In holding spots, you do not see what is going on under the surface—nor do you want to see it—thus the reason to blind cast. Stay back a bit, for the same reasons mentioned before: you may not see what is going on in this slightly deeper water but the fish may nevertheless detect your presence. It may not move out but will likely shut down. How many times did I hear: "Found the fish but they would not take."? Sometimes they will not eat, period. Most of the times they would have had a look at this strange critter swimming funny, if not to eat it, at least to chase it—a predator is hardwired to do that—if they had not detected your presence.

Work the holding spots systematically. Again, remember that your fly line makes a terrible noise on landing. While staying way back makes sense for the reasons already mentioned long casts tend to hit the water hard. Not the fly. This appears not very different from a mullet jump and the fish seem used to it. It may even attract them. But the fly line. Those long casts may impress your friends but they do not impress the fish. Try my method: get closer to the holding spot, but on your knees. Nothing in there can see you when you are on your knees. Make short casts first, dry-fly style, as delicately as you can. And extend your cast progressively. This way you are minimizing your chances of lining or spooking fish that would be close.

Use weighed flies that you will let fall to the bottom before the retrieve if there is not too much grass. Most of the time chain-eye flies will do the job. Just wait long enough to let them fall all the way to the bottom. In deep water, in current (Turtle Mound, Haulover Canal) or if you are using a bushy fly you may use lead eyes. Vary your stripping speed. Moreover, be careful at the line pick-up at the end of the retrieve. A surface-bound escaping prey will often trigger an attack from a fish that was following the fly but not otherwise committed. Big trout are notorious for doing that, sometimes going for the fly when it is almost airborne.

Approaching Water

Never walk in like into a supermarket. Your catch of the day may be 10 feet from shore, only showing tail sporadically. It may be with three dozen others... Stay away from the shoreline—I insist, stay *away*—sit and relax and observe for at least 10 minutes before entering water. You may be amazed.

Because of their excellent hearing, fish tend to detect our presence when we walk along the shoreline. Looking for fish in an area that you know will hold them, wading silently in open water 200 feet from shore will actually increase your chances of seeing fish undetected.

If going to a spot by motor boat, cut the motor 600 to 800 feet away (or more in very calm water) and pole the rest. Coming by canoe or kayak is the same approach as on foot. If you anchor, do it away from the fishing grounds, unless you want to lose the big one that will tangle in your anchor rope. Same elementary precaution when you fish with others: stay back the full length of your back line, or be prepared to pay the price.

Approaching Other Anglers

Here the rule is simple: DO NOT. At any time. Under any circumstances. Do not approach another angler. Period. This is a game of stealth that is the closest thing to approaching a deer. The last thing any serious angler needs is company. Bad blood has developed between guides and kayakers who try to follow them to fish the same school. The guides are at the right end of the argument. One day, a guide will run out of patience and it will not be pretty.

Fishing for Black Drum

Generally, what goes for redfish also goes for Black Drum—it is just much more difficult… Finding them is the first thing. Indeed, these fish are sometimes seasonal visitors to our wading territory. Other times there will be just a few blacks swimming with the reds. Most of the time they will show up in schools of fish in the 22- to 30-inch range (4 to 10 pounds). They can be found anywhere in the Indian River Lagoon system, including on the flats and in the usual fishing spots in our wading territory. Scientists estimate that a significant proportion of our Black Drum spawn inside the Indian River Lagoon system for the same reason as for our Red Drum: the inlets are too far apart. Some older fish migrate to the ocean for spawning, travelling the Intracoastal Waterway. This migration is well known by the locals who target those big Black Drum.

Although slow moving and generally impossible to detect, let alone to catch most of the time, blacks will have their bouts of aggressiveness. At times they will charge the fly like a red and will attack just about anything. This will happen mostly with the smaller specimens… and to wade fly-fishers blessed by the gods of fishing. Most of the time however you will catch them on blind casts, systematically working areas of deeper water with a weighed fly stripped slowly on the bottom.

There are several of these environments in the parts of the lagoons covered in this book but, so far, I have found only a few productive spots accessible on foot, and even these are not always productive. One such spot is a small bay of Mosquito Lagoon south of Parking Lot 5 that, with all my imagination, I have named the Black Hole… (See page 97). Other spots are Glory Hole (see page 106); the Big Bay in Dummit Creek, across Sendler Education Center (see page 157); and Turnbull Creek (see page 178).

When blind casting for Black Drum make sure the fly goes all the way down. Let it rest for a few seconds and then strip slowly. Repeat until tired. When blacks are tailing and showing some willingness to play the game you can sight fish them like reds. The approach is the same, although blacks are not nearly as spooky.

A tailing Black Drum will be easily told apart from a tailing redfish: the tail is translucent, while redfish tails are of a darker hue; it is usually straight up while redfish tails are usually at an angle; and it will move so little while redfish tail will swagger. As long as the tail is straight up the fish has its head in the mud and sees nothing. Save your casts. When the tail finally goes down, figure out where the head is—easier said than done, but the odds are 50%—and cast a small weighed fly directly in front of the fish. Let the fly go down to the mud and then retrieve it so that it passes inches away from the nose of the fish. Strip the fly as if it were trying to escape, but not too quickly. This will trigger the attack… some times. Remember that the fish has poor eyesight. In fact, it relies mostly on smell and sound for feeding: a bad start for catching them with a fly that has no smell and makes no noise. Now is the time to take out of the box those little rattle flies that you did not know had a purpose.

Dalen Mills proudly showing a nice Black Drum on Tiger Shoals in January 2012.

Fishing for Spotted Seatrout

We call them trout, short for Spotted Seatrout, and this is the number-two game fish that you will pursue in the lagoons. Here, I must distinguish between small and big trout, since they are not the same for sportfishing. I define small trout as being less than 18 inches. They generally live in large schools in (relatively) deep water, which would be three feet in our wading environment. Although they will generally stick to the bottom, they will feed in the entire water column. They will attack anything shown to them, in any fashion, at any time. You just have to find them. I will not delve further on the sport of catching small trout, for we are on the hunt for *big* trout. Big trout means up to approximately 30 inches (10 pounds) in the area covered in this book: an impressive, fierce looking fish, all mouth with menacing teeth. A big trout is a loner, although it will occasionally swim with one or two other big trout and with reds. A trout is a predator and will attack just about anything that moves, including its own, on some days. Trout can also be fussy fish that will not touch a fly for the following two weeks. Catching trout is mostly a game of chance. You cannot see them most of the time—and if you do, forget it. They have very good eyesight. You will catch trout on the feed, often in schools of mullet, and on blind casts in the holding spots. You increase your chances a lot by going to those spots that have proven to hold trout regularly. Spotted Seatrout are not as territorial as their freshwater eponyms. However, I believe that they are quite sedentary and will tend to stay in the same area for long periods. They feed very early in the morning and will generally keep feeding on an overcast day. Most often all action will be off by 8:00 AM on a sunny day. You may keep catching some in the sun, but this will be mostly from the white spots and deeper holes and will likely be opportunistic as opposed to aggressive feeding.

Trout eat big, very big. In theory, you can show trout a big fly. In fact, sometimes only a big fly will trigger the bite. I do not use them because I find most big flies to be *uncastable*, noisy, and poor swimmers. In addition, big flies may spook reds. I stick to size four and six hooks and generally use the same flies as for reds. Reds and big trout are often found in the same environment. However, trout will more likely attack a surface fly, like a popper or a gurgler, since they are built for it: the mouth is straight in front of the fish. Being of the family of the weakfish, they have a very delicate mouth and you should not force them too much. Their frontal conical teeth look worse than they are (for the tippet that is—watch your fingers when you unhook them). What causes trout to cut the tippet so often is the combination of those very sharp small teeth—very much like Bluefish and Snook—and the shaking of the head—very much like bass—on top of the water when it is hooked. And they often succeed. Hooking a big trout is not easy; landing a big trout is a feat.

Occasionally trout will show tail. A trout tail is black and round. Trout do not show a tail for the same reason that reds do. It is not eating in the mud. Trout will show a tail when it is cruising on top of the water, like an emerging submarine. Although a cruising trout is rarely a fish that you will catch it may indicate that the area harbors a few of them. Hunting trout on the shallow flats when they sometimes roam in group, terrorizing the neighborhood like a pack of wolves, is a lot of fun although your success rate will not likely be high.

Ron Stidnick is proudly showing a sizeable trout caught in Turnbull Creek on a bright cold winter day.

Blind casting in the holding spots and in the white spots is the best way to catch trout. You can also sight cast to feeding trout. It is sometimes impossible to differentiate a trout boil from a mullet boil. Shoot at the mullet, one of them may turn out to have a round black tail, a toothy mouth and an attitude. This is the time to be careful with your line pick-up at the end of the retrieve. Trout are notorious for following the fly until it escapes. They will then dash in on it at lightning speed, sometimes taking the fly as it gets airborne. In response to this behavior I often practice the *pick-up interruptus*… At the end of the retrieve, instead of picking up your line for a back cast, stop the movement just before the fly leaves the water and let it hang there a few seconds. Sometimes, I even make it dance near the top of the water. This erratic behavior will often trigger the bite from a fish that was following but not eating, until the fly escaped.

Trout in the Winter Thermal Refuges

This is Central Florida and sometimes it gets cold in the winter. Actually cold. Although it may come as a shock to the unaware visitor this is nothing new to the fish. They react predictably by seeking deep, warm, and sheltered spots exactly as any other animal would do, including humans.

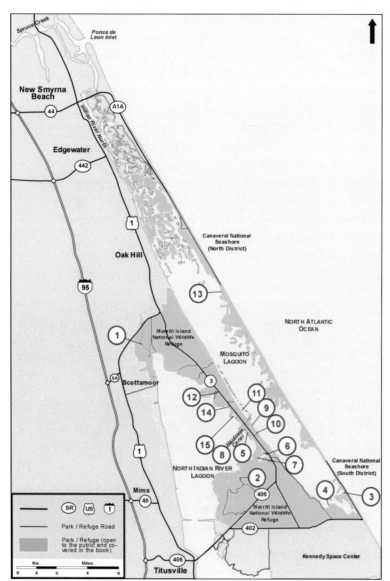

As a rule, cold weather and low water levels go together. Clear and cold water also go together. Therefore, finding the deeper spots becomes much easier. Finding sheltered spots also comes as a natural for fly-fishers. Finding warmer water is a little more challenging. Generally, you will find it over black mud. Indeed, cold days are sunny days and the sun warms the black mud. The deeper the mud, the longer it will retain the heat. The fish know this and will congregate by the thousands on these areas. In short, the four characteristics of a winter thermal refuge are: deep water, black bottom, sheltered from wind and waves, and easy access to the open waters of the lagoon. Find these spots and you will likely find an abundance of fish during the coldest periods of the winter, as reliably as clockwork.

Braving the cold early in the morning is no more appealing in Central Florida than anywhere else. You will be relieved that the bite is delayed several hours. Starting your fishing day at eleven in the morning is the way to go on these cold winter days. Early in the day—and this can be past noon—there will be very little indication of the concentration of fish in these winter thermal refuges. Trust me, the fish are there: trout in all sizes, including surprisingly big ones, sometimes mixed with reds that tend to be on the small size. Sometimes, a few blacks will join the fray.

This is all blind casting. Simply cast in the deepest water, let the fly sink all the way to the bottom, wait a little, and retrieve very slowly, in small strips. Sometimes, I make the fly dance on the bottom with the tip of my rod. What is likely happening down there is a bunch of fish lying against the bottom. They are not seeking food. But if one half-decent bug shows up inches from their mouth, they will hit it. Be alert: sometimes the take will be delicate, not unlike freshwater nymphing. Later in the day, as the water warms up a little, the fish may become more aggressive and you may actually spot them feeding. Then a more aggressive "trout strip" (see text box), including the *escaping bug*, are the ticket. You will be amazed by the number of fish that you can catch on one of these cold winter days.

Here is a short list, in their approximate order of reliability, of some of the winter thermal refuges of the lagoons that are accessible on foot, with the corresponding number on the map and page number in the book:

1. The middle section of Turnbull Creek — page 181
2. Marsh Bay Creek in North Indian River Lagoon — 152
3. Eddy Creek in South Mosquito Lagoon — 118
4. The mouth of Max Hoeck Back Creek in South Mosquito Lagoon — 145
5. Granny Cove in North Indian River Lagoon — 159
6. The ditch in Dummit Creek along Sendler Education Center — 156
7. The deep middle section of Dummit Creek in North Indian River Lagoon — 157
8. The ditches south of Bairs Cove in North Indian River Lagoon — 163
9. The second canal south of Haulover Canal in South Mosquito Lagoon — 131
10. The entry basin of the Old Haulover Canal in South Mosquito Lagoon — 135
11. The ditch along the shore north of Haulover Canal in Mosquito Lagoon — 130
12. The west ditch of Patillo Creek in North Indian River Lagoon — 169
13. The Trout Hole off Parking Lot 5 in Middle Mosquito Lagoon — 91
14. The deep-water basin off Live Oak in North Indian River Lagoon — 166
15. The middle of Duckroost Cove in North Indian River Lagoon — 165

THE TROUT STRIP

Spotted Seatrout are mostly caught blind casting the deeper holding spots. As is the case for most predators the action of the fly is a significant factor in inducing the fish to attack. Any critter escaping is worth attacking. Typically, the trout strip consists into letting the fly fall to the bottom after the cast. Both the landing of the fly and its hitting the bottom will draw the attention of the fish. Then three successive fast and long strips will cause the fish to chase the escaping fly. A long pause will allow the fly to fall back to the bottom, mimicking a shrimp diving for cover or a disoriented or wounded baitfish. Repeat the three strips and the pause until the fly is approximately 20 feet from the tip of the rod. Instead of picking up the line for a back cast, do a *pick up interruptus*: start the line pick up but stop the movement just before the fly leaves the water and let it hang there a few seconds. Sometimes, this is irresistible for a predator. Then, you can finally pick up the slack and do the regular line pick up, back cast, false cast, and final forward cast.

Wading the Lagoons

Wading is not the most popular way of fishing the lagoons for good reasons: access is limited and the bottom is sometimes soft. At best few people have the strength to go all day in the worst of these conditions. Others are afraid to do it for reasons that belong to urban legends more than to reality. This book shows you how and where. You will not find much other printed material on wading the lagoons. Some anglers and nearly all guides use flats boats with powerful engines. They reach their destination quickly using deeper "travel lanes" and then push the boat over the shallow flats from an elevated platform above the motor with a long push pole. This is called "poling". It is efficient because the guide can see far and into the water from the high platform and can position the boat within casting distance of fish. There are several good fly-fishing guides in the area. Among others I recommend Captain Nick Sassic (386) 479-3429, and Captain Scott A. MacCalla (321) 795-9259. They work together and you can visit their web site at: mosquitolagoonflyfishing.com (as of this writing). I also highly recommend Captain John Kumiski's Spotted Tail Charter Service (spottedtail.com (407) 977-5207 as of this writing). John Kumiski is the author of several books on fishing the Indian River Lagoon system, and specifically fly-fishing for redfish. These excellent guides, as well as several others specializing in fly-fishing, will take you to the same fish, in comparable locations, but in a different way than described in this book. As *boat people*, with the best guides around, you will most likely see schools of fish that will likely behave differently than those precious few that you will hunt down on foot. From a boat you will actually see the fish, probably lots of them. While wading you will see only signs of their presence, if that, and you will do your best *not* to see them in the water and therefore not be seen by them.

Same fish in the same areas; very different approaches.

Using a boat to reach a wading area makes perfect sense, as long as you understand the limitations of navigating the lagoons. The lagoons are very shallow and the water levels change quickly and dramatically, making it difficult and often impossible to navigate if you do not know your way. At the very least, get a Top Spot map, available at most bait shops. You can launch your boat from a number of locations. One convenient boat ramp for a significant area of Mosquito Lagoon is the County Ramp at the northern entrance of Canaveral National Seashore, between the guard booth and the gate. The unimproved ramp at Parking Lot 5 is restricted to smaller vessels and to all-wheel-drive vehicles and only in high water. Bears Cove Boat Ramp at Haulover Canal is large and modern and gives boaters an easy access to both lagoons in all water levels. Four other official boat ramps located in the Park and Refuge give boaters access to the lagoons: WSEG, Beacon 42, Bio Lab and Eddy Creek. Some of these ramps can be challenging in low water. Outside the Park and Refuge you can launch boats at Scottsmoor Landing north of Titusville and at Parrish Park east of Titusville on North Indian River Lagoon; and at River Breeze Park and a few private fish camps on the west shore of Mosquito Lagoon. At Bairs Cove, Beacon 42 and Bio Lab Boat Ramps you must pay a small fee (self-ticketing) unless you have the mirror-hang tag associated with an annual pass. If you have a very light boat and an all-wheel-drive vehicle, you

Captain Nick Sassic is poling his flats boat with clients soon to be hooked on something big. Photo credit Capt. Nick Sassic.

may be able to use a few natural ramps: Parking Lot 5, Patillo Creek, Live Oak, Dummit Creek at Sendler Education Center, Old Haulover Canal, Rookery Island (north shore of Haulover Canal on North Indian River Lagoon) and Turnbull Creek off US 1. Of course, every boat ramp—improved, unimproved, and natural—and several other locations, all mentioned in this book, can be used to launch carry-on crafts.

Canoes are used by some anglers and do a good job in high water. However, they are less practical in low water in this territory because they generally draw too much water and you will end up dragging them over the shallow flats.

Kayaks are becoming very popular and for good reason since they will give you the capacity to

Dalen Mills is poling his kayak; not easy and not for every kayak, but a very efficient way to find fish.

carry more equipment than just walking, move quicker from one spot to the next, and reach areas across deep channels that you cannot wade. Recent developments in lithium batteries have brought efficient electric motoring to the kayaking world, allowing paddlers to increase their range while maintaining the capacity to navigate the skinny waters of the flats. These new electric motors and batteries are very much appreciated by their users when they face a long return trip against the wind in open water. Some anglers have mastered the art of fishing from a kayak. However, kayaks are generally not adequate fishing machines. And the addition of the high-pitch electric motor just made the powered kayak one of the noisiest underwater devices. Learn to turn it off well ahead of your destination or accept to *fish in nothing*. When it comes to the actual fishing, wading is mandatory most of the time. Indeed, approaching fish in a kayak, as in any other floating device, can be a daunting challenge, especially in the wind or on a moving fish when you will definitely run out of hands to do the craft handling and casting simultaneously.

Light boats are also a valid transportation alternative in the lagoons. Light means that you can navigate in four inches of water, drag it over sand bars and launch it from marginal ramps. Still, the boat has to be able to withstand the bursts of bad attitude that the lagoons will sometimes throw at you in open water. One of the best combinations is the Gheenoe,[17] a locally made hybrid between a canoe and a flats boat that you can fit with a small gas motor, an electric motor, or a combination of both. Of course, paddles, oars, and push poles are mandatory. The boat is transportation. At the limit it can be used for scouting for fish, but the actual fishing is best done on foot, away from the boat. Unless you are sharing the spot with alligators…

There are several *wadeable* and productive areas of Mosquito Lagoon and North Indian River Lagoon accessible on foot from the Park and the Refuge. A disproportionately large part of this book focuses on the North District of Canaveral National Seashore, off New Smyrna Beach, from Parking Lot 5. This is the best destination for waders because it provides an easy access to Tiger Shoals, arguably the best fishing territory of the lagoons. Indeed, a rough truck road called Klondike Beach Trail runs from Parking Lot 5 all the way to the South District on the barrier island. This road services the Park, NASA installations, and the dikes. Now, this is the interesting point: the dikes *are* roads. Therefore, not only can you cover a good distance southward easily on the truck road, you can also walk long distances along the shoreline on solid and dry ground (save

---

[17] Gheenoe is the registered name of an excellent fishing machine that combines low draft, stability, roominess and lightness. It is made in Titusville, Florida by Gheen Manufacturing. Talk to your local boat dealer or fishing store or to a member of the famous Gheen family at 321-267-4953, gheenoemfg@aol.com or visit on the web at www.gheenoe.net (as of this writing).

for the first two miles where the dikes have been removed). There you have it: easy access to one of the best fishing grounds in the world where, in all likelihood, you will be alone… But maybe not. Indeed, the place can be busy at times and the access limited. At Parking Lot 5 you must compete for parking spaces with people using the beach as well as anglers fishing the lagoon. While this is arguably the best wading spot, the rest of the two lagoons covered in this book is a vast territory and several of the fishing accesses shown in this book are known only to a handful of people (until now…).

Since ninety percent of the game is to find fish this book includes detailed maps showing those areas that are most likely to hold fish at various times. While there may be fish everywhere I have pointed those areas that have been the most productive for me over the years. Of course everything in the lagoons is subject to seasonal changes. All these spots are reasonably accessible on foot. There is no walking in the underbrush where you would tear your waders in no time and there is no dangerous channel crossing or sinking hole, although there are spots that you will want to avoid, mostly by going around them from the open water away from shore. None of this is easy going and there will be some walking to get there (up to one hour) and some slugging.

Talking about slugging: you will be wading in the mud, anywhere from one to nine inches deep, maybe more, depending on your weight. Get used to it. I have pointed out in the book the general conditions that you will find in each area covered. However, within these general areas, there will be exceptions in the wading conditions. For example, one small bad spot that you have to go through to reach an otherwise good wading area. If you cannot, for any reason, handle walking and wading in mud stay in the areas specifically identified as hard pack and listed on pages 48 and next. None of these hard-pack or hard-bottom fishing spots is nearly as good for redfish as the "soft" spots. However, it is better than going all the way to the areas shown in this book only to realize that you just cannot do it. On the other hand, if you are built like a cat and have strong legs you will have no difficulty getting used to the mud. On the bright side most of the walking to and from the fishing spots is on hard ground.

The author wading the lagoon. Photo credit John C. Gamble.

Wading the lagoons alone could be a dangerous sport. At certain times and in certain areas. I have done 99% of the exploring for this book alone. I belong to one of the best fishing clubs: the Mid-Coast Flyfishers[18] of New Smyrna Beach. I have the privilege of fishing with a tight group of friends called the Gang from Five (GFF…). I enjoy very much the company and I appreciate the security of one or several partners. Still, when I explore new fishing grounds most of the times I do it alone. There is something about the patience and perseverance that only the lonely can do. As for the safety aspect of it, this is another matter altogether. If you do not fish with a friend, which I recommend, at least let somebody know where you are. And stay away from the bad spots and from the reptiles.

For many, including myself, the camaraderie of fishing with friends is an important part of this noble sport and I am blessed to have friends who share my passion. My friends also have another quality: they are good. Good in the sense that they find and catch fish. But also good in the sense that they know how to fish in group.

Finding the fish is a big part of the game and a group of waders spreading out and scouting for fish is a very efficient fish finder, not only for this day but also for the next few days. Indeed, fish in one area today means fish in this same area tomorrow and the following days. By spreading out initially groups increase their chances of a successful hunt for days to come. Take two-way radios along.

While there are clear advantages in fishing in group there are serious problems with it, especially in the winter. In our lagoons in the middle of the winter, when the water is low and clear, one wader on the shallow flats is a major threat that will be spotted by a school of wary redfish long before the wader can see the school, let alone try fishing it. Two waders are a crowd. A group of waders is a sure-fire ticket for a big vacuum where hundreds of redfish were previously schooled up. And do not get me started on trying to get near big trout… A gang approach does not work. No more than you would consider tracking a deer in group. Still it is very much possible to fish, and catch, while enjoying the company of your friends. Here is how you can do it:

On the shallow flats each wader must be alone, meaning that there has to be enough distance between waders for a spooked fish to settle down in front of the next wader. A spooked redfish will often run more than two hundred yards; this gives you an idea. Even keeping long distances between waders, there should be no communication other than visual or by whispering in a two-way radio.

A group of waders that are well spread out and working very quietly will have an excellent chance of spotting a school on the flats. Typically, the school will detect one wader before the wader can see it and it will take off. Now is the time for the other waders to freeze, even go down, and watch where the school will settle. And now is the time for all waders to show that they understand this game… by waiting and letting the school settle. I know it is tempting to chase the school but one hundred wary redfish will give you no more bites that one single wary redfish. And

---

[18] Founded in 2002, the Mid-Coast Flyfishers is a fly-fishing teaching club based in New Smyrna Beach that numbers upward of 80 members. This is one of the most active fly-fishing clubs in Florida. Club members routinely terrorize Red Drum and Spotted Seatrout in Mosquito Lagoon and North Indian River Lagoon, Snook in Tomoka River and Basin as well as Shad in the St. Johns River. The club is very involved in Project Healing Waters Fly Fishing, Inc. dedicated to the physical and emotional rehabilitation of disabled active military service personnel and disabled veterans through fly-fishing and associated activities, including education and outings (www.projecthealingwaters.org as of this writing). The author is an honorary member of the Mid-Coast Flyfishers. Visit at www.mid-coastflyfishers.org (as of this writing).

one spooked redfish at the outskirt of a school means one hundred redfish taking off in unison, never to be seen again. In the arithmetic of the low waters of the winter on the flats, there is likely to be a one-hundred-fish school in the area… and not one other fish. You blow the school, you are done. And contrary to *boat people* if you came on foot you cannot run to the next area, you are stuck there.

At times, in a little deeper water, a group of waders will succeed in cornering a school without blowing it. This has happened several times with my friends and we all have found memories of these moments in paradise. You can do it too, if you follow the rules: stay low, remain quiet, and *stay back*. This is where the group is as strong as its weakest member, the one who will take one more step… You cannot be close to a school and, contrary to the spin casters, you cannot cast a fly line *into* the school.

While the clear mono of spin casters lands silently and is invisible to the fish your fly line makes a significant sound on landing and is a threat from the sky to the fish. Often, the little *plop* of the spin casting lure seems to be associated by the redfish with a mullet jumping. And good spin casters will often cast *beyond* the school. Good spin casters will clean fly-fishers any day on schools. Sorry, but this is the way it is.

You can play with a school a long time if nobody makes the fatal step forward and everybody casts at the outset of the school, catching the occasional fish that strays outside the pack. In the tiny brain of redfish the fact that each of their companions chasing this strange bug is not coming back does not seem to register. But show them a shadow and panic kicks in.

Fishing large white spots and holding spots in relatively deep water is something that you can do as a group. Indeed, since blind casting is the only way for the wader to find fish in these environments, the more the merrier. Once somebody is hooked up you can presume that there are more fish in the same general area and groups can congregate around the hot spot, congregate in the sense that you can see each other, not eat the same lunch. The minimum distance between waders should be the full length of the fly line. You can all cast to the same spot, but you must be spread out around it. Since this is deep water, the fish are not likely to spook. But it helps tremendously if the group takes a break after one wader has fought a fish.

Finally, one of the most fun ways to fish in group is on Spotted Seatrout in the winter thermal refuges. By definition, these are deep areas and the fish do not see you or your friends. Trout are not likely to make long runs when hooked, but why take a chance? Spread out just a little and enjoy the fun of sharing these moments with your friends.

Hard Bottom

Wading Mosquito Lagoon and North Indian River Lagoon is not the nightmare that some urban legends would have you believe, but it is rarely easy. In some places the bottom is reasonably good in the fishing areas but the access is difficult. In other places the best fishing is in the soft areas. This is not for everybody. Nevertheless, a few areas accessible on foot have a hard-packed bottom that anybody capable of walking on dry pavement can reach and wade. These are not the best spots to catch redfish, but they are often teeming with Spotted Seatrout, sometimes relatively big ones. Here they are, in the order covered in the book, with the corresponding numbers on the map next.

1-The Deep-Water Trough North of Parking Lot 5. This spot at Parking Lot 5 of the North District of Canaveral National Seashore should be your first choice for access and you may be pleasantly surprised at times. From the ramp and old pilings to First Point North over a distance of approximately 700 yards a deep trough hugs the shore. The deep water is approximately 50 yards across and the bottom is firm. It will become softer as you move closer to First Point North. This trough is deep enough to prevent wading across in normal water level and will harbor fish of all stripes, depending on the season and a number of other factors.

Very early in the morning casting around the old pilings at the ramp will sometimes yield spectacular results. However, most of the times I suggest you walk north along the shore and begin fishing as close as you can to First Point North, finding your own level of comfort between the soft grassy bottom and shallow water at First Point North and the hard-bottomed deep water south of it. Big trout are often present in this transition area, sometimes swimming among the mullet, and generally you cannot see them. Blind cast the place with a weighed fly and be ready for pleasant surprises. If it is calm you should consider keeping the lowest possible profile (try kneeling) since these old mothers have good eyesight.

This spot is described on page 90 and shown on the detailed map of page 91.

2-Castle Windy off Parking Lot 3. From Parking Lot 3 of the North District of Canaveral National Seashore take the Castle Windy Trail to the lagoon. This is just a seven- or eight-minute walk, but bring the bug repellent. At the lagoon, you will be on a sand bar that juts into the deep-water channel. This is the old channel and it was the major navigation route on Mosquito Lagoon before the Intracoastal Waterway. This deep water is mostly occupied by schools of small Spotted Seatrout, although I have caught slot-size trout at times. You may have to look for them a little, but you will eventually find them and it will be non-stop action on a weighed fly that you will let fall to the bottom and "trout-strip" (see page 43). The bottom is very firm and this is very easy wading. The major difficulty will likely be to find a comfortable position where you have enough room for a back cast without being too deep in the water.

This spot is described on page 109 and shown on the detailed map of page 110.

3-Eldora Loop. The shoreline between Parking Lot 6 and Eldora State House in the North District of Canaveral National Seashore is a good fishing spot and all three Parking Lots 6, 7, and 8 provide a practical access. The old channel is right along the shore and you can wade on hard bottom and cast to deep water that may harbor fish of all stripes, but mostly schools of small Spotted Seatrout. Between Parking Lot 7 and the Eldora fishing dock old pilings provide some obstacles in an otherwise regular and featureless shoreline. Big trout may be caught early in the morning among those pilings. During the coldest days of the winter, when the water temperature falls into the 50s and low 60s, you may hit a bunch of big trout in the deep channel off the old pilings.

This spot is described on page 111 and shown on the detailed map of page 112.

4-The Sand Bar at Turtle Mound. Turtle Mound is an environment similar to the two above as far as the ease to wade and the relative absence of redfish. At Turtle Mound you will regularly find Spotted Seatrout, Weakfish, Silver Seatrout, Sand Perch, and Bluefish, all mostly small but there could be some pleasant surprises. You could also hit the occasional Ladyfish and Crevalle Jack in season. I recommend a visit to Turtle Mound to anglers new to wade fly-fishing or new to fly-fishing in salt water. This is the ideal setup to get a sure footing, practice your cast, your stripping and hook set. Use a weighed fly, anything will do, and a heavy shock tippet or steel wire if Bluefish are present.

This spot is described on page 113 and shown on the detailed map of page 114.

5-Eddy Creek. Eddy Creek is a good year-round fishing spot on Mosquito Lagoon off the South District of Canaveral National Seashore. You can walk on the south shore of the bay on hard sand, wade on firm bottom and cast to deep water right along the shore all the way from the dock to the island and around the point. The area close to the dock is the deepest; however, the entire south half of the creek is a deep channel and is one of the winter thermal refuges of the lagoons. During cold snaps, trout will congregate by the thousands in the deep areas of Eddy Creek, earning the place the unequivocal surname of "The Trout Hole". In the coldest periods of the winter, this will likely be your best bet.

This spot is described on page 118 and shown on the detailed map of page 120.

6-Dummit Creek at Sendler Education Center. This is at the southeast end of North Indian River Lagoon. A deep ditch runs along the shore of Dummit Creek at Sendler Education Center. The west part of this ditch, from the natural boat ramp to the point, can be waded from shore on hard sand bottom. It will harbor mainly schooling-size trout most of the times; however, it may harbor a few big trout in the winter when they have to take refuge in the deep water. Dummit Creek in this general area harbors both redfish and Black Drum and some may roam the deep water of the ditch at any time.

This spot is described on page 155 and shown on the detailed map of page 156.

7-The Peninsula at Granny Cove. A deep ditch runs along the shore of the peninsula at Granny Cove on North Indian River Lagoon and it can be fly-fished from land at a few places around the peninsula. So is the west shore of the peninsula along the lagoon where you will be standing on the hard pack. The deep ditch is a winter thermal refuge and can provide spectacular fishing for trout and mid-sized redfish during the cold days of the winter. At all times, it harbors schooling-size trout.

This spot is described on page 159 and shown on the detailed map of page 160.

8-Haulover Canal North and Rookery Island. The north side of the canal on North Indian River Lagoon is open to the public by an access road called Birds Island Road (shown only on some maps) that parallels the canal from the remnants of the old bridge to the lagoon. Along this road there are a few open spots with enough room for a back cast. You can cast a sinking line and weighed fly while standing on firm ground and catch anything that swims in the lagoons and will take a fly. You will find all the room that you need at the western point called Rookery Island and cast to both the deep water of the canal and varying-depth waters of the approach, again while standing on firm bottom. I never had much success there. But you may hit it right.

This spot is described on page 163 and shown on the detailed map of page 160.

9-Road along Clifton Cemetery. A few hundred yards south of Live Oak a small unnamed one-lane dirt road gives access to the dike south of Live Oak on North Indian River Lagoon. This road runs along historical Clifton Cemetery and becomes a dike road (now closed) at the lagoon. Park at the turn around, where the dike road is blocked, and find your way to the lagoon between the palm trees. You will see old pilings and a small spoil island, unmistakable signs of an old dock. Indeed, there is a deep channel on the south side of the old pilings. You can wade on the hard ground along the spoil island and cast to the channel. To get to the spoil island, just walk straight to it from shore aiming for the middle of the spoil island. This is a little deep, but the bottom at this exact location is firm sand (it is much softer on either side of this spot) and you should easily make it in low and normal water levels. You will likely hit trout and reds in this channel every time you fish it. Just hope for fish small enough that you can winch them out of there quickly, because those pilings will cut your leader/tippet before you know it.

This spot is described on page 166 and shown on the detailed map of page 167.

10-Patillo Creek. As an environment seriously modified by man Patillo Creek on North Indian River Lagoon offers a few opportunities to wade on hard ground and cast to deep water. The difficulty will be to find a spot with enough room for a back cast. And you may get some dirty looks from bait casters. To explore the various opportunities of this complex area go to page 169 and go through the entire section.

11-Turnbull Creek. As another environment modified by man the headwaters of Turnbull Creek offer a few opportunities to wade fly-fish on hard ground. You can cast right off the natural boat ramp. Sometimes the fish are there. Or you can walk just a few hundred feet from the ramp on the truck road and fish one open spot right off the shore. At times these two spots will harbor schools of trout, mostly small, but there could be some bigger ones, especially in the winter. However, the fish are not always in this area.

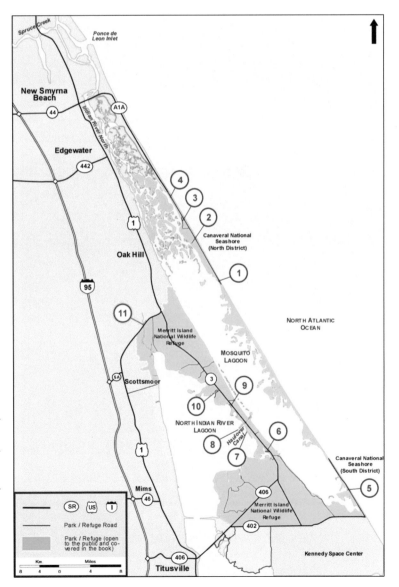

On the west side of US 1 the deep ditch harbors fish of all stripes, including Tarpon and Snook. This is private property and the access may or may not be possible. If you can make it to the junction of the creek with the man-made ditch you will find a sand bar that allows wading on hard sand half-way into the creek and ditch and cast to deep water on either side. This is one opportunity to target juvenile Tarpon on foot. This is a long ditch and Tarpon and Snook tend to congregate in a few specific spots. They may not be in this area of the ditch. Nevertheless, trout in all sizes are usually in this area.

These spots are covered in the headwaters section of Turnbull Creek, starting on page 187.

Fishing Seasons

The Indian River Lagoon system straddles the two climate zones of Central Florida: temperate and sub-tropical. Mosquito Lagoon and North Indian River Lagoon are the northern part of this system and are definitely temperate. You may be fishing in your winter underwear in the morning and drip sweat in the afternoon. For most of your friends in the North a winter trip to Florida means shorts and sandals. This is *Central* Florida and, given the proper conditions, one day it could snow…[19] Not that it is miserable all the time. In fact, fall and spring are phenomenal; winter is sunny, a little bit on the cool and windy side but very interesting. While summer can be quite hot the East Coast benefits from the cooling sea breezes and the early hours of the morning can be comfortable. In 2004, the area was struck by four back-to-back hurricanes…

Spring

By far the most beautiful season is spring, which I would place from mid-March to the end of May. Nature truly wakes up in the spring in Central Florida and you will see all manners of flowers and shrubs blooming. In April the cactuses will bloom, all at once, a magnificent show. One of the best places to observe this is as you walk the truck road / Klondike Beach Trail and as you drive the paved road in the North District of the Park. The weather is fairly predictable in the spring; however, there are still regular cold fronts, with rain and wind that will prevent you from fishing. The nights are generally cool, in the lower sixties and even fifties, thanks to the low water temperature of the ocean. The days will warm up to the mid-eighties under the increasing power of the sun. The dress code is a little complicated in the spring. Typically, you may need several layers in the early morning and keep peeling off during the day. Lagoon water temperature will typically be in the low sixties in the morning and will warm to the high seventies in the afternoon. The water levels will tend to be normal (around 0.60 feet on the height gauge at Haulover Canal—see page 56) or on the low side. Typically, winds will be calm in the morning, rising during the day, but will generally remain at a level acceptable for fly-fishing. If you fish from the Park and make it to the gate at 6:00 AM the switch to Daylight Saving Time allows you to get on

Wild spring flowers blooming along Klondike Beach Trail off Parking Lot 5 of Canaveral National Seashore. Beauty is a bonus for the long walk.

---

[19] On January 24, 2003 flurries fell around Titusville and Cape Canaveral. Between January 5 and January 15, 2010 night temperature dropped below freezing *every single night*. On January 10, 2010 the daytime temperature rose to a frigid *maximum* of 37°F.

those big trout in the dark.

Indeed, spring is prime-time fishing in the lagoons. Big trout come along the shore to feed on mullet in the morning. The schools of reds are breaking up and you will see singles and small groups cruising and busting bait near the shoreline and tailing on the flats. With the return of the baitfish, other predators will follow, such as Ladyfish and Crevalle Jack. If and when Black Drum show up in your preferred wading territory it will often be in the spring.

Summer

Summer in Central Florida is no different from most of North America: hot and humid—much more comfortable along the ocean—with the occasional shower in the afternoon. Summer simply lasts longer here in the South.

The water levels in the lagoon will fluctuate; however, hurricanes aside, not nearly as much as in the winter. Typically, the water levels will fluctuate between 0.20 to 1.20 feet on the height gauge at Haulover Canal (I consider 0.60 to be the optimal). The water temperature will remain above 80°F. Typically the morning water temperatures will be 80°F to 88°F while the afternoon water temperatures will reach 86°F to 91°F. The fishing will slow down as the water temperature reaches the high eighties. The water will lose some of its clarity as algae bloom; this is becoming a recurring and serious problem. In addition, floating grass will be abundant at times, to the point of preventing fishing some areas along the shore. Finally, expect an abundance of mosquitoes near shore and on shore.

Fishing traffic will be reduced, not that it has to be. Indeed, algae blooms aside, fishing the lagoons can be excellent in the summer; it is simply different. Reds are no longer schooling but scattered everywhere. They tail. They also tend to run bigger than in the winter in the wading areas. They eat differently. Indeed, the lagoon is now full of baitfish.

Fred Althouse is showing a 34-inch red caught in the summer of 2005. "You had a hard time catching a slot-size fish; they were all too big" says Fred. Photo credit Fred Althouse.

I have noticed that my fellow fly-fishers use bigger flies in the summer than those that I use in the winter. It makes sense since the idea is to imitate a baitfish, as opposed to imitations of shrimp or crab that are typical redfish food in the winter.

Fall

Fall is a beautiful season in Central Florida, not the least because there is very little traffic. Except on holidays and weekends you will generally find space at the beach parking lots of the Park at all hours of the day. I place this season from October to the end of November. This is a season when the weather is reasonably constant. In the fall the warmer water of the ocean compensates for the lower angle of the sun and the shorter days. The nights are pleasantly mild while daytime temperatures will remain in a comfortable 75-85°F range. The water level in the lagoons may play tricks on you: sometimes it rises to levels that make fishing difficult. However, the water

Snow-covered bushes (or maybe not...) along the truck road off Parking Lot 5 of Canaveral National Seashore. Fall can be a surprisingly pretty season.

temperature will remain quite stable in the mid-seventies, again due to stabilizing effect of the ocean, lower angle of the sun and shorter days. These shorter days will enable the early-rising angler to sneak up on reds having breakfast along the shore in the first light. Typically, winds will be calm in the morning, rising only to moderate levels during the day. There is often a light convection wind early. This is a local adjustment in the air masses of different temperatures and it will often die before the dominant wind of the day rises.

Although not as spectacular as spring I also consider fall to be prime-time for fishing Mosquito Lagoon and North Indian River Lagoon. You will see reds, singles and small groups, tailing on the flats. In high water you will find them busting baits along (and inside) the shoreline.

Winter

This is *Central* Florida, not South Florida. We have a winter here and it is a very interesting time. Typically, winter will be from December to mid-March; however, it can vary by a few weeks at either end. One phrase dominates the weather as well as the fishing patterns: cold fronts.

Typically, the cycle of cold fronts will be from 5 to 10 days. This cycle is the weather-maker and should be at the center of your fishing plans, if you can afford the luxury of short-term planning. If you cannot, cold fronts will make or break your trip to Central Florida.

The days preceding a cold front are warm, mostly cloudy, with shifting winds, generally light. Air temperature will rise to the mid-seventies and low-eighties, the water temperature will rise to the low seventies, and the water level will rise. Generally, fishing will be good.

Then the front will sweep through. Sometimes, you can see the line of clouds moving in from the north or from the west. The wind will pick-up suddenly and air temperature may go down several degrees within a few minutes. The cold front may or may not carry enough moisture to produce rain. If it does, it will generally fall all at once. In any case one thing is for sure: the wind will be strong and gusty and you have no business near the water.

After the front a high pressure system will move in. This means a glorious blue sky but very cold temperatures and a strong north or northwest wind. It may *freeze* in the morning.[20] This high pressure system will literally blow the water out of the lagoons. The water level may fall by *one foot* and the water temperature may fall by 15°F over a two-day period. You have no business near the water.

The second day—or third, depending upon the power of the front—will be a *day made in heaven*. Truly. The sky will remain perfectly blue with sunshine all day. The winds will have fallen

---

[20] On December 25, 1983 temperatures dropped to 19°F in Daytona Beach and 10°F in the western parts of Volusia County. On January 21, 1985 temperatures again dropped to 15°F in Daytona Beach and 11°F in West Volusia. Before these two back-to-back killer frosts, 15,000 acres of land were cultivated as citrus groves in Volusia County. The business was wiped out. The vegetation around Mosquito Lagoon and North Indian River Lagoon was also dramatically affected. You can still see some skeletons of dead mangrove trees dotting the marshes and the shorelines of the lagoons.

the night before and will remain calm, sometimes even too calm. This will be a very cold morning again, with air temperature in the low fifties (and lower) and water temperature to match. Both the air and the water will warm up during the day, but only to the sixties. Dress warmly and go fishing! This is the time for winter underwear and several layers of clothing (you may have to peel off some during the day). Those of you who are not early risers will appreciate that the bite will typically be delayed to the afternoon, the fish coming back to life as the water temperature rises over the flats.

The following days may bring more of the same if the next cold front is far off, or there may be increasing cloudiness and some warming in both air and water temperatures leading to the next cold front. In either case these are good fishing days.

Fishing can be spectacular in the winter but sometimes you may have to bundle up. Ralph Hasnosi with other members of the Mid-Coast Flyfishers in Marsh Bay Creek on a glorious January winter day.

Winter is excellent fishing time—that is, between the cold fronts—and it offers more challenge than in the other seasons. Water will become very clear and will often stay cold and low for weeks. The fish adapt to these conditions. Trout will congregate to the deeper spots (I call them winter thermal refuges) and will give you a good bite if and when you can find these spots, which you should with the help of this book—see Trout in the Winter Thermal Refuges on page 42. Reds will school up and chasing these schools on the flats will be a fantastic fishing experience. You will also find them in the white spots and in the deeper holding spots, sometimes in great number. Winter is not the season when you will see them *tailing* as often as in spring or fall. However, when the water warms up a little in the afternoon fishing can be absolutely fantastic.

FROM FRESH TO SALT: WIND

Unless you fish on lakes, the wind is generally not a factor in fresh water and is certainly not a factor if you do small streams in deep wooden valleys. However, in the vast expanses of salt water wind is a major factor for all anglers and even more for fly-fishers. In theory, wind interferes with fly casting and makes sight fishing impossible. There is some truth to this. But it is not the entire story.

True, the wind interferes with fly casting. But just a little. Firstly, you must learn to cast against the wind. Obviously, these will be short casts, which is all you need, if and when you will need them (keep reading). Instead of cursing the wind position yourself with the wind at your back *and* side and make your casts at a 45-degree angle so that the wind carries your fly in front and away from your head. You can cover white spots and holding (deeper) spots better with the wind than without it.

True, the wind makes it difficult to find fish and sight cast to them. On a windy day you must know where the fish are holding and fish these spots (generally the same place as the last time you found them). You will also see them. Indeed, wind means current and current means food being carried by the current... in other words: dinner bell. Therefore, the fish will likely be actively feeding. Big fish actively feeding in skinny water. You will see them, even in the wind.

And there is a bonus. The rough water surface becomes a shield for the fish. They do not see much of what is going on up in the air and they figure that the same is true in the opposite direction. You will get close to the fish and they will not spook.

Countless times I could not see a living thing in calm, still water in the morning, only to find myself surrounded by numerous fish actively feeding after the wind had picked up later in the day. So the next time you want to curse the wind, think again.

Water Level and Temperature

Most of the time the water level is the number one variable for fishing conditions in the lagoons. The conditions will vary tremendously whether you visit the lagoons in high, normal or low water. Normal variance is approximately 1.5 feet; maximum variance is approximately 2.5 feet. This is enormous, considering that most reds are caught in 12 to 18 inches of water, and many in much less.

You can consult the water level and temperature on the Internet prior to your trip to the lagoons from real-time observations at Haulover Canal. The Internet address is: http://waterdata.usgs.gov/fl/nwis/uv?02248380 (as of this writing). The stream gauge is under the bridge. Certain combinations of wind and tide sometimes funnel water in or out of the canal and amplify the changes in level. Aside from these temporary distortions, I find the observations at the Haulover Canal stream gauge to be consistent with conditions everywhere in the lagoons. From my observation, 0.60 feet on the *height gauge* (see text box on page 58) corresponds to *normal* water level. Note that zero (0.00) is not "no water". It is simply the 1929 agreed mean sea level (NGVD 29). The scale goes down to negative numbers. Indeed, in mid-January do not be surprised by readings down to –0.40 on the height gauge.

The two graphs on page 57 were taken directly (and unedited) from the USGS Internet site. I have chosen November 2003 as a particularly striking example of the influence of cold fronts on the water levels in the Indian River Lagoon system. You can see the significant daily changes, some being amplified by wind, as well as the impact of the cold fronts, not only on the water temperature (to be expected) but also on the water levels.

The water level in the lagoons is subject to short-term influences and seasonal cycles. Aside from wind that causes temporary fluctuations the principal short-term influence is barometric pressure. The graphs next speak volumes of the correlation between cold fronts (cold, dense air behind the fronts) and the dropping water levels. When the water leaves the lagoons it goes into the ocean, whose water level has already dropped due to an increase in barometric pressure. Of course the ocean water has to go somewhere and it will rise where the barometric pressure is lower, which could be quite far away. Therefore, the principal short-term influence is *relative* barometric pressure in the entire stretch of ocean that is subject to the weather system. The lagoons and the ocean tend to have the same level. Given the lag due to the great distance between

This is Mosquito Lagoon at Target Bay off Parking Lot 5 of Canaveral National Seashore in the fall (top) and in the winter (bottom). One could hardly believe that fish were there to be caught a few weeks before the bottom picture was taken.

Ponce de Leon and Sebastian Inlets, it may take a day or so for the lagoons to adjust to a change in the mean ocean water level. But it will adjust, always. This is simple physics.

Aside from the gravitational forces of the moon and planets on the amplitude of tides mean sea level seasonal cycles and inter-annual variations are caused by fluctuations in coastal ocean temperatures, salinities, winds, atmospheric pressures, and currents.[21] This is the predictable cycle of higher tides at certain times of the year and lower tides at other times. The water level in the lagoons simply adjusts to the gradual changes in the mean ocean water levels. The water tends to be higher in early fall and lower in the winter.

The next two graphs on page 58 demonstrate the seasonal trends of the ocean and their direct impact on the water level in the lagoons. I have selected data from NOAA's Port Canaveral Station, as it is the station situated the closest to the lagoons. It is roughly midway between Ponce de Leon and Sebastian Inlets. The graphs show that water levels in the lagoons and in the ocean are correlated and one should logically estimate that the driver is the ocean.

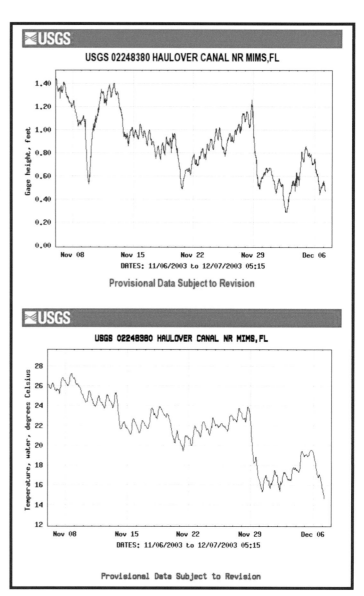

The Haulover Canal stream gauge gives the water temperature in both Celsius and Fahrenheit degrees.[22] Daily variations in the water temperature will sometimes be amplified on the very shallow flats. This is particularly the case in the cold winter mornings when the actual water temperature on the flats can be as much as eight degrees F colder than what the stream gauge will read in the deeper water of Haulover Canal. There can also be a difference on sunny afternoons when the water will warm up more on the flats. However, at most other times, personal observations generally concur with measurements at the Haulover Canal stream gauge.

According to various sources, including the Smithsonian Marine Institute at Fort Pierce and the Florida Museum of Natural History, the preferred water temperature for reds is 56°F to 85°F, with the lower temperature limit being 39°F and the upper temperature limit being 93°F. In other words, Red Drum will take just about anything.

For trout the range is much narrower. The preferred water temperature would be 59°F to 81°F; the lower temperature limit would be 45°F

---

[21] Source: NOAA (National Oceanic and Atmospheric Administration).

[22] To convert quickly and roughly from Celsius to Fahrenheit when both scales are not shown, multiply the Celsius degrees by 2, add 32 and adjust by subtracting 2 or 3 in cold temperature and 4 or 5 in warm temperature. The exact formula is [°C × 1.8] + 32= °F.

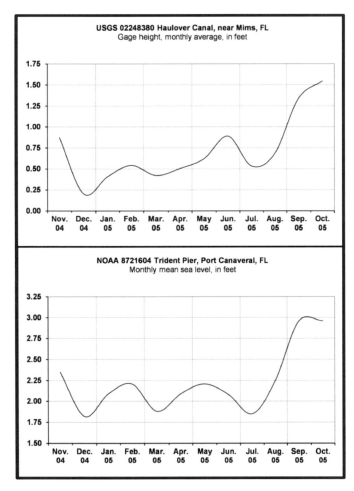

USGS 02248380 Haulover Canal, near Mims, FL
Gage height, monthly average, in feet

NOAA 8721604 Trident Pier, Port Canaveral, FL
Monthly mean sea level, in feet

and the upper temperature limit 88°F. Spotted Seatrout are sensitive to the drops in the water temperature.

For Black Drum the preferred water temperature is 54°F to 91°F; however, there is little scientific information on their minimum or maximum tolerance. Based on anecdotal evidence and personal observation Black Drum is a sturdy fish tolerant to a wide range of water temperature.

I rarely fish in water colder than 48°F or warmer than 85°F. I have had success in cold water, between 50°F and 60°F; however, the bite will often be delayed to early afternoon when the water temperature rises a little bit on the flats. The fish seem to become lethargic when the water temperature drops below 50°F or rises above 85°F. In sustained low water temperature I have experienced the disappearance of Spotted Seatrout from vast areas of shallow water. They move to the deeper holes and some of these, that I call Winter Thermal Refuges, are identified in this book on page 42. Reds however generally stay in the same areas, assuming they have adequate water level, and often keep biting, even though in theory they should be affected by the cold water temperature.

Wading the Lagoons is a unique experience and it is never the same. Remember that conditions change dramatically from one season to the next. For example, most of the area that you will be fishing in high and normal water levels in spring, summer or fall will be dry in the low-water period of the winter; the water temperature will drop below 50°F; fish location and behavior will be quite different. What you read and hear from others may reflect their experience of one specific time and place. Do not be surprised if you find a very different environment.

NGVD of 1929 and NAVD of 1988

The National Geodetic Vertical Datum of 1929 (NGVD 29) is the theoretical mean sea level established in 1929 for Canada and the United States. All surveyed elevations refer to this "0" benchmark. In 1991 this benchmark was replaced by the North American Vertical Datum of 1988 (NAVD 88). This new benchmark takes into account additional data, includes Mexico and is based upon the International Great Lakes Datum of 1985. In Florida, the new base is generally 1.0 to 1.4 feet higher. Therefore, the number from the new standard is lower.

As of this writing, the USGS stream gauge at Haulover Canal still refers to the NGVD of 1929 and all water levels mentioned in this book still refer to the (old) NGVD of 1929. The water level recorded on the first graph on the web page (GAGE HEIGHT, FEET) is exactly the altitude of the water above the *theoretical* mean sea level of 1929. A second graph on the same web page (STREAM WATER LEVEL ELEVATION ABOVE NAVD 1988, IN FEET) is the new measure. At Haulover Canal, the new base is 1.25 feet higher. In other words, a *normal* water level of 0.60 on the old base of 1929 corresponds to –0.65 feet on the new base of 1988.

Sources: United States Geological Survey (USGS).

Other Topics

The Dikes

You will notice that long sections of the shoreline of both lagoons have dikes that are part of mosquito impoundments. In the 1920s the government tried to reduce the number of mosquitoes by building impoundments. Indeed, salt marsh mosquitoes do not lay their eggs in stagnant water like other breeds of mosquitoes, but instead on the moist soil of the slightly higher grounds above the water level. The idea was to keep these areas flooded with dikes, thus preventing mosquitoes to breed without the use of pesticides. To produce the impoundments a canal was dug on the impoundment side and the material used to build a dike. Operational culverts would allow water inside the impoundments during periods of high water and closing the culverts would keep the water inside when the water level in the lagoons receded. The idea was a good one but the first dikes dug by hand shovels were not very good: they were costly to maintain, were often damaged by storms, and tended to lose water by seepage. The availability of the power shovel in the 1950s allowed for the building of much better dikes and impoundments, complete with pumps where required. The first (modern) impoundments in Florida were built in Brevard County in 1954 with other counties soon following. By the 1970s, in excess of 40,000 acres of Florida's coastal wetlands had been impounded.[23]

What you will see today along the shoreline of both lagoons are the new impoundments, built after the 1950s. They can be described as follows, starting from the open water:

- New regular and featureless shoreline, most of the time steeper than the natural (pre-diked) shorelines; during periods of high water redfish will come swimming right along the dike;

- Dike, approximately five feet high with a rough dirt road on top; the material used to build the dike/road comes from digging a ditch inside the impoundment; over time the mangroves have taken over the sides of the dike but there are openings left and generally the areas around the culverts are open; the top of the dike has been a road at some point, either for the construction and maintenance of the dike and culverts or as a Refuge public road open to motor vehicles. Roads that were closed recently to motor vehicles are good enough for biking. The older roads may be taken over by tall grass and low bushes in some areas but generally it is possible to walk on them.

- Ditch, approximately 30 feet wide and three to five feet deep; unfortunately, just deep enough to prevent wading across; very muddy bottom and populated by alligators, except along the barrier island; in certain areas at certain times the ditch can be fly-fished with success;

- Flooded marsh or, in other areas, mangrove right up to the inner edge of the ditch.

Note that there are only two impoundments with a pump in the territory covered in this book: one is at the southern end of L Pond Road; the other one is south of the Bio Lab Boat Ramp. The remaining impoundments of the lagoons—some dikes have been removed, see later—have culverts whose control mechanisms consist of a valve or a blockage of wood planks.

The flooding of the salt marsh prevents mosquito eggs from hatching. This also provides a high-quality habitat for ducks during their migration. The diked salt marshes of the lagoons are prized hunting grounds, complete with access roads and unimproved ramps that allow for the

---

[23] Source: Smithsonian Marine Station at Fort Pierce.

launch of boats in the ditch inside the marsh. Some of these access roads can be used by waders to access the lagoons or to fish the ditches and the ramps can be used to launch carry-on crafts to fish the ditch or to paddle to spots that allow for the transport of the craft over the dike to the lagoons.

This is the story of the dikes, and several are still in operation. They were a major hit on the ecosystem of the lagoons. The fish adapted to this environment over the years and some spots inside the dike were nothing short of fantastic during the winter. Some are still good, particularly for juvenile Tarpon. In some places and at certain times the gushing of lagoon water through the culverts in rising water is a magnet for fish living in the ditch inside the impoundments. These prime fishing spots are accessible on foot.

Although impoundments are effective in controlling mosquitoes there are serious ecological problems with them:

- Degradation in water quality inside the dike; actually fish are sometimes dying in the summer for lack of oxygen in an artificial environment that is no longer connected with the normal mixing and oxygenation in the lagoons;

- Isolation of several fish and other species from their normal nursery habitat; according to biologists from the St. Johns River Water Management District, the biomass being generated in those areas where the dike was removed is several times larger than it was before removal of the dike;

- Interruption of nutrient flow from the marshes to the lagoons and vice versa; interruption of the natural cleaning function of the marshes;

- Unnaturally high water salinity is some areas and unnatural high and dry grounds allowing for plant species that should not be there;

- Unnatural low water salinity in other areas, allowing for the proliferation of alligators; now if you were not concerned by the other impacts, as a *wade* fly-fisher, you should be concerned by this one.

In the late 1990s, authorities[24] began to eliminate the dikes. The goal is to return parts of the lagoons to their original state. In the two lagoons covered in this book sections of dikes were recently removed at Eddy Creek and north of Parking Lot 13 (southeast end of Mosquito Lagoon–pages 119 and 123), at Grassy Point (east shore of North Indian River Lagoon–page 175) and south of Parking Lot 5 on Mosquito Lagoon (page 91), among others. This last area is of particular interest and illustrates best the impact of dike removal on the fishing and on the wade fly-fisher.

In the early part of the removal, starting just south of Parking Lot 5, you can observe that the former ditch was filled and that bays and creeks were widely reopened with just small segments of ditch left around the openings. The Trout Hole (page 91) and the Black Hole (page 97 and illustration next) are, in my opinion, successful restorations and the fishing success attests to that.

As work progressed from north to south there was gradually less removal of the dike and less filling of the former ditch. Long sections of half-filled ditch were left. South of Bay of Two Islands (page 101) instead of restoring the entire opening at the bays and creeks, the operator simply cut through a narrow channel. An opportunity to give back to nature or even to improve upon it was lost.

---

[24] I use "authorities" as a generic word for the staggering number of public bodies involved with the lagoons in one way or another: St. Johns River Water Management District, Volusia County Mosquito Control, Canaveral National Seashore, Merritt Island National Wildlife Refuge, U.S. Fish and Wildlife Service, Florida Fish and Wildlife Conservation Commission, Florida Department of Environmental Protection's Office of Coastal and Aquatic Managed Areas (East Central Aquatic Preserve Field Office), Environmental Protection Agency, NASA, just to name a few.

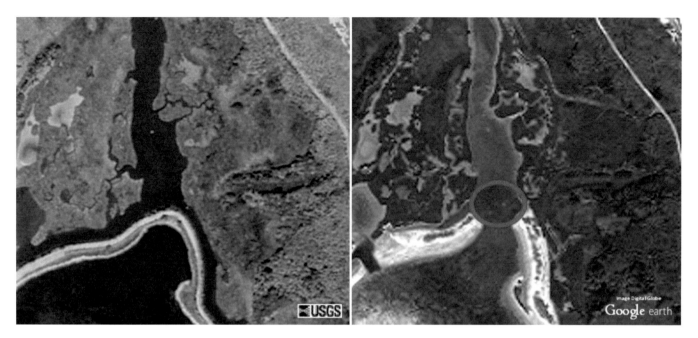

A good illustration of successful dike removal is the entrance to the Black Hole, on Mosquito Lagoon from Parking Lot 5 of Canaveral National Seashore. The left aerial photograph was taken before the removal of the dike. The right aerial photograph was taken after the removal of the dike. The spot circled in red at the entrance of the bay on the right photo is the old ditch: deep water, soft bottom and one good holding spot for fish.

The aerial photos show the old ditch at the entrance of a typical bay—here the Black Hole—where dikes were removed. When wading from open water to shore in an area where the dike has been removed **remember that you will cross the old ditch**, which may be only partly filled back; you will find deeper water as well as a very soft bottom. Be careful. If you begin to sink in black mud in water above your thighs, back off immediately. As these new environments mature and acquire more bio-diversity and as the fish adapt to these new environments, new fishing spots may appear.

You may also notice that some small ditches were dug in the flood plains: the purpose of these is to harbor small fish that will eat mosquito eggs and larvae. This alternative method of mosquito control has minimal impact on nature; it works and is the preferred one these days. When you encounter these ditches, have no fear in crossing them. Usually, you can walk right in and find a firm bottom. (Usually… You may wish to check it out before.)

Sinking and Channel Crossing

There is no reason to worry about sink holes in much of the wading territory: follow instructions on a few channel crossings. Generally, there will be black mud along the shore among trees and stumps. You will sink one foot (or deeper depending on your weight) and this is harmless. If you sink more, consider going around and trying another approach.

Despite all elementary precautions you may accidentally hit a soft spot, either on shore or in water close to shore. Step back quickly. In the worst case, fall back and crawl or paddle away. Do not insist and be fooled by the proximity of shore: the closer to shore, the deeper you will sink. All soft spots are along the shore, around islands, in the old channels, in recently back-filled areas and other places, most often where man has interfered with nature. There are no mud holes on the flats. Mud holes are, to some extent, part of the urban legend. We like to boost of having survived such dangerous perils. There is most likely less than one percent truth to it. That being said, I have been scared a few times. Given the extensive exploration that I did, alone in uncharted territory, it was bound to happen. Be careful and you will be safe.

As a rule, aside from the cold winter days, you should be *in* the water before sunrise. The Refuge is theoretically open at sunrise. Since there are no gates or control in the morning, you can get in as early as you want (you cannot stay overnight). Canaveral National Seashore opens at 6:00 AM. Be at the admission gate five minutes before six. Unless you have an annual pass, the entrance fee is $5.00 per vehicle (all fees and regulations are as of this writing) and $35.00 per vehicle for an annual pass that gives access to the two Park districts and the four fee areas of the Refuge: Beacon 42 Boat Ramp, Bairs Cove Boat Ramp, Bio Lab Boat Ramp and Black Point Wildlife Drive; remember to ask for the mirror-hang tag. Consider the cost of the annual pass the bargain of the century.

Be on the fishing grounds, actually in the water, before sunrise if possible. The early-morning feed on the flats, often close to the shoreline, will generally last until one hour after sunrise. This is heaven on earth for the fly-fisher and you will likely see more fish in this period than during the rest of the day, however long you make it. Exceptions to this are overcast days when the fish may continue feeding and the coldest days of the winter. Indeed, when the water temperature plunges into the fifties fish can be sullen in the morning and only come alive when the sun warms up the water in the afternoon.

Often mornings will be calm, with the wind starting to pick up around nine or ten. By twelve there is often a 10- to 15-MPH wind. The fish may have left the flats or may still be there and eating, but you will no longer be able to see them, let alone give them a good cast. In this situation you may consider working a few deeper spots and white spots, blind casting with the wind at your back. The wind seldom calms down early enough in late afternoon to allow for the typical evening fishing session that is so cherished in the North.

The Refuge closes at sunset. Again, since there are no gates and few controls, you may consider leaving on your own terms, within reason. The Park *gates* close at 6:00 PM. Closing has been delayed to 8:00 PM during Daylight Savings Time in the past but not as of this writing. You must check this in advance. In both districts, allow 15 to 20 minutes driving time from the most removed parking areas to the gates. Do not speed, for consideration of wildlife and your wallet. The rangers take pictures.

In the Refuge parking is not a problem. In the Park parking is restricted to the designated spots and fills quickly in season and on weekends. This is one more reason to get there early. If you carry a car-top craft, get a permit at the admission booth and you will be able to park in the ramp areas, even if the regular parking lot is full. These car-top permits are limited, first come, first serve. They will ask you to leave your driver's license at the admission booth, to be given back to you upon your return. Check the admission booth closing time, which may be earlier than the gate closing time. On the other hand, if you have a light boat or canoe on a trailer, no permit is required and you can still park in the ramp areas even if the regular parking is full and all of the car-top permits have been handed out. On weekends when the weather is nice, carrying a canoe, kayak or light boat on a trailer may be the only way to get into the Park if you are not an early bird. Once at the ramp do not leave your craft on the trailer… That would be pushing your luck.

Fishing Licenses and Regulations

If you are a Florida resident, aged between 16 and 64 inclusive you need a no-cost[25] saltwater shoreline fishing license. The rules are: you must fish from shore (or from a structure attached to land) and this includes wading. However, fishing from a boat, a carry-on craft or reaching the fishing grounds in any vessel, you need a Florida resident saltwater fishing license. As of this writing the cost is $17.00 per annum, plus a small handling charge if you are buying by phone or on the Internet. There is a five-year license at the cost of $79.00. No license is required until age 16. Any resident 65 years or older can obtain a no-cost license from any tax collector's office.

If you are not a Florida resident, you need a Florida non-resident saltwater fishing license. There is no exemption if you are 65 or older, but there is an exemption until age 16. As of this writing the cost for one year is $47.00, the cost for seven days is $30.00 and the cost for three days is $17.00, plus a small handling charge if you are buying by phone or on the Internet.[26] In all cases if you keep Snook (see the very stringent regulation below) you must have a Snook tag that costs $10.00 ($50.00 for a five-year license).

Everybody can fish without a license on Florida Free Fishing Days. For saltwater fishes these were the first Saturday and Sunday in June, the first Saturday in September, and the Saturday following Thanksgiving, as of this writing. Residents and non-residents do not need a saltwater fishing license when fishing from a licensed charter boat.

You are allowed to keep:

- One Red Drum between 18 and 27 inches;

- Four Spotted Seatrout between 15 and 20 inches, including one above 20 inches;[27]

- Five Black Drum between 14 and 24 inches, including one above 24 inches;

- Ten Flounder above 12 inches;

- Ten Bluefish above 12 inches, measured at the fork of the tail;

- One Snook between 28 and 32 inches; out of season from December 15 to January 31 and from June 1 to August 31. Check the regulations on this one: following the cold-weather-related fish kill of 2010, Snook was off-limit for one complete season. The closing was extended into 2013 on the West Coast but lifted on the East Coast. There may be more of this in the future.

No Tarpon can be harvested and any Tarpon longer than 40 inches must be released in the water; one Tarpon per year can be harvested with a $50.00 tag and only for the purpose of a potential IGFA record.

All measurements are to the *tip* of the tail unless otherwise specified (Tarpon, Bluefish). Regulations dictate that you have to *compress or squeeze the tail* to measure a fish when the regulations call for "tip of tail" measurement. This way of measuring fish will add approximately one

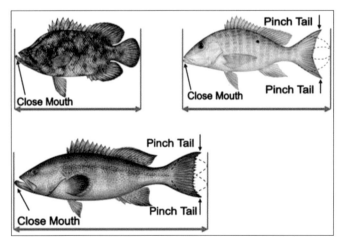

Most fish of the lagoon must be measured to the tip of the tail. Image from Florida Fish and Wildlife Conservation Commission.

---

[25] Buying your license by phone or on the Internet involves a small handling fee.
[26] There are a few more specific exemptions; see the web site of Florida Fish and Wildlife Conservation Commission at http://myfwc.com/fishing (as of this writing).
[27] For years Spotted Seatrout was out of season in November and December; trout is now open year round.

inch to the larger redfish and cause the release of a significant number of them. Indeed, we all know that the redfish in our lagoons were genetically modified years ago to measure exactly 27 inches (the legal limit) during a long stage of their lives under the previous regulations… Until evolution works its course again (according to Darwin), all these fish now measure exactly 28 inches and have to be released!

These fish are all excellent to eat. Keeping one fish is often enough food for the entire family. Keep your fish alive all day on a plastic chain that you will drag behind you. (Not in alligator territory, please.) Be careful with a trout, which is very delicate despite its ferocious look. Fish must be kept alive. If it dies it has to be on ice within one hour. Catch and release becomes very practical and is the sporting way to play with these wonderful partners.

You are not allowed to fillet a fish in the Park. There is a rudimentary fish-cleaning table at the County Boat Ramp in the North District of Canaveral National Seashore. As of this writing this was the only one in the territory covered in this book. There is no running water, so bring a bucket.

Pole and Troll Zone

Since 2006, the use of motors is prohibited in that part of Mosquito Lagoon that also happens to be our best wading territory. The restricted area matches Tiger Shoals. It lies south of Parking

Lot 5 of Canaveral National Seashore and extends south past Preachers Island. It is marked by buoys. Two running lanes allow boats to motor in from the deep water. The running lanes are marked and restricted to boats drawing less than twelve inches of water. Inside the Pole and Troll Zone (and off the running lane) all gas motors must be shut off. Electric motors are allowed. A much smaller area at the WSEG boat ramp is similarly restricted to motors, with the running lane matching the only navigable channel from the ramp to open water.

The Pole and Troll Zone was established to protect the sea grass and to improve the fishing experience. No more motoring over the skinny water to bump up the fish and disrupt our stealth approaches. This is excellent for waders and boaters alike and benefits the entire fishery. The one side effect is that there is some increase in the traffic in the areas remaining open to motors.

You may witness cheaters. Take a picture of the offending boat on power, enlarge the tag on any photo editing application, and send it to the Park/Refuge authorities with a few details such as date, time of day, location, etc. While charges are unlikely to follow, warnings may be just as effective. In fact, just pointing that camera sends a powerful signal to the offender.

Controlled Burns

Nature has its own way of controlling the density of the underbrush. Every so often lightning starts a wild fire and burns the place to the ground. To prevent those catastrophic events (from man's point of view) man used to put out the brush fires at their early stages. The unintended consequence was the buildup of combustible material resulting in the next fire to be of catastrophic proportions. Besides, the Florida scrub-jay, a bird on the list of threatened federal species, needs burned underbrush to exist. A better solution was found and is in practice today: the management of the underbrush by controlled burns. The idea is to burn small, defined areas of the Refuge periodically before an excessive amount of combustible material builds up. Firefighters working with helicopters and specialized equipment do this regularly in the winter. Most of the times the main access roads remain open, but traffic may be delayed a bit because of the smoke. Side roads will be closed in the areas of the controlled burns and you may be denied access to your fishing

destination on this day. If you happen to be very early and reached your fishing destination before the burn, you will likely be signaled by helicopter or otherwise to leave the area. They will find you. In any case those controlled burns involve small areas and the fire runs out or is put out at the end of the day. I have been there before, during, and after these burns and never experienced anything more than minor delays, and I have yet to hear of injuries or serious threat to people's lives.

This smoke is from a controlled burn near the Old Haulover Canal. The return trip may be delayed a bit.

Closures for Launches

Since the end of the space shuttle program the Park and the Refuge no longer close for the launches at Cape Canaveral. This may change in the future as the space program evolves. Check on the NASA web site and time your visit with one of the scheduled launches. If you time it right and are lucky you may have a front-row seat to one of those spectacular events. And you can keep fishing. There is an urban legend about fish feeding right after the launch on buried critters dislodged by the vibration. Good if it ever happens to you.

Security

It is unlikely to happen if you have read this book and followed the instructions, but you may need help while in the Park or in the Refuge.

Kayak fishing with NASA launch pads in the backdrop. In the south end of Mosquito Lagoon you have a front-row seat.

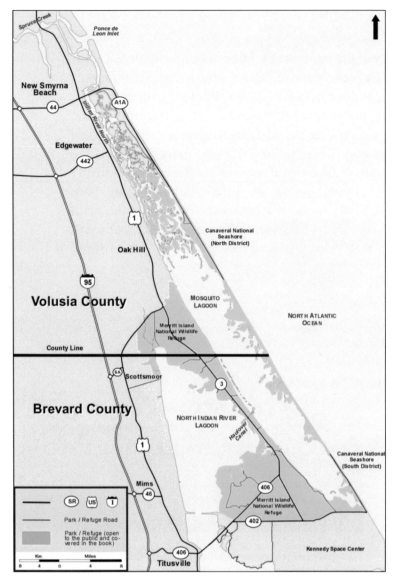

For non-emergency matters during normal business hours call the Park Visitors Center at (386) 428-3384; if you are in the Refuge call (321) 861-0667. For emergency assistance at any time, dial 911 **AND** specify whether you are in Volusia County or in Brevard County. In the Park the North District is in Volusia; the South District is in Brevard. In the Refuge the county line is at the WSEG Boat Ramp on Mosquito Lagoon and at the mouth of Turnbull Creek in North Indian River Lagoon. (See map). You must then indicate your position by referring to official and known locations, such as Parking Lot 5 of the North District of Canaveral National Seashore—if that is where you are. (Nobody but the readers of this book and members of the Mid-Coast Flyfishers may know some of the names in this book.) You must also specify whether your exact location is accessible by boat (depending on water level), by ATV, by airboat, or even by helicopter. All these emergency transportations are available from the Counties or from the Park and Refuge.

Wildlife

Canaveral National Seashore and Merritt Island National Wildlife Refuge are a paradise for birds. Over 310 species have been reported. Water birds are particularly abundant. You will certainly see ospreys diving on mullet from hundreds of feet high, brown pelicans smashing on them from a few feet above the water, and white pelicans fishing while swimming in great numbers.[28]

You cannot miss the ospreys. Like you, they are fishing and (maybe not quite like you…) they are catching. The osprey (*Pandion haliaetus*) is a large, hawk-like bird that is commonly found along the coast. It reaches a length of approximately 22 inches, with a 54-inch wingspan. The beak is short and hooked. Body color is black or dark brown over the back and upper wings, with a broad black stripe running from the nape of the neck through the eye. The crown is white, as is the throat, breast underbelly, and legs. The tail is brown, banded with white. The feet have

[28] Main source Smithsonian Institute.

large, sharply hooked talons. In flight, the wings are distinctly kinked at the elbow. The kinked wings and the white underbelly help differentiate ospreys from bald eagles, which have straight wings and black bodies. When hunting for fish, the osprey spots its prey from the air, hovers over it and then dives, talons first, to snatch it up, much like a bald eagle would. You have seen it before and you will see it a lot in the lagoons. I never tire of watching it.

The brown pelican (*Pelecanus occidentalis*) is a large shore-bird that reaches a length of approximately 40 inches, with a wingspan of over 90 inches. The bill is long, with a bare throat pouch on the underside. Bill color is typically dark (bright yellow during breeding season). Body color is generally a dark silver-gray to brown, with a white neck and yellow crown. Immature birds are entirely dark brown. The brown pelican is listed as endangered throughout most of its range. However, it has been *delisted* due to recovery in Florida and Alabama. Brown pelicans are generally restricted to the coastal zone and are only rarely found in freshwater areas. They utilize beaches, estuaries and marshes for feeding. Nesting occurs in colonies in mangroves and other estuarine trees. When feeding brown pelicans spot prey fish from the air and make swift, plunging dives from 50 feet or more to capture their prey. However, in the shallow waters of the lagoon, you will mostly see them diving from a very low height. You will see many of them around when you wade. Inasmuch as they make quite a racket you should tolerate them because they are good indicators of baitfish and therefore of game fish.

White pelicans are particularly interesting. The American white pelican (*Pelecanus erythrorhynchos*—it pronounces as it spells…) is a large, white bird with black wing tips. It reaches approximately 50 inches in length and has a wingspan of over 100 inches. Larger specimens can

Osprey. Photo by John C. Gamble.

Brown pelican. Photo by John C. Gamble.

John C. Gamble, Wildlife Photographer

The author thanks his friend and fishing partner John C. Gamble for the superb photos of this section. John was a founding member of the Mid-Coast Flyfishers and is an amateur photographer as well as a seasoned fly-fisher. View his stunning recent work at http://johncgamblephotography.blogspot.ca/ (as of this writing).

White pelicans. Photo by John C. Gamble.

Feral hogs. Photo by John C. Gamble.

weigh up to 13 pounds and reach a wingspan of 9½ feet. The bill is long and orange, with a throat pouch on the underside. Primary and outer secondary feathers are black. The legs and feet are orange. They migrate in colonies from the interior of western Canada and the northwestern United States. They do not dive on fish as our resident brown pelicans do. Instead, they float on the surface, duck their heads into the water and scoop up fish. You will often see them flocking in great numbers on schools of baitfish, surrounding and disorienting their prey as they deliberately flap their wings and pummel the surface of the water. From a distance, this looks like a snow storm, racket added.

Among the other most likely bird species that you will see in the lagoon are herons, egrets and ibis, as well as the ubiquitous gulls, cormorants, and turkey vultures.

There are deer in the Park and in the Refuge. I have rarely seen them and when I did it was only from the road, never near the water. You will see rabbits, raccoons, turtles, river otters, etc. You may see feral hogs, or wild pigs. You will most likely hear them trashing the underbrush as they move out of your way. You will likely see their tracks on the road and on the soft ground along the shore. While they inhabit Florida, wild boars are unlikely visitors of the lagoons and you will be glad for it.

If you walk the truck road / Klondike Beach Trail off Parking Lot 5 of Canaveral National Seashore, you may see *my* bobcats (*Lynx rufus*). I could not tell at first whether this was always the same or different individuals. The answer came in the fall of 2004, as I met the two offspring. *My* bobcats are wild and wary animals. Still, they are curious and will take a good look at you before vanishing in the underbrush. You will have plenty of time to have a good look back—even take a picture if you carry a camera with a zoom—if you freeze on first sight. It is ironic that I spent a significant part of my life in the woods up North and never saw one. Here, I see them very often. Indeed, the walk on Klondike Beach Trail offers unique opportunities to see wildlife. Given the impenetrable underbrush, animals use the trail extensively.

Bugs, Snakes and Others

Mosquito Lagoon earned its name rightfully and North Indian River Lagoon is right along for mosquitoes. Mosquitoes will bite you. Have a good supply of insect repellent and you will not be bothered most of the time. Wading in the lagoons away from the shoreline there are no bugs. Occasionally conditions will become just right for the breeding of a bumper crop of mosquitoes. If you happen to walk at such a time you will need a head net and the most powerful repellent. And you will walk fast and be happy to reach your destination. Fortunately, these conditions do not develop often from fall to spring. Summer is a different story, as mosquitoes are often very numerous and very aggressive.

Bobcat. Photo by John C. Gamble.

There are dangerous snakes in the Park and Refuge, including the diamond-back rattlesnake. Hopefully you will never see them, let alone step on them. Be particularly attentive when walking the truck road / Klondike Beach Trail from Parking Lot 5 of Canaveral National Seashore. Snakes are sometimes encountered in those sections of the road where the tall grass has taken over. This is one more reason to opt for boot-foot waders, although gravel guards will also provide some form of protection. Keep a cell phone on you at all times, in a sealed plastic bag. The Park, the Refuge and the County are well equipped for rescue missions and they know about snakes in the emergency rooms of the private clinics and hospitals of the area.

Wade often enough and eventually you will step on a stingray and it will hit you with its dart. You may be lucky enough for your boot-foot waders to protect you. If not, it will hurt but you should be able to walk back. Since the venom is protein-based, soaking your leg in warm water will break down the venom and ease the pain. You need to go to a clinic or hospital to have the wound cleaned and get preventive shots.

I have never seen alligators in the North District of the Park and this is one good reason that I give this area a disproportionately large place in this book. Same with the South District of the Park: there should not be any alligator north of Eddy Creek (page 119). Note that big trout are called "Gators" but this is another story. Alligators are everywhere else in the Park and Refuge. Florida currently has one million of them and it is estimated that there are approximately 5,000 in the Park and Refuge…

Alligators kill *just* a few people every other year. Why I am not comforted? Urban legends aside, the real story is that these reptiles, which can reach an impressive size, are dormant or very slow during most of the winter. In late spring, which is mating season, and during the summer do not go wading around them. And do not assume that they will not come into salt water.

Alligators across the ditch along Bio Lab Road of Mosquito Lagoon. In the cold and low water of the winter, one can reasonably expect them to stay on "their" side. At any other time, one should be very careful, "my side" notwithstanding…

ALLIGATOR ATTACKS

As of November 2013, the latest available statistics as of this writing, 357 *unprovoked* attacks on humans have been documented in Florida since 1948, with 235 resulting in major injuries and 22 resulting in deaths (a 23rd death occurred in October 2015). Generally, people fishing have accounted for 10% of alligator attacks while people wading/walking in water accounted for an additional 5% of attacks. Simple arithmetic suggests that *wade* fly-*fishing* can be a dangerous sport in certain places at certain times…

Alligators are most active when temperatures are between 82°F to 92°F. They stop feeding when the ambient temperature drops below approximately 70°F and they become dormant below 55°F. Alligators are dormant throughout much of the winter season. During this time, they can be found in burrows (or "dens") that they construct adjacent to an alligator hole or open water, but they occasionally emerge to bask in the sun during spells of warm weather. Alligators can dive for up to two hours in exceptional circumstances; however, the normal dive lasts 15 minutes. The probabilities are for the fly-fisher to first see an alligator when it is lying on the bank. The gator is most likely to slide in the water and disappear. Observe attentively and you will likely see the eyes popping up within just a few minutes. Sometimes, the animal will observe you for hours. When in the deep water they can move around with total stealth.

Alligators breed in late May or early June. This is a period when male alligators can be aggressive. Later, in August and September, females guarding the nest become dangerous.

Female alligators rarely exceed nine feet in length, but males can grow much larger. Approximately 5% of all alligators reach a size of 12 feet. The Florida state record for length is a 14-foot, 5/8-inch male from Lake Monroe in Seminole County. Florida state record for weight is a 1,043-pound (13 feet, 10½ inches long) male from Orange Lake in Alachua County. Scary as they may be, super-sized beasts are not automatically the deadliest. Indeed, a significant number of deaths are caused by alligators measuring *only* between six and nine feet.

Sources: Florida Fish and Wildlife Conservation Commission;
Ricky L. Langley, MD, MPH. 2005. *Alligator Attacks on Humans in the United States*. Wilderness and Environmental Medicine, 16:119-124.

EQUIPMENT AND FLIES

Equipment

The fly rod must handle heavy fish and should be "fast action" or "tip-flex" for long, powerful casts. I will make an exception to this: those who struggle with *loading* a stiff rod should use a more flexible rod. It is better to enjoy the fishing and sacrifice some distance. The combination of rod and line must be heavy enough to allow for casting upwind. The minimum combination is a nine-foot seven-weight rod outfitted with an *eight*-weight weight-forward floating (WF-8-F) line. I think the optimum combination is 9-9-9 (9-foot rod, 9-weight, 9.0 flex on the Orvis[29] scale) if you can handle it. I have used a longer rod, useful when you are keeping low on the water. However, it has its drawbacks, and I find that few fly-fishers use a rod longer than nine feet. I now use a lighter seven-weight rod because years of casting have taken a toll on my arm and shoulders. In fact, this seven-weight rod is my default rod on everything salt or fresh water except on the small freshwater trout. While the seven-weight will easily handle big fish in the open water, restraining a fair-size Tarpon or Snook in tight quarters can be a bit of a challenge on anything less than a nine-weight rod. In all cases the fly rod must have a fighting butt.

The reel must have a solid drag system, be saltwater-proof, and contain as much backing as possible (minimum 100 yards). Tip: cut out the back 10 feet of the fly line and replace it with extra backing.

FROM FRESH TO SALT: FLY REELS

Salt water will destroy a reel unless it is specifically built to resist corrosion. If you plan to fish extensively in salt water, buy a saltwater reel. However, for the occasional trip, you may use a quality freshwater reel as long as it has the required specifications: a solid drag system and adequate line and backing capacity. Wash it in fresh water and lubricate it as often as possible. However, be aware that in the not-very-long run, some parts of your reel will most likely be affected.

The quality of rod and reel is not a significant factor as long as basic requirements are met. Top-of-the-line equipment will add to the enjoyment and will certainly be gentler on your arm and

---

[29] Founded by Charles F. Orvis in Manchester, Vermont in 1856, Orvis is America's oldest mail-order outfitter and longest continually-operating fly-fishing business. Privately owned by the Perkins family since 1965, today Orvis is an international, multi-channel retailer. In 2013 Orvis acquired Scientific Angler and Ross Reels from 3M Corporation. Orvis sporting services include fishing and shooting schools, an international sporting and eco-travel agency, and the Orvis-endorsed network of lodges, outfitters, and guides. The award-winning website offers more than 5,000 products and every fly shown or mentioned in this book can be entirely tied with Orvis fly-tying material and tools. Orvis donates 5% of pre-tax profits every year to protecting nature, supporting communities, and advancing canine health and well-being. With a unique matching grant program, Orvis and its customers have raised and donated more than $14 million to protecting nature over the past 25 years. Source: The Orvis Company Inc., www.orvis.com (as of this writing).

shoulders but will not make a significant difference in your rate of success. The line however should be of high quality; otherwise, it will deteriorate quickly in the salt water. There are other considerations as well. First and foremost, the line must be able to make long casts against the wind, which means a heavy, long belly and a relatively small diameter rear section. In addition, if you are going to fish the lagoons in the winter you will likely find cold water sometimes, and very cold conditions at times. A single-core monofilament tropical line will have *reel memory* in the cold water. It will coil, tangle, and make your life miserable. I use and enjoy Scientific Anglers' Mastery Series Saltwater Specialty Taper Floating line. This line has a braided multifilament core that is suppler, has less memory and achieves better floatability than the tropical lines of the same brand. The highest authorities at Scientific Angler recommended this line for winter use. However, the same line that does such a good job in the winter will not pass the test in the summer. You need a tropical line in the warm water and no line does both winter and summer fishing in the lagoons. The fly line must have a smooth fishing. In the salt water fishing is stripping, and the line will rub against your finger all day. Special textures and cracked fly lines will draw blood quickly.

In theory a sinking tip or intermediate line could be of some use when working the deeper spots. In practice it is not. Carrying an extra spool is adding weight and changing line every time you change environment is highly impractical.

FROM FRESH TO SALT: FLY LINES

Saltwater lines have a special coating that protects the line from salt water. If you plan to fish extensively in salt water, buy a saltwater line. However, for the occasional trip, your freshwater bass, salmon or steelhead line will do just fine, as long as it meets the minimal specifications: floating and weight forward. Just wash it in fresh water and clean it every day and before storing.

Leaders should be nine-foot, one-piece tapered, 12 to 15 pounds. While it is perfectly acceptable to build your own leader the more knots the more it will catch weeds. I never use the last two feet of the manufactured leader. No machine should be trusted to achieve a perfect 40-pound and 12-pound in the same length of material. I always attach a tippet. The leader-tippet combination should be 10 feet or more (I use 11 feet). Tippet should be the best material money can buy, minimum 12-pound test. And there should be some elasticity to the leader-tippet combination; otherwise you may break it on the hook set. The fluorocarbon leader-tippet combination 1X is an excellent choice. I will not re-stoke the debate between nylon and fluorocarbon. The more expensive fluorocarbon is a better material because it is less visible, more resistant, sinks quicker, and does not absorb water. However, fluorocarbon tends to slip more at the knots and I find that it sometimes breaks without cause. The best quality nylon leader-tippet is a combination that works for me and any high-quality brand will work for you. I strongly recommend using glue on the knots.

FROM FRESH TO SALT: LEADERS

Saltwater leaders are no different and serve exactly the same functions as freshwater leaders. Rigidity is important, the leader must be invisible to fish, of course, and be long enough for the fish not to see the fly line. None of this is specific to salt water; all of this applies to any fishery where the fish are big and spooky.

You need waders. Wet wading is rarely an option. The water can be surprisingly cold in the winter, mud will sneak inside your shoes and there is the danger of stepping on the ubiquitous stingray. Waders must be chest-height to allow you to get down and hide. And they must be breathable for obvious reasons; neoprene is not an option. You will tear your waders every so often when walking around the stumps and in the low bushes, which you will have to do. The compromise on price *vs.* comfort is all yours. The boot-foot type prevents infiltration of mud and sand between boot and stocking foot and offers some protection against stingray in the water and snakes on the ground. It works for me and I will not wear anything else if I can help it, but not for some of my heavier friends who claim that they will sometimes tear boots trying to pull them out of the mud. If you go with the boot-foot type of wader the boot must be tight with your foot to resist the suction of the mud. If you go with wading shoes, they must have an excellent guard to prevent the mud and gravel from infiltrating between the shoe and the sock. And you will not have the same protection against stingray and snakes. Felt soles are optional and will give you a slightly greater foot base in the mud, more so if the entire sole is flat. Spikes are useless. Felt-sole boot-foot non-neoprene breathable waders are increasingly difficult to find and increasingly expensive. As of this writing you could still find one model at the leading outfitters.

Everything has to be carried and will remain on your back all the time. Vests must be short so as to remain above water when you go down. I slip my rain / cold-weather jacket in the back pocket of my vest. All your gear must go in the vest or other packing device worn high. I use a belt pack, the type trekkers use, to carry drink, lunch, sunscreen, and insect repellent. All this stuff must be either waterproofed or be insensitive to water since it will be under water regularly when you get down to hide from fish. You may not need it, but it would be wise to carry a head net for protection against mosquitoes while walking to the fishing spots.

A scoop net is a great asset, especially if you are planning to keep fish or to take the picture of a lifetime. It does its primary purpose. It also provides the much-needed third (or fourth) hand required for putting a fish on leash when away from shore. A medium-size wading scoop net with a magnet will do, the lighter the better. Size is not critical: as long as the head and two-thirds of the body of the fish get into the net, this is sufficient. You will not fit a very big red in a net if you catch one anyway.

A stripping basket is a great asset and, for me, better if it is folding. I use it for its primary purpose only occasionally. Indeed, I find that it hinders my stripping. Most of the time I am happy using it as a resting-place for the reel when changing fly or handling a fish. When not required, my basket folds back on my waist and disappears—not really: it looks like a girdle, but who cares. One pull at the Velcro strap and it springs back to shape, ready for use. Others prefer the non-folding type. They are much more efficient; however, this is like carrying a kitchen sink all day. And it may be a nuisance when you go down on your knees to hide from fish. While excellent stripping baskets are readily available finding the folding type is a challenge.

If you plan to keep a fish you need a plastic stringer to keep it alive and in tow while you continue to fish. On a big fish that you intend to keep, use two hooks. And do not for one moment consider wading in alligator areas with a fish in tow on a stringer…

The dress code varies immensely with the weather. Avoid any bright color: it really makes a difference for the fish to see you. In the coldest days of the winter you will need winter underwear. Trust me. In every season, you must protect your skin against the sun.

The subject of flies is a never-ending debate. We all have this miracle-doer that will not fail us… until it does. After buying and tying hundreds of different flies—actually using much less—I have come up with the following simplification.

Reds and trout eat shrimp, crab, and baitfish, depending on the season, availability, and *opportunity*. All fish are opportunistic. I use only a few flies and most of the time my choice of the fly is not dictated by the food to imitate but by the *fishing conditions*: how deep is the water; how much water there is above the grass; what is the nature of the bottom, etc. (I also tend to be lazy and fish with yesterday's fly, as it so conveniently comes readily tied on my tippet… but this should not be a consideration.) Most classic saltwater patterns are effective in the lagoons and the choice will largely be dictated by the conditions at the time of your visit.

Agent Orange. A very light shrimp pattern.

In very shallow, grassy areas, where the fish are spooky and where any weighed fly would immediately catch grass use little unweighed flies such as an Agent Orange as a shrimp pattern, or a Bucktail Deceiver as a baitfish pattern, in size six or even smaller. The Agent Orange is an old classic developed by Winston Moore for bonefish at a time when there were no flies used with such bold colors. The Bucktail Deceiver is Lefty Kreh's version of the classic deceiver. Entirely made of bucktail this is one of very few baitfish patterns that will swim in very shallow water. It has proven fantastic for me on redfish chasing finger mullet on the shallow flats in early spring.

Lefty Kreh's Bucktail Deceiver. A very light baitfish pattern.

In slightly deeper water, say up to 18 inches, I use a McVay's Gotcha as a shrimp pattern, either with the light tan wing of the original version or with the orange wing. The man responsible for the creation of the Gotcha is Jim McVay, a retired oil driller who claims to have caught several thousand bonefish on it in the Andros Island group. This fly swims on its back and, with the bead chain eyes, it will sink moderately. It will dive much deeper with heavier eyes. This fly casts well, lands relatively quietly (with the bead chain eyes), swims well, and will catch reds, trout *and* blacks (with the orange wing). I even use it extensively, in smaller sizes of course, on American Shad in the St. Johns River. If there is an all-around fly, this is the one.

Another one of my favorite all-around flies is the Kwan. Miamian Patrick Dorsey originated this fly for bonefish and trade-marked it Dorsy's Kwan Fly—thus contributing to the misspelling of his name forever. The Kwan was originally developed to imitate the blennies and gobies of the Florida Keys and the pattern was immediately successful on bonefish. Soon, it was tried by anglers elsewhere and proven effective for every species of shallow-water game fish. Kwans are now tied for, and widely used on redfish everywhere, including in the lagoons. For some of my fishing friends this is the go-to fly on any fish and I have seen it successfully

McVay's Gotcha. An all-around fly.

catching Tarpon, trout, reds and blacks. I use it in all kinds of situations, including on trout. Many a fly tier takes liberties with the pattern and you will find Kwans in many shapes, colors and sizes. I favor the classic pattern of brown, white (natural or beige) and tan, with or without eyes, bead chain eyes as well as lead ones. I will use a Kwan in any water where I can make it swim. This fly will dive naturally and with bead chain eyes or without eyes it can be just dropped near a fish, without stripping.

Kwans swim with the hook down and therefore catch grass. I cannot use them everywhere I would like. The no-eye version will stay higher in the water, but will catch grass if it sees any. I have tried the heavier eyes for deeper water and found that if you tied the eyes *under* the hook it swims as intended. The chartreuse version also works well and, according to my kayaking friend Dalen, has saved the day a few times. I have tried the version with legs and found that the legs add nothing to the effectiveness of the fly. Others, in other environments or circumstances, may draw a different conclusion. I have tried the Kwan with a weed guard and found that the fly catches grass anyway, and keeps it once it has it. The shape of the fly makes it prone to catch grass both at the hook *and* at the eyes. Again, others may have had a different experience.

Patrick Dorsey's Kwan.

The Kwan does not cast very well. It catches the wind and kites. You have to watch for the tail not to wrap around the hook (even if it is tied correctly) and you have to straighten the body and eyes occasionally. It is not the easiest fly to fish with, but it is deadly on reds *and trout* and I will use it whenever I can. Strip it in short bursts, sometimes (when you can) allowing it to fall to the bottom. In the very clear, low water of the winter, when the fish become very spooky, make sure the Kwan that you are using offers a small profile, both from the body and the tail. I have had big fish bolting from the sight of a size-four Kwan. In the winter, I will sometimes switch to a size-eight Kwan…

For a baitfish pattern in medium-depth water I find the Clouser Minnow to be a very effective pattern on trout, redfish as well as Snook and Tarpon. Developed by renowned author and fly-fishing expert Bob Clouser of Pennsylvania this multi-use fly has become a classic and is shown to fish of all stripes everywhere. Since this fly swims on its back snags are reduced to a minimum. I tie it with bead chain eyes and my preferred color is a dash of natural-brown bucktail (from the top of the tail) over white. I have had days when trout destroyed several of these flies. This fly has become my go-to pattern in much of my winter fishing in the salt as well as on freshwater bass. And I know at least one guide who uses only this fly. If the water is not clear you may have a better luck with darker colors, such as black and purple.

My own sparsely tied Clouser Minnow in size six seems to catch everything, including juvenile Tarpon.

I use Borski's Bonefish Sliders in deep water (more than two feet), in mud holes and in white spots as a mud-minnow imitation— among others, you have to ask the fish—the saltwater equivalent to the freshwater Muddler Minnow. Well-known Florida Keys resident Tim Borski designed this bonefish fly as an imitation of a goby or other small fish that dwell on the flats. I use it with yellow-painted lead eyes for a quick sink, a puff when it hits the bottom, and a small trail of smoke as it slides upside-down in the mud or sand. It can also be tied with lighter eyes such as epoxy with silver

Borski's Bonefish Slider.

casing. I believe it must be tied with eyes, for both the look and the swim. Same as for the Kwan, I favor a small profile in the clear and shallow water since I had big reds bolt at the unexpected sight of a Borski's Bonefish Slider. This fly is also very effective on freshwater bass.

Fly-fishing in salt water is relatively new and most of the flies were developed for fishing bonefish in the sandy flats of the Florida Keys. A fly sliding on its back on the sandy bottom among the sparse grass (where there is any) will remain relatively clean and will be spotted by fish some distance away. The lagoons are not like that. Many of our most productive areas are in effect the exact opposite of the clean flats of the Keys: so thick with grass that, at times, it is almost unfishable. Picture nine inches of thick grass covered with four to nine inches of water, depending on the season, and you have fish Nirvana and… angler Hell. In this perfect *tailing* environment, swimming a clean fly is almost impossible. Placing it within the very limited range of vision of a tailing red without spooking it is even less probable. To make it even more difficult on the fly-fisher, when the water level fluctuates, dead grass will float on top and some will even suspend in the water column. I have seen days when you could not strip a fly six inches without catching a clump of salad…

Brown Bang suspender. Hackle, bucktail, and spun deer hair on a fine-wire hook. The name is from a similar fly developed by my friend Fred Althouse. In the suspender *version it floats until moved. Do not call Orvis for it…*

Something had to be done. I came up with a line of "suspender" flies. The idea was to have a fly that I could cast near the tailing reds, leave it floating while the reds are slowly moving closer, and turn it into an escaping baitfish when a redfish comes within sight, all that time remaining free of grass. The fly had to be small and still big enough to be visible, stay on top like a dry fly until moved, and finally swim just inches below the surface. It would not hurt if it could resemble a baitfish or a shrimp and look edible. These flies work… sometimes. Indeed, they are good at avoiding the bottom grass, but ineffective against the floating and suspended grass. Second, while the fly is swimming high in the water column, tailing reds are looking down in the grass. Sometimes they only see the fly when it is too close and they spook. Sometimes they do not see it at all. Finally, tailing reds are looking for crab and other creeping bugs, not for baitfish, and will sometimes simply ignore this questionable baitfish imitation. The "suspender" may not work all the time, but at times it is the only fly that I can use.

I tie a close relative of the suspender for Tarpon. The head is a little bigger to push more water and the tail is limper. Tied on a very light hook, this *quasi-popper* floats on landing, pops on the first few strips, and swims just under the surface film. Although Tarpon theory suggests that all-white should work best, I have better success with light brown grizzly tail and rust brown head. Tarpon have a mind of their own and I will not try to educate them.

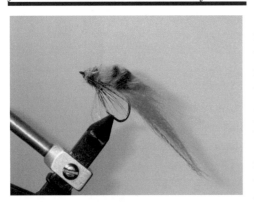

The author's own craft-fur shrimp is a very light and realistic shrimp imitation for the low and crystal-clear water of the winter.

In the low and crystal-clear water of the winter big fish roaming the flats of the lagoons become very spooky, more so if they are schooled up. I developed my own craft-fur shrimp[30] a few years ago as a realistic shrimp pattern that would land as softly as a feather and swim above the grass in inches of water. Snook and Tarpon in the creeks have hit it as well. Smaller, much smaller versions have also been successful on reds schooling or tailing and

---

[30] Tim Borski, renowned fly tier and painter, has trademarked a Fur Shrimp that is often called Craft Fur Shrimp; Lefty Kreh, a fly-fishing legend, also ties a Craft Fur Shrimp; these are excellent flies and I am not trying to steal the name; my fly is simply a shrimp imitation made of stacked craft fur and underfur with a head of spun deer hair.

refusing larger flies. This fly has no flash and no weight. On the first cast the dry craft-fur shrimp will suspend until moved. Once water logged it will sink at a slow rate. One main attraction is the slight wiggling of the tail even in the slowest of movements. This is often my default fly in the winter.

I always carry a gurgler in my fly box for *emergencies*. I have successfully used the improbable gurgler on reds working the shoreline in inches of water where no other fly would go. Given the position of their mouth, it is not natural for reds to eat looking up. However, in inches of water, this is much less a consideration.

And there is the spoon fly. There is some controversy surrounding the half-fly half-lure spoon fly. If you tried to cast some of them upwind, you probably have already settled the issue by promptly *throwing* it downwind as far as you could, no line attached… I am sorry to say, but sometimes redfish will not eat anything but a spoon. The only spoon fly that I use is John Cave's Wobbler. I will sometimes use it in a small gold Mylar version in white spots and deep spots.

Spotted Seatrout is a predator that will eat anything that it can get when it is small. Typically these fish are loosely grouped in similar sizes in deep-water spots. They will attack anything at any time as long as it is shown to them deep enough. Any fly with solid eyes that you cast, let sink to the bottom and retrieve in quick strips will catch these small trout… and will get destroyed.

A big trout is a different animal. It is a top predator that will keep to the slightly deeper spots of the flats. It is a fish eater and it will eat surprisingly big prey. In theory large flies make sense on these fish, and I have used some in the past with relative success. Still, my regular flies are size four and six—and increasingly even smaller. Although I do not deny the trout's natural inclination for a bigger bite I use the same flies on reds and big trout since they often cohabit. The smaller hooks of size four and six make the fly lighter, allowing a better presentation and, when tied without eyes, some of them swim above the grass. I would not hesitate to use size-two hooks in deep water, on Spotted Seatrout, Snook, and Tarpon. However, in very shallow water I find that a large fly will sometimes intimidate even a big red. Smaller hooks unfortunately increase your chances of bites without hook sets.

I have had days when big trout would only hit a red and white Seaducer. Go figure. I always keep one or two of the weird-looking baitfish imitations in the fly box for *emergencies*. It is also an excellent pattern for Tarpon and Snook and I have watched redfish eating it with gusto as well.

Seaducer.

Finally, have some fun and use a gurgler or a popper on trout. Contrary to poppers cast to Bass, Pike and Pickerel, the landing splash of a popper may not work for you here (gurglers land more quietly). While small trout in deep water will be attracted by the surface sound, big trout in skinny water may bolt at anything falling from the sky. But get the gurgler or popper to cross over the hiding spot of a big trout and watch the explosion. Contrary to Red and Black drums, the mouth of the Spotted Seatrout is adapted to attack a surface prey.

Black Drum is the oddball for flies. As a rule, to be broken anytime, Black Drum do not chase food. While they will jump at the opportunity of eating a shrimp or even a baitfish that does not escape fast enough Black Drum are typically bottom grazers. A weighed crab pattern stripped slowly on the bottom is the key. While using a *black* fly on *Black* Drum sounds like an urban legend there is proven merit in using dark colors. Most classic crab patterns will do and I will often use a Redfish Toad that will also catch redfish. Strangely, the orange-wing McVay's Gotcha is also very effective on Black Drum, which again makes it an excellent all-around fly.

Snook are a baitfish eater and I find that any trout fly will catch Snook, the better if it swims on top and is retrieved quickly. Tarpon is a fussy animal. As the top predator in the area that they colonize juvenile Tarpon eat baitfish almost exclusively, but only if and when they decide to do so. A top-water fly that pushes water seems to get their attention when the water is warm and the fish more aggressive. My experience in the colder water of late fall and early spring is different. The deeper the fly the better; the quicker the strip the better; and, hear this, the *smaller* the fly the better... Again, the Clouser Minnow in white and natural brown is a very effective baitfish imitation. For juvenile Tarpon, I tie them in size *10* with brass eyes on a size-six Mosquito hook, the same as my Shad flies.

Aside from the special situations and special fish, such as Tarpon above, I think any fly that decently imitates a shrimp, a crab or a baitfish will catch fish in the lagoons, as long as it swims well and is well presented. The weight of the fly is very important. In deep holes and in white spots, flies must be weighed because you want them down quickly. The puff of smoke that they make when they hit the bottom and the trail of smoke that they leave as they slide along the bottom are what you want. On the shallow flats use flies without eyes, with smaller bead chain eyes, or clip the eyes off. The ability of the fly to swim above the grass and remain clean becomes the most important criteria. I do not always use weed guards. Some weed guards may work better than others. I find that sometimes when the fly catches grass the weed guard keeps it on the hook. Without the weed guard the grass shakes loose most of the time with a false cast. Of course false casting makes noise and is for windy days only.

Unless you take the time to wash your flies in fresh water and dry them thoroughly every time never use a fly that has been used in salt water for more than a week. Breaking a corroded hook on the only fish of the day will break your heart.

PART II

WADE FLY FISHING AREAS OF THE LAGOONS

A Word on Maps

All the maps in this book are custom-traced from various sources. Mapping the lagoons is complicated. There is a very thin line between flooded marsh and the adjoining shallow grass flats. Consider that most of the wading territory has less than two feet of water at normal water levels. The water levels rise and drop during long periods, moving the shoreline, transforming fishing areas into wet pasture, only to cover it back with water again in the next season. Islands appear where there were none and become peninsulas until the water comes back up again. To further complicate matters men built dikes and then recently took some of them out, changing the shoreline each time. Therefore, the solid line that you see on my maps is a *rendering* of the approximate location where an inch of water over grass becomes shore mud in normal water level.

There are dirt roads and tracks everywhere in the Refuge. These serve a number of purposes, including access for the controlled burns, but most are closed to the public. Showing them on the maps would clutter them and serve no purpose. Indeed, the maps that I have drawn include the minimum for general orientation: the dominant shoreline, the major islands, the roads open to the public, etc. Do not use them for any other purpose than access to the fishing areas described in this book. And do not, ever, use these maps for navigation.

The aerial maps that I use as background of the large-scale detailed maps showing the fishing areas are recent, accurate and complete, but show the areas at a specific water level. You will likely visit the place in a different water level.

The Order of the Book

Coverage of the wade fly-fishing territory accessible on foot begins with the **northeast** part of **Mosquito Lagoon** situated in the North District of Canaveral National Seashore (the Park) off New Smyrna Beach. First covered is the area accessible from Parking Lot 5. Situated at the south end of the road Parking Lot 5 is your prime destination and is the focus of this book. The coverage is from north to south. (Lower arrow **1** on the map next; page 83 in the book.)

In the same chapter we cover the north end of the Park. This is a marginal subarea and is mostly an alternative when Parking Lot 5 is full. Coverage of the north subarea is from south to north, which is the natural return way from Parking Lot 5. (Upper arrow **1** on the map next; page 109 in the book.)

The second part of the territory covered is the **southeast** part of **Mosquito Lagoon** in the South District of Canaveral National Seashore. It goes from south to north, which is the natural way of entering the Park from Titusville or from Kennedy Parkway. (Arrow **2** on the map; page 115 in the book.)

The third part of the territory covered is the **southwest** part of **Mosquito Lagoon** that you access from side roads off Kennedy Parkway and from Bio Lab Road. This is in Merritt Island National Wildlife Refuge (the Refuge) and the coverage is from north to south. (Arrow **3** on the map; page 125 in the book.)

The fourth part of the territory covered is the entire **east shore of North Indian River Lagoon** from the Refuge. Coverage of this large area begins with the southernmost accessible areas off L Pond Road and progresses north along the east shore of the lagoon, first off Kennedy Parkway, later along Shiloh Marsh Road as one progresses toward the north. Turnbull Creek at the north end of North Indian River Lagoon is the last area covered in the book. (Arrow **4** on the map; page 149 in the book.)

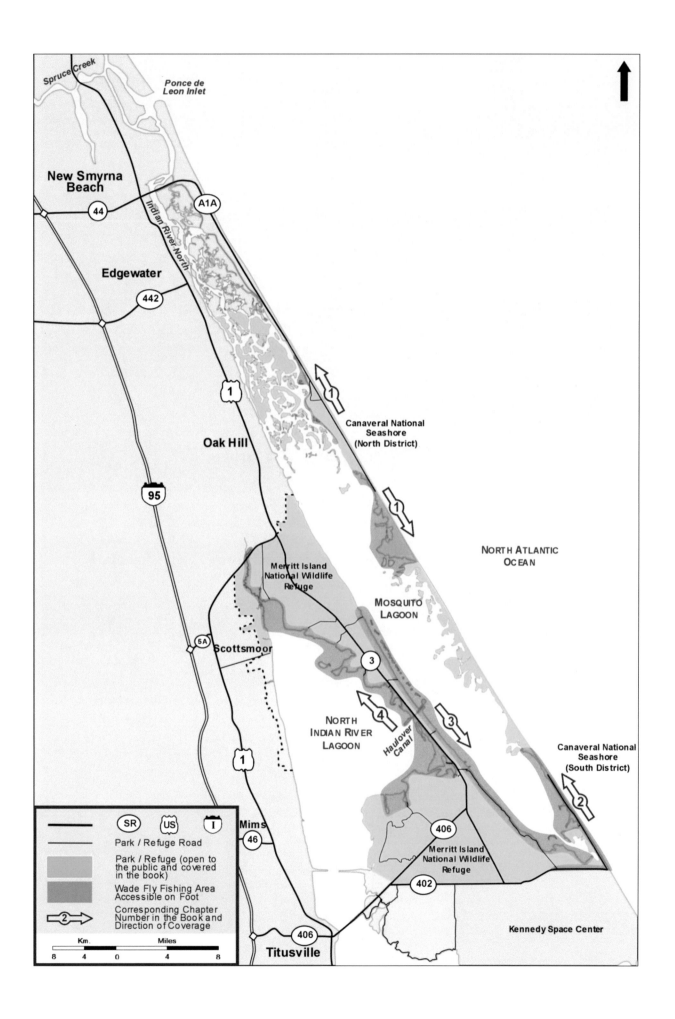

1 – NORTHEAST MOSQUITO LAGOON IN THE PARK

South of Bethune Beach[31] (an unincorporated community in Volusia County south of, and generally associated with, New Smyrna Beach) Mosquito Lagoon is in Canaveral National Seashore (the Park). Also called Apollo Beach, the North District of Canaveral National Seashore is off State Road A1A. Since this is one section of State Road A1A that dead ends, it gets relatively little traffic and many area visitors will miss it. Other visitors who make it to the Park gate are clearly lost... The locals know the place very well, either for its nude beach (south of Parking Lot 5), its steep beach that gives surf casters unique access to deep water, its busy County Boat Ramp, and its unrivalled access to Mosquito Lagoon off Parking Lot 5. Visitors will appreciate the uncrowded beaches, historic Eldora, access to nature and the interpretation activities of the Park.

The North and the South Districts of Canaveral National Seashore are contiguous in geography. The narrow 12-mile-long barrier island is not breached (as of this writing) and you can walk from one end to the other, in theory. In practice the North and the South Districts are separate and driving from one to the other involves a significant trip back to the mainland and around Mosquito Lagoon, and a rather confusing one. To reach the South District you must first drive through Merritt Island National Wildlife Refuge, with its own Visitors Center, security and maintenance headquarters. By necessity the North District has evolved as a semi-autonomous entity with its own self-contained facilities.

The County Boat Ramp is situated inside the Park, meaning past the admission booth but before the gate that is closed at night; therefore, it remains accessible before and after Park hours. The parking is reserved for boat trailers. Vehicles without trailers can park at Parking Lot 1 across the road (but access to the beach is not allowed after Park hours). The short section of State Road A1A just before the Park guard booth is posted as no parking. The Visitors Center is situated three-quarters of a mile south of the Park entrance.

Parking Lot 5 of the North District—the reader will understand that all parking numbers in this chapter refer to those of the North District—is, by far, the best wading access in the North District of Canaveral National Seashore. Other accesses in the North District of the Park, between Turtle Mound and Parking Lot 3, will get you to a river-like environment—this is the old channel—where you will find trout, mostly small, but very few reds at the best of times. You cannot wade across the channel to reach the typical lagoon environment inhabited by reds. Unless you have a floating device and intend to cross the channel and explore the vast territory beyond—not covered in this book because it is not accessible on foot—or unless you have other reasons to do otherwise, go to Parking Lot 5.

This chapter begins with the coverage of the vast and very important territory accessible from Parking Lot 5. Coverage is from north to south. A second part of this chapter, starting on page 108, deals with a few spots accessible from the north end of the Park.

---

[31] Bethune Beach was the only beach that African Americans were allowed to use in Volusia County during the first half of the last century and is named after the famous black educator Dr. Mary McLeod Bethune, founder of Bethune-Cookman College.

Parking Lot 5

The area of Mosquito Lagoon accessible from Parking Lot 5 of the North District of Canaveral National Seashore deserves a disproportionate share of this book. It is by far the best and most accessible wading territory. And it is free of alligators.

Parking Lot 5 is at the south end of the road. It is the site of the old Mosquito Lagoon House of Refuge that became a U.S. Coast Guard Station in 1915 and disappeared in the late 1940s (see text box next). There is an unimproved ramp on the lagoon. You can use it to launch a light boat from a trailer, but only the lightest of boats and only with a four-wheel-drive vehicle. People use this ramp to launch carry-on crafts.

To access the fishing areas north of Parking Lot 5 you will walk along the shoreline. It is a one-hour walk to the practical limit of the wading territory. To access the fishing areas south of Parking Lot 5 you will use the truck road / Klondike Beach Trail that starts at the ramp, assuming it is open to the public. If not, you will follow the shoreline—and make a few shortcuts—as shown on the large-scale detailed maps of this chapter.

To fish the lagoon south of Parking Lot 5 you need a Refuge Fishing Permit. Indeed, even if there were no signs to this effect as of this writing you will eventually enter Merritt Island National Wildlife Refuge. The actual territory of the Refuge begins a few hundred yards south of the ramp. The permit is free and self-procured on the Internet. Go to www.fws.gov/merrittisland/

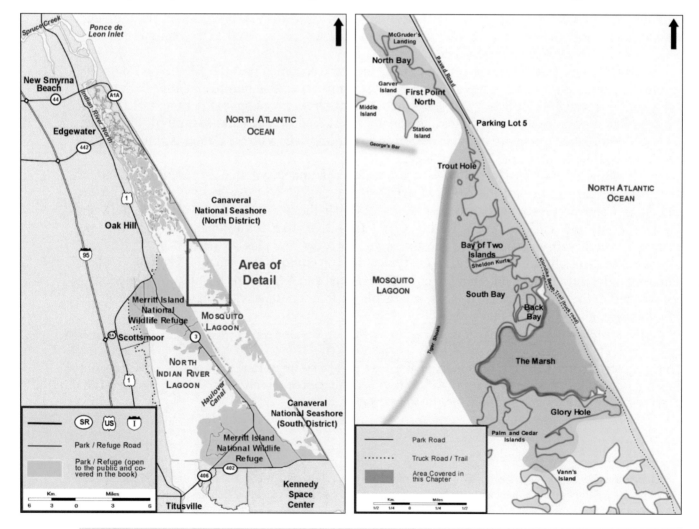

and look for *Fishing Regulations* (as of this writing). One of the features of this permit is that you will sign on having read the regulations for the Pole and Troll Zone.

A quick word on names at Parking Lot 5: you will not find many "official" names on maps. I belong to a dedicated group of wade fly-fishers who literally lived at Parking Lot 5. It was imperative in our communications that we defined and referred to locations precisely and concisely. We came up with names as short and descriptive as possible and they became normal *parlance* among my fishing friends. These names are not official and will likely be shared only by readers of this book.

The general area south of Parking Lot 5 is Tiger Shoals and this is an official name. Tiger Shoals begins precisely at the Trout Hole, which coincides with the boundary of the Refuge, and extends a significant distance toward the south, past Glory Hole and Preacher's Island. The Pole and Troll Zone (see page 64) matches Tiger Shoals. The entire area inside Tiger Shoals is shallow and can be waded in low water.

MOSQUITO LAGOON HOUSE OF REFUGE

The Houses of Refuge in Florida were a series of stations operated by the United States Life-Saving Service along the coast of Florida to rescue and shelter ship-wrecked sailors. Five houses were constructed on the East Coast in 1876, with five more added in 1885. Mosquito Lagoon House of Refuge is among this second group. The houses were manned by civilian contractors who lived in the houses with their families. Most of these houses remained in service as life-saving stations until 1915 or later. Some of the locations became United States Coast Guard (USCG) stations after the Life Saving Service was merged into the Coast Guard in 1915.

Mosquito Lagoon House of Refuge. Image from United States Coast Guard.

The Mosquito Lagoon House of Refuge was constructed in 1885 at the location of what is today Parking Lot 5 of the North District of Canaveral National Seashore. Its first keeper was Jacob Summerlin and it had five other keepers until dissolved into the USCG service in 1915. However, the Mosquito Lagoon House of Refuge continued to function as before. The house was manned through World War I and by World War II it had become a Life Boat Station. An observation tower was constructed to look for German submarines, which were sinking merchant marine vessels up and down the East Coast in the early years of the war. In 1945 the facility was decommissioned and sold, but was apparently abandoned and became a target for vandals. The structure burned down between 1948 and 1950.

No visible signs of the house and dependencies remain today. The old foundations of the house are buried under the pavement of the road a short distance before the turn around. The only remains are the old pilings of what was the dock on Mosquito Lagoon and the century plants (agave – *Agave americana*) that were presumably planted by one of the housekeepers. These non-native plants live up to 30 years—not one hundred as the name suggests—and bloom once in their life with the erection almost overnight of a spectacular stalk that can reach several feet. The descendants of those plants can still be seen blooming in the spring around Easter.

Sources: Jennifer Faith McKinnon. 2010. *The Archaeology of Florida's US Life-Saving Service Houses of Refuge and Life-Saving Stations*. Electronic Theses, Treatises and Dissertations. Paper 2530. Florida State University;
Susan Parker. 2008. *Canaveral National Seashore, Historic Resource Study*. Edited by Robert W. Blythe. National Park Service. Atlanta. www.nps.gov/history/history/online_books/cana/cana_hrs.pdf (as of this writing);
United States Coast Guard; and
Personal research.

Other official names (either from topographic maps, navigation maps or old maps) include: McGruder's Landing, Garver Island, Station Island, Middle Island, George's Bar, George's Slough, Sheldon Kurts,[32] and Glory Hole.

Each name on the small-scale location map—and in large typeset on the large-scale detailed maps—represents a *general* fishing area. Within these general areas, there are "fishing spots" (usually of deeper water) where the fish are holding when not feeding on the flats. General fishing areas will therefore encompass shallow flats, white spots (also called sand spots) and deeper holding spots. Depending upon various factors—such as wind, water level and water temperature—fishing may be restricted to blind casting white spots and deeper holding spots. This is why their location is so important and they are shown on the large-scale detailed maps.

You reach North Bay and all areas *north* of Parking Lot 5 by walking along the shoreline, which is mostly hard-packed shells. An old channel runs along the east side of Station Island and is used by boats as a running lane. You cannot wade to George's Bar and Station Island across the old channel because it is too deep but you can easily wade to Garver Island, the next island to the north, from North Bay because the old channel crosses over to the west side of Garver Island.

The Trout Hole area is just south of the parking lot and you reach it without using the truck road by walking first along the shoreline and then by walking in the shallow water one hundred yards away from the soft shoreline. There is no need for a Refuge Fishing Permit if you do not wade past the two islands.

All other areas to the *south* can be reached by walking on the truck road / Klondike Beach Trail, assuming it is open to the public. This truck road is not a dike road. It is a service road on the barrier island that connects to the dikes at various points and is only used periodically to service the dikes and the culverts located further south. It is chained but there were no signs restricting access or suggesting regulations as of this writing. Nevertheless, you need a Backcountry permit available at the admission gate at a cost of $2.00. Some sections of the road may be overgrown by grass and you should watch for snakes. You will appreciate the additional, but still limited, protection of your boot-foot waders. Some sort of maintenance of the truck road will be done if and when equipment is rolled in to repair or maintain the dike and culverts. The truck road runs from one hundred to a few hundred yards away from the lagoon, separated by an impenetrable underbrush or the marshes of the mosquito impoundments. It connects with the lagoon and the dike (or what used to be the dike) at three points in the territory covered in this book: at Target Bay (Bay of Two Islands), at Back Bay and at Glory Hole. These are identified as "exits" on the large-scale detailed maps of each section of this chapter.

If the truck road is off limits to the public you will follow the shoreline and make a few shortcuts, as shown on the maps next. This is not as bad as it sounds. But reaching the southernmost fishing areas described in this book without using the truck road is not practical.

While this book does not cover the territory south of Glory Hole, there is nothing to prevent the enterprising wader from going further south. There are several other exits giving access to the lagoon. I find this more walking than fishing. I have not explored these areas and, from the aerial maps, I think you should be careful and wary of some soft spots. And remember that the Park gate is closed at 6:00 PM. You have a long way to go back.

---

[32] The jury is still out on the exact spelling of the second part of this name. The name Sheldon may relate to Arad Sheldon, one of the early settlers of Oak Hill, or to his descendants. The name appears in historical records. The road leading to the Mosquito Lagoon House of Refuge (today's Parking Lot 5) appears in an old document that predates the construction of the House of Refuge as Arad Sheldon's Trail; however, this is not well documented. The name Sheldon's is commonly mentioned by guides and anglers of the lagoon and mostly refers to what I call South Bay in this book. The combination of Sheldon Kurts, or Sheldon Kurt's, or Sheldon and Kurt(s), or ('), or (s'), etc. is also sometimes mentioned by guides but does not appear in any of the historical documents that I could find. I found the spelling "Sheldon Kurts" handwritten on an old map on the peninsula—not on the bay south of it—and this is the name that I have used in this book.

North Bay is the only area north of Parking Lot 5 where redfish will be found regularly. It is not accessible by the truck road / Klondike Beach Trail; therefore, no Backcountry permit is required. Instead, walk along the shoreline toward the north for approximately 20 minutes. It is mostly shells and hard pack with the occasional trail sections next to the shoreline and the occasional detours into the water to avoid trees and stumps. You will hit some mud at a few places but this is minor. I rate this walk as easy and accessible to anyone capable of walking in waders for 20 minutes.

As you walk, observe carefully. You may be occasionally rewarded, especially as you get closer to North Bay and as the deep water and hard bottom at the beginning of the walk gradually turns into the shallow water and grass bottom that is typical redfish environment. You can fish for Spotted Seatrout along the way (see First Point North next).

North Bay is not an official name, of course. The name McGruder's Landing appears on an old map and most likely refers to the deeper water along the shore past North Bay, and not to the shallow, mud- and grass-bottomed bay itself. I called it *North* Bay because this is the practical northernmost wading point from Parking Lot 5.

North Bay is a fairly large area that holds reds and trout. Almost all of it is grass over mud: you will sink a little. If you are not fit for mud, you can fish the white spots between the sand point and Garver Island (see **2** on the large-scale detailed map next) or you can walk all the way around

North Bay along the shoreline and go to the Trout Sloughs (see **7** on the map). The walk around North Bay is not difficult. In high water do not hesitate to cut through the flooded area: it is reasonably hard. Same thing at the cut to the Pond: walk straight across the cut. It is hard bottom.

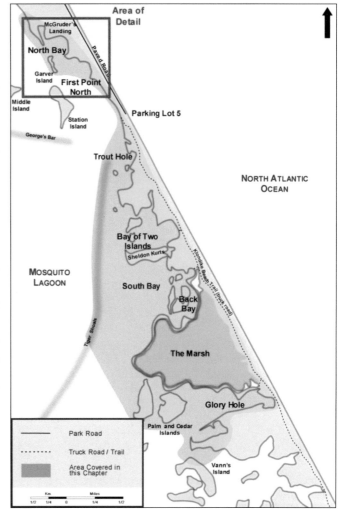

North Bay is relatively shallow and becomes *unfishable* in low water. In periods of high water, it may be hard to find the fish if they are not moving and the (otherwise easy) walk along the shore may be a little more difficult. I have often found reds busting bait along (and inside) the shoreline in high water and this has produced memorable fishing experiences. However, I would generally suggest that you make North Bay your destination when the water level is around 0.60 on the height gauge at Haulover Canal. I would make one exception to this: the white spots between the sand point and Garver Island (see **2** on the map) and the adjacent deeper area south of the point (see **1** on the map) hold fish (reds and trout) in low water. Occasionally the drop-off west of North Bay (see **4** on the map) may also hold fish in low water, but this seems to be infrequent.

All of North Bay can be productive in normal water level. You will not likely see schools of reds.

North Bay and the sand bar at the entrance from the south.

You may find small groups of reds and they will likely be a little spread out—as opposed to tightly together in schools—and they will often be tailing.

When the water level is high work all the eastern shoreline for reds busting bait around the stumps. Wade and stalk one full casting length from shore and sight cast very light flies, gurglers or poppers to reds moving in inches of water. The odds are not in your favor but the chase does not get more exciting than this.

Trout may be found in the deeper area at the northeast corner of North Bay (see **3** on the map); they are usually big.

The Pond (see **5** on the map) will hold reds in both normal and high water. The deep-water shoreline around the bushes is always worth investigating since it provides excellent cover for reds busting bait. Most of the bottom in the Pond is soft mud: it makes for difficult wading and the water will not be clear when there is a high wind. However, it is relatively well protected from most normal winds. I have rarely seen trout in the Pond, even if the black mud and deep water are the normal attributes of a winter thermal refuge.

North Bay is protected against the east winds, like most of the wading territory accessible from the Park. There is reasonable protection against a north wind in some areas, notably in the Pond, along the northern shore of North Bay and at the deep spot south of the sand point. The west wind is generally no nicer in North Bay than in most of the wading territory. However, the Pond and the white spots between the sand point and Garver Island are welcome exceptions and you may find acceptable fishing conditions in those two spots when the predominant west wind makes most of the rest of the wadeable territory of the Park inhospitable.

A trip to North Bay in favorable water levels will rarely be disappointing. However, when

John C. Gamble in North Bay with a bent rod and the resulting nice redfish. In the background Garver Island.

all else fails in North Bay you can always pick up a few trout in the Trout Sloughs. These are troughs on both sides of the sand bar, some 200 yards north of the northern point of North Bay (see **7** on the map). A white PVC pipe some 200 feet from shore marks the location of the sand bar. Wade on the sand bar toward the pipe and cast weighed flies on either side. Small trout and small reds hang out in the deeper water; mid-sized trout will also be there regularly. This is why my friends who discovered this spot named it the Trout Sloughs. When you go there you will know that it is appropriately named. While this is not a genuine winter thermal refuge you will likely find a concentration of fish in the deeper spots when the water gets very cold. This is the only fishing spot from Parking Lot 5 where you will see tidal current.

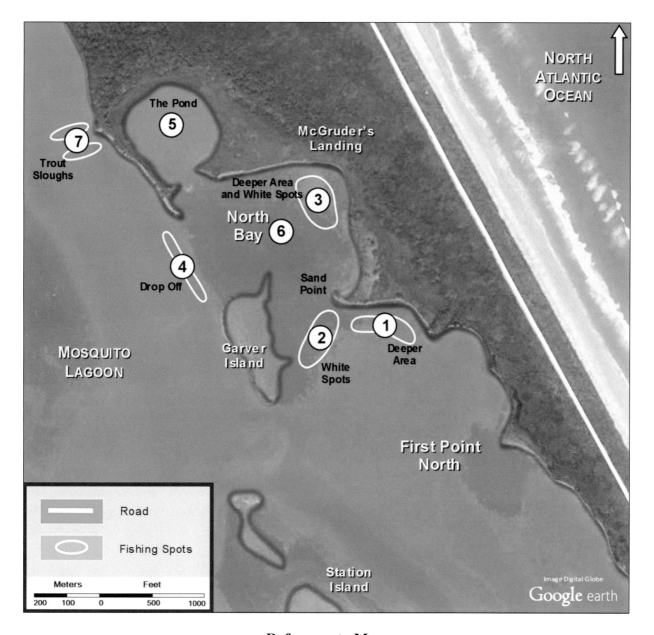

Reference to Map

1. Deeper area south of the sand point (before entering North Bay): mostly trout and the occasional red; soft bottom; seasonal.

2. White spots southwest of North Bay between the sand point and Garver Island: mostly reds and the occasional big trout; good wading; good in most water levels.

3. Deeper area at the northeast corner of North Bay: reds and trout; soft bottom with some white spots; good in most water levels, except very low.

4. Drop-off west of North Bay: reds and trout; hard bottom; may hold fish in low water; seasonal and irregular.

5. The Pond: mostly reds and mostly big ones; soft and muddy bottom, difficult to wade; good in normal and high water only.

6. North Bay (all of it): reds, singles and small pods, occasional trout, mostly big; grass over soft bottom, difficult wading; good in normal water (too shallow in low water).

7. Trout Sloughs: trout, mostly small, some mid-sized; hard bottom; good in all water levels.

From the ramp at Parking Lot 5 going north there is a deep trough right along the shore with hard packed bottom and shell shoreline. This looks like a natural channel, either from an ancient epoch when water level was lower, or from one of the many inlets that were opened and closed by storms in more recent times. This is the easiest access, easiest wading, and one of the few places where you will regularly find Flounder swimming among trout. Generally, trout will be small in the deeper water next to the ramp, getting bigger as you progress toward First Point North. The most regular spot seems to be the northern third of the area. In the coldest days of the winter, the entire deep-water trough sometimes becomes a thermal refuge for fish, mostly medium and big trout but also small and medium reds. It does not seem to happen every year and I cannot tell what triggers the fish to adopt the place, or not. Since this is very close to the ramp not giving it a try would be unforgivable. You can do it from the shoreline: just wade into the trough until you have space for a back cast. Do not assume that the fish will be far into the open water. The deep water starts close to shore and the fish are often well spread out, including close to shore. This is all very easy wading on firm bottom, becoming a little softer as you reach First Point North, and very accessible. Blind cast weighed flies that you will let sink to the bottom and try various strip retrieves. At times, the fish will react to a few fast strips followed by long pauses: this is the typical trout strip (see text box on page 43). At other times, especially when the water is very cold, the fish will react to a very slow strip and only to a fly placed between its eyes. For some wade fly-fishers this is the only accessible area in Mosquito Lagoon and may be well worth the trip if trout is your target, especially during the coldest period of the year.

For serious big trout at all times First Point North is the place. It is just a short walk along the hard packed shoreline north of the ramp. As the name suggests it is the first point (the first big one, with mud and stumps) along the otherwise regular shoreline from Parking Lot 5. You can walk to it directly, or fish the deep trough along the shore all the way, as described above.

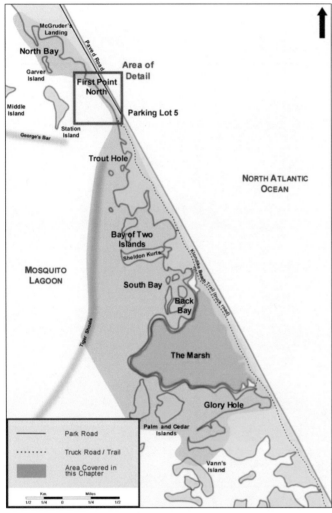

First Point North; photo taken half-way from the ramp.

There will likely be fish there in all seasons and at all times of the day, but prime fishing time is very early in the morning in normal water level during spring, when finger mullet gather in the area and big trout come near the shore feeding on them. They will likely be just south of (before) the tip of the point, where the water is less deep and the bottom softer, a mixture of grass and sand. This is not your typical redfish environment. Nevertheless, you may be surprised from time to time. One of my largest reds came from First Point North on a foggy morning when a whole school had settled right along the shoreline.

Past First Point North the bottom becomes softer but there is generally deep water within 100 feet from the shore, including one much deeper spot in the last small bay before North Bay. Success in these spots is variable and seems to be a random affair. It is generally trout only and they are often swimming among the mullet.

From this point we will cover the area *south* of Parking Lot 5. This area is called Tiger Shoals. The shoals run from the Trout Hole—the sand bar in line with the second island is the northernmost limit—south past Glory Hole and Preacher's Island. At its widest it stretches surprisingly close to the Intracoastal Waterway on the other side of the lagoon. The buoys delimitating the Pole and Troll Zone are on the outside of the shoals (see map on page 64). The vast area inside Tiger Shoals is mostly shallow grass flats and the bottom is relatively soft. For the fish, this is prime feeding ground and waders have access to the entire area in low water. While possible on foot, the practical access to Tiger Shoals is from a boat or carry-on craft because of the sheer size of the place. However, the area near the shore is easily accessible on foot and arguably provides the best wade fly-fishing of the lagoons. The shoreline of Tiger Shoals is covered next from Parking Lot 5 to, and past Glory Hole, a three-mile walk on the truck road / Klondike Beach Trail. All this area south of the Trout Hole is within Merritt Island National Wildlife Refuge. The Trout Hole is the first fishing area south from Parking Lot 5.

Trout Hole Area

The Trout Hole was named (by me) when I began to find big trout regularly coming into the deep ditch along the shore early in the morning in pursuit of mullet. This ditch is the remnant of the dike and mosquito impoundment that used to run along the shore south of Parking Lot 5. The dike was removed in 1999 and the ditch was filled with the dike material. However, in those areas facing small bays and creeks the ditch was not entirely backfilled. This created new environments where fish are now holding, more so at times of low water. The Trout Hole—and the Black Hole that we will see in a few pages—are excellent illustrations of the potential for holding fish in such deeper spots where the ditch was not completely filled back. The Trout Hole and the Black Hole always deserve a visit. See page 59 for a discussion on the removal of the old dike and its impact on the fishing.

The Trout Hole *area* is a diverse habitat that holds fish in all water levels. This is, with First Point North, the closest fishing area to Parking Lot 5 and is ideal for a quick run. Since it is so close to the parking lot, visible and accessible, expect some traffic. When we refer to the Trout Hole *area*, it should be taken as the entire area north of the two small islands inside the sand bar.

You can only access the Trout Hole area from the water. An old path from the truck road has closed and can no longer be used. There is no need for a Backcountry permit to walk to the Trout Hole area. Walk along the water from the ramp; this is all hard pack on the shore and a small sand bar near the shore. Before you get to the first little cove (small pond north, no. **5** on the map on page 94), wade toward deeper water and keep progressing south. This is all nice sand (sort of) as long as you stay away from the shore. Follow the blue dotted line on the large-scale detailed map of page 94. To get to the deep ditch along the shore (the Trout Hole *proper*) you must go through the heavy grass and softer bottom. But you may be content just to work the large area of deep water between the sand bar and the grass (no. **3** on the map) and you may do very well there, especially in low water. This is one of the few spots that you can do if you cannot handle mud.

Like most of the wading territory along the east shores of both lagoons the Trout Hole is well protected from east winds; there is some limited protection against the north wind right along

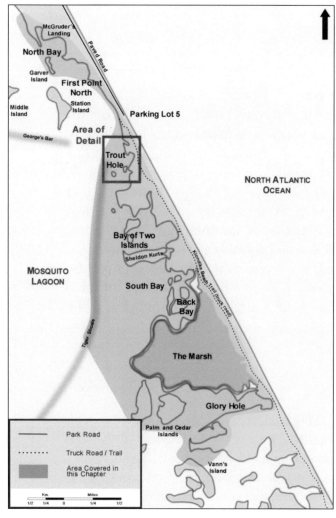

the shore, at the Trout Hole proper. Otherwise, you are on your own against the west wind and you will find that some northwesters are bad enough to muddy the water.

The Trout Hole *area* is a diverse environment and it will hold both reds and trout in all seasons and water levels. As the name suggests one of the prime spots is the deep ditch along the shore (see **1** on the large-scale detailed map next). During low- and cold-water periods in the winter trout and reds to a lesser extent will often find refuge in this old ditch. This is a winter thermal refuge, one of many identified in this book. However, I have seen times when the fish were not there and I cannot explain why. When the water warms up and rises, the fish can move around freely, but big trout (as well as reds) will often visit the place in the early morning for breakfast, more in the spring but at any other time as well.

In high water reds will be everywhere in the area. However, you will more often find them along (and sometimes inside) the shoreline, busting bait and swimming in very shallow water. You will also find reds and trout regularly in the big white spot nearest to the point and you will find mostly reds in the shallower and smaller white spot nearer to the first island (see **2** on the map).

In normal water level (around 0.60 feet on the height gauge at Haulover Canal) you will often find reds on the grass flats, in the white spots closer to shore and in the deeper spots along the shore. Schools, sometimes surprisingly large, will roam the area. However, it is in the low-water winter months that the Trout Hole becomes such a good spot. Aside from the big trout that take refuge in the deep ditch along the shore reds and trout will congregate and stay in the large deep-water area between the sand bar and the grass flat along the shore (see **3** on the map). You will frequently catch them tailing in the morning and late afternoon at the edge of the deep water. Schools of reds will roam the area. These fish may be difficult to catch but they provide excellent sport. Blind casting a weighed fly in the deep water will often bring results.

The small pond north (no name—see **5** on the map) will hold single reds at times. The entrance is shallow and very soft and the deeper water inside has a soft muddy bottom; not good wading. The small pond south (no name—see **6** on the map) holds small trout and small reds at times. The entrance is deep water over soft muddy bottom (this is the old ditch) and you will not want to wade in it but instead swing toward open water to avoid it. This should be a winter thermal refuge. However, I very rarely find reds or big trout holding in the deep water at the entrance of this small pond and I cannot explain why they have not adopted this spot.

Note that from this point toward the south the lagoon is in Merritt Island National Wildlife Refuge. The northern limit of the refuge is in line with the two islands and you should be able to see the first buoy and post of the Pole and Troll Zone. You need a Refuge Fishing Permit, free and self-procured on the Internet. Go to www.fws.gov/merrittisland/ and look for *Fishing Regulations* (as of this writing).

Trout Hole, viewed from open water. The remnant of the deep ditch along the shore is the key of this spot and it is a well-hidden feature.

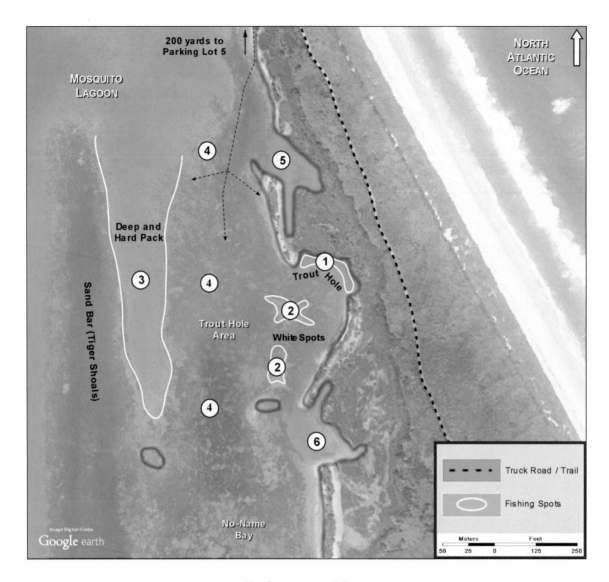

Reference to Map

1. Trout Hole (proper): remnant of the pre-1999 ditch inside the dike; trout, big ones; very muddy and soft near shore—do not wade near ditch or attempt to cross it; access from the sand point, wade away from shore and cast toward shore; seasonal, excellent in spring; winter thermal refuge for big trout.

2. White spots between point and first island: trout and reds; sand bottom, but soft to get to; better in high water.

3. Large area of deeper water and sandy bottom: trout and reds, including schools in winter; mostly good wading bottom; good in all water levels, can be excellent as fish refuge in low water.

4. Trout Hole area in general (other than specifics above): reds and trout, big ones; shallow water over a mixture of grass and mud, difficult wading; good sight fishing in normal and high water.

5. Small pond north (no name): very shallow and soft bottomed entrance, deeper water inside, difficult wading; occasional red, mostly small.

6. Small pond south (no name): deep area where old ditch was—do not cross, muddy bottom, difficult wading; small trout and small reds in the low-water winter months.

No-Name Bay

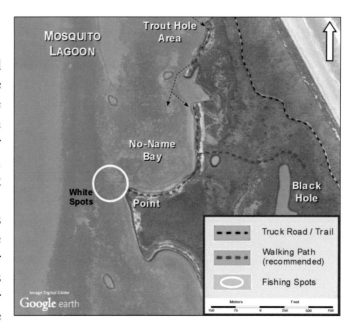

South of the Trout Hole lies a large shallow and grassy area *named* (by my friend Dalen) No-Name Bay... The area does not always have fish because it is too shallow in low water. However, when conditions are right, No-Name Bay can offer exceptional redfish tailing. Look for a water level between 0.60 and 0.80 on the height gauge at Haulover Canal.

Access to No-Name Bay by foot is as bad as it gets. From the Trout Hole, follow on shore to the entrance of the small pond south. Enter the water approximately 150 feet *before* the point—it gets softer as you progress towards the point. Wade near the small island and then turn south. See the blue dotted line on the map.

You can wade and find fish in the vast expanse of No-Name Bay all the way down to the point. It is all thick grass over mud and difficult wading. You can also explore it from the shore where you can walk on firm ground once past the first small pond. This can be a good spot for redfish in normal and high water levels. In the lowest water of the winter all the shallow flat of No-Name Bay becomes wet pasture.

If you made it that far, you should check the white spots at the point (this is the southern end of the bay, as shown on the map). These white spots are the only deep water in the area and are a magnet for fish, more so in low water. In fact, this is just about the only spot in this area where there is enough water to hold fish in low water. Be careful as you enter the water from shore: the white spots are close to the shoreline and you do not want to disturb the fish.

Again, if you made it that far, you may wish to take advantage of a shortcut to the Black Hole (covered in the next subsection). There is an old path between No-name Bay and the Black Hole that was made by the machine that dug the mosquito-control ditches when the dike was removed. Depending on the growth in the vegetation you may not easily find this path. But once you find it you will be able to use it year after year. The approximate location is shown as a red dotted line on the map. The key to finding it from No-name Bay is the little round pond: the path is north of this little pond. It will take you to the head of the Black Hole. Go around the head and follow along the east shore of the Black Hole some distance from the water. At this point, there is no more path, but you have a visual of the area and you will easily find your way. You will cross a few ditches that look menacing, but are not really. You will sink less than a foot (for some, this is menacing... your call). You can access the Black Hole anywhere or keep going and fish George's Slough, Target Bay, and all areas to the south described in the next subsection.

Millions of fiddler crabs on a sandy shoreline of Mosquito Lagoon. Redfish will cruise the shoreline in inches of water looking for a crab meal. Photo Dalen Mills.

The name "Bay of Two Islands" is from the locals who named the area after the two islands that hide most of the bay from the open water. It is strictly oral; there is no written evidence of the name. The only deep-water access is along the peninsula called Sheldon Kurts. Once inside Bay of Two Islands there are three well-defined fishing areas: the Black Hole, George's Slough and Target Bay. The Black Hole is at the northern end of the bay and was named by me. George's Slough is the slightly deeper area between the big island and the shore and the name appears on topographic maps. Target Bay was named by me after the *Target Rock*, a name given by the locals to the remnant of the concrete-filled airplane body that still lies in a cleared patch between the lagoon and the ocean. It was used as *target* practice for fighter airplanes during World War II. You may still find spent shells in the area. This is one of the narrower sections of the barrier island and it may have been the location of a temporary shallow inlet that opened in the eighteenth century.

Entrance to the Bay of Two Islands from open water. To the right, Sheldon Kurts Point.

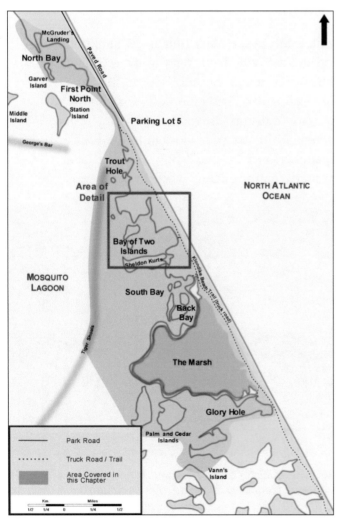

Bay of Two Islands has Red Drum, Spotted Seatrout and Black Drum. This is the sector where you have the best chance at a grand slam (by the local definition). It is a diverse area, with flats of various depth, white spots and deep spots. The area is very much influenced by water levels and the presence and quantity of fish are subject to significant seasonal fluctuations.

The main access to Bay of Two Islands is by the truck road / Klondike Beach Trail, assuming it is open to the public. From Parking Lot 5, take the trail and walk south. You can exit either at the Black Hole or at the Target Rock. Accessing the area at the Black Hole is a wise choice if you intend to fish it; and/or to fish George's Slough; and/or to fish the big white spots; all shown on the large-scale detailed map next. Walk the truck road / trail approximately 16 minutes and exit at a path to the Black Hole. Contrary to the exits next that are (or were) actual roads, this is just a path in a very small clearing in the bushes and it may not be readily apparent. The bushes may be slightly overgrown near the road, but you will clearly see the Black Hole in the distance. Walk in the low bushes and tall grass, either along the mosquito-control ditches or cut straight, bearing closer to the tree line to your left (in either case, you should see some footprints, if not a well-defined path). The last few hundred feet may not be a clearly defined path if you aimed directly at the Black Hole. Choose your own route. The mosquito-control ditches are not deep and the bottom is (reasonably) solid. You will sink in mud a little, but nothing to worry about.

You may also choose the Target Rock "exit". The Target Rock "exit" is not what it used to be. Being no longer a truck road (because the dike has been removed in this area) it is now down to a path that the mangroves are invading. You may have to pick your way. It gives you an easy access to Target Bay and Sheldon Kurts Point. It is also a longer but easier way to get to the big white spots, George's Slough and the Black Hole, without the mud: walk along the northern shore of Target Bay where it is all hard pack. Just before the point, avoid softer spots by swinging toward the open water.

If the truck road is closed to the public you can access the area by walking along the shoreline from the Trout Hole area, either following the shoreline south of No-Name Bay, or through a shortcut in the low bushes and tall grass, as described in the previous section. In all cases the paths are shown as a red dotted line on the large-scale detailed map next.

In periods of normal and high water schools of reds will occasionally roam the entire area while singles and small groups will tail on the shallow flats. When blacks are present they will likely be found around the deep spot at the entrance of the Black Hole (thus the name given to this spot), just inside as well as just outside. They will also sometimes go far up the creek where they will easily be spotted tailing. Trout will be found mostly in George's Slough and in the deeper spots, inside and outside Sheldon Kurts Point. Reds will be found regularly in the big white spots in normal water level. Sometimes schools will settle there.

In periods of low water reds may abandon the shallow flats altogether. Trout will congregate in the deeper spots: at the entrance of the Black Hole, in George's Slough and in the deeper spots at the point, both inside and outside the bay. These are low-water fish refuges and, at times, the fish will be literally stacked in those areas, not that they will be easy to take. At all times and in all conditions these deep-water spots may hold fish and should be blind cast.

Since the establishment of the Pole and Troll Zone (see page 64) the entire Bay of Two Islands is almost off limits for boats. Indeed, boats have to be poled or trolled all the way from beyond the shoals (a 600-yard journey just to get to Sheldon Kurts Point) or drifted from the Trout Hole or from South Bay. With the wind at their back, boaters may find it an easy *one-way* glide; the return trip may not be as easy. Waders and kayakers have the place almost to themselves.

Black Hole

See **1** on the large-scale detailed map next. I named it such because this is one among very few spots in the wading territory covered in this book where I could expect to find Black Drum regularly in the spring. The Black Hole is probably the best example of the positive impact of removal of the dike a few years ago. See "The Dikes" page 59.

When they are there Black Drum will hold in the deep ditch at the entrance of the Black Hole and will venture out in the shallower areas, both inside

Black Hole in the winter. The deep water in the bushes along the shore attracts single reds looking for baitfish.

the creek and outside. You will see them tailing and your heart will race out of control. The first year after removal of the dike I had Black Drum there all winter and was delighted in the anticipation of more of the same in the years to come. This did not materialize. I suspect that my first-year Black Drum were the ones that were previously trapped behind the dike. They did not see the point of leaving the place right away after removal of the dike. Since then, I have not seen Black Drum there other than in April. I have reports that they stay during spring and sometimes the entire summer and into early fall. I have rarely seen them in late fall and during the winter.

However, there is more to the Black Hole than the seasonal Black Drum. Indeed, the remnants of the deep ditch is a holding spot for reds and trout, some of the latter quite big. The shallow mud flat inside and the deep water in the bushes along the shore attract single reds looking for baitfish. At all times and in all water conditions, the Black Hole may yield excellent fishing. It is well protected from most winds and should be blind cast anytime you come by. The ditch is soft, deep mud. This black mud captures and retains heat from the sun and allows the spot to sometimes act as fish refuge during the coldest days of the winter. But not always, for reasons that I cannot explain. The ditch itself is off limits to wading. If you get too close, you will sink seriously. To get inside the creek walk on land in the bushes on the east shore. Inside the creek you will find some soft mud along the shoreline but it will become firmer as you get away from the shore, not that it will ever get comfortable.

George's Slough

See **2** on the map. This is one area that I did not have to name. The name appears on topographic maps. As the name implies, this is a deeper area (in a relative, *lagoon* sense) and it holds fish most of the time. In the low water of the winter George's Slough sometimes becomes the refuge of choice for trout inhabiting the general area and the fishing can be spectacular. Remember that big trout are very wary fish. Reds also hold in George's Slough, sometimes entire schools, but most often individuals and small pods. George's Slough has always been one of my favorite destinations. Most of George's Slough is grass over soft bottom, but not uncomfortable to wade, with the occasional small white spots and a large bare spot in the middle, the result of the hurricanes of a decade ago. The area is reasonably protected from all winds; it has excellent protection against an east wind.

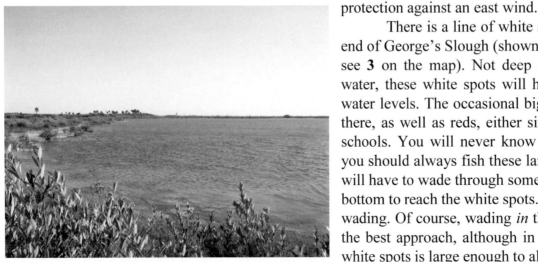

Target Bay in high water. Photo taken from the southeast shore in normal water level. This area will almost disappear in the lowest water levels of the winter.

There is a line of white spots at the southern end of George's Slough (shown as Big White Spots, see **3** on the map). Not deep enough in very low water, these white spots will hold fish in all other water levels. The occasional big trout will be found there, as well as reds, either singles, small pods or schools. You will never know what to expect, but you should always fish these large white spots. You will have to wade through some grass over soft mud bottom to reach the white spots. Once there it is easy wading. Of course, wading *in* the white spots is not the best approach, although in this case the line of white spots is large enough to allow it. Nevertheless, make your first casts away from the edge of the white spots. And in low water, keep as low a profile as you can.

Target Bay

See **4** on the map. Target Bay is the first large expanse of water that you will meet if you exit the truck road / trail at the Target Rock. Target Bay is very shallow and will generally not hold fish in low water. In normal water, you will usually find reds in the deeper water along the eastern shore and in a large white spot in the middle. In normal-high and high water, reds may be anywhere, as is the case for the entire wading territory. Target Bay is mostly covered with grass, so when the water level is just right, it is a good tailing area. However, the presence and quantity of fish remain seasonal in Target Bay. Generally, if you cannot see anything after a few minutes move on. There are rarely any trout in Target Bay. Most of Target Bay is grass over mud and difficult to wade.

Deep Water at the Entrance

See **5** on the map. The only deep-water access to Bay of Two Islands is between the south island (the smaller of the *Two Islands*) and Sheldon Kurts Point. This is a deep area, again in relative lagoon standards. This deeper area also has some small white spots. This is a fish refuge in low water, especially for trout. At times, this area can be spectacular. It has some protection against most winds. The grass bottom is quite soft and the white spots are small and must be fished from the grass.

White Spots off Sheldon Kurts Point

See **6** on the map. There are several large white spots just off Sheldon Kurts Point extending several hundred feet in a southwest direction. The white spots are easily accessible from shore and they are reasonably easy to wade. This may be one of the few fishing spots for those not quite up to serious mud. It is not second choice either. These white spots hold reds, sometimes schools, as well as trout, some large ones. It is a fish refuge in low water and is protected against east winds. Blind casting theses white spots will often yield spectacular results.

The Cut

See **7** on the map. Shallow and gradual on the Target Bay side, the cut between Sheldon Kurts Point and the mainland is deep and very spongy at the location of the old ditch before removal of the dike. This small spot of deep water sometimes holds redfish, mostly in low water. This is one spot that is sheltered against most winds and can be blind cast in adverse weather. The best access is from Target Bay: just wade toward the cut on the hard-bottom shallow water until you get approximately one hundred feet from the deeper water. I suggest you progress slowly, even kneeling as you get close to the deep. Sometimes the fish are right at the drop off. Blind cast the entire area and do not hesitate to cast a heavy fly that will sink. In a south wind you may work the spot from the other side; however, getting there is a bit tricky and can only be done in low water. In this area if you feel that you are sinking uncomfortably, back off. There is some seriously deep mud.

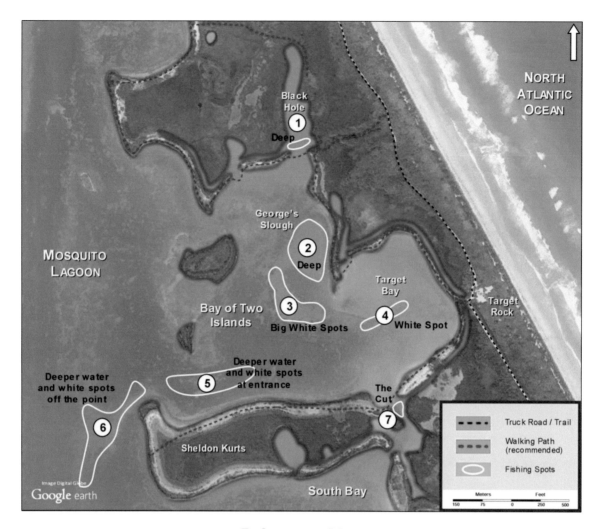

Reference to Map

1. Black Hole: reds and trout, blacks seasonal; remnant of ditch from mosquito impoundment at the entrance—do not cross ditch, access inside creek from east shore; difficult wading; blind cast deep water of ditch in all water levels; sometimes ditch becomes fish refuge in low water.

2. George's Slough: reds and trout, some big; large deeper area soft but *wadeable*, all other areas grass over soft mud and difficult to wade; good in normal water levels; deeper area can be excellent in low water as a fish refuge.

3. Big White Spots: mostly reds, some big trout; good sandy bottom, but some slugging through grass on mud to reach the white spots; good in all water levels, except very low; spectacular at times when schools of reds settle in.

4. Target Bay: reds almost exclusively; grass over soft bottom, difficult to wade; normal and high water only; habitat almost disappears in low water; strictly sight fishing except for the white spot in the middle.

5. Deeper water at entrance: mostly trout, some big, and occasional reds; grass over soft bottom, difficult to wade; white spots too small to wade in; good in normal water, can be spectacular in low water as a fish refuge.

6. White spots off Sheldon Kurts Point: easy access and white spots large enough to be waded; reds, including schools, and trout in all water levels and almost all the time; can be spectacular in low water as a fish refuge.

7. The cut between Target Bay and South Bay: can be fished on hard ground from Target Bay side but stay back from the soft mud; very tricky approach from any other angle; red and trout in the deep water at the intersection with the old ditch.

South Bay was named (by me) as the southernmost point easily accessible on foot from Parking Lot 5. I named Back Bay the backwater behind the spoil islands of South Bay. When it comes to names, there is no end to my imagination… Some locals call it Sheldon Kurts. On the old map where I found the name Sheldon Kurts refers to land, not water. As for the exact spelling… (See footnote 32 on page 86.)

Access to South Bay and Back Bay is easy via the truck road / Klondike Beach Trail, assuming it is open to the public, through either the Target Rock or the Back Bay "exits". If you cannot walk the truck road you can walk along the shoreline from the Trout Hole Area to reach Target Bay, as shown on the large-scale detailed map of the preceding page. This is a longer walk; however, you could be rewarded in the morning with redfish tailing close to the shoreline. From the Target Rock "exit", follow the south shoreline of Target Bay and walk on the cleared area where the old dike used to be. Crossing one shallow slough, the cut to South Bay and the old ditch is easy because they are not deep. This will get you to the northeast end of South Bay. From there you can reach the middle of South Bay by following the shoreline along Sheldon Kurts Point and entering the water near the point. Or you can go straight south and follow the shoreline along and between the spoil islands to reach the shallow end of South Bay and the old ditch of Back Bay.

If you come from the truck road you will find that the Back Bay "exit" is a real road, since the dike still exists from this point toward the south and some kind of truck road must be maintained to service the dike and the culverts. From the Back Bay "exit", you can go west, following the ditch to reach the northeast corner of South Bay. Or you can walk on the dike road, going south around Back Bay and all the way to the southern shore of South Bay. This dike is cleared of bushes from time to time. You may find it covered by tall grass, but it should be walkable all along Back Bay and South Bay. You can reach the southern point of South Bay, marked by the *mailbox*—a box on top of a white post; it is in fact a mosquito trap—without getting wet. You can also push it and walk all the way south on the dike road to Glory Hole, but this is a long way.

South Bay

South Bay is big (approximately one mile across) and it is the most productive flat for reds in the entire area covered in this book. If you are to see reds tailing anywhere chances are it will be in South Bay. And if you are to hit schools of reds, again chances are that it will be in South Bay. But there is a price to pay. Aside from the long walk expect serious mud. The first two to three hundred yards from the north shore will be daunting. It is not the black mud that you find at the Black Hole or in the Trout Hole. This is worst: soft bottom under thick grass… If you are not up to it do not go to South Bay. Or reach it in a boat or kayak and wade the middle, where the wading is easier.

In high and normal water levels you may find groups of redfish close to the shoreline, especially in

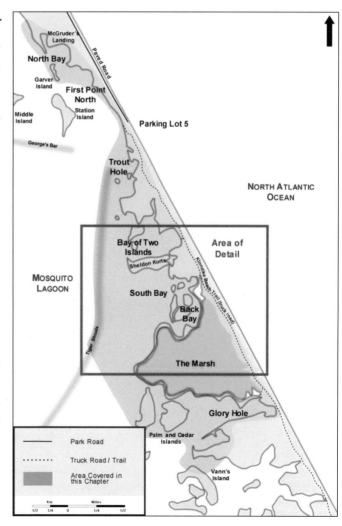

the early morning hours, along the southeasterly spoil islands where schools sometimes settle for their morning feed.

The cut between Target Bay and South Bay (see **1** on the large-scale detailed map next) is a microenvironment worth exploring in all conditions but even more in normal and high water. The ancient ditch and the more recent partly filled ditch are deep-water holding spots for reds, while the surrounding flats provide a rich hunting ground. The wind often creates a current between Target Bay and South Bay, which attracts bait and predators. There is always a sheltered spot at the cut that can be fished on windy days.

You should also try the Pond along the north shore (see **2** on the map). It sometimes holds fish in normal and high water and may provide shelter on a windy day. Cross the cut right in the middle, it is hard bottom; cross the soft-bottomed old ditch (inside) near the stumps along the west shore of the Pond.

In periods of low water fish habitat will disappear along the shore of South Bay. However, you will often find schools of fish as well as singles roaming the slightly deeper water in the middle of the bay, along an imaginary line between the point of Sheldon Kurts and the *mailbox* on the southern shore. There are good white spots and areas of slightly deeper water as well as shallow flats from the above-described line to the edge of the shoals. If you go the distance and cover the territory you will rarely be disappointed. This area is the only part of South Bay where you have a reasonable chance of catching trout (see **3** on the map next).

Again, this is a vast body of water. Wading across South Bay may take a few hours. If this is not your idea of having fun, getting to the middle of South Bay in a boat—no motoring, this is inside the Pole and Troll Zone—or a carry-on craft is not a bad idea. Once you find the fish there is no substitute for wading. And you will find the bottom surprisingly friendly as long as you stay away from the shores.

Back Bay

Back Bay is very shallow and will provide good fishing for reds only in normal and high water. During the low-water periods of the winter Back Bay is closed for business. However, the old ditch (see **5** on the map and picture below) and, to a lesser extent, the white spot at the southern entrance from South Bay (see **6** on the map), provide adequate environments for both reds and trout in all water levels. These two areas should be worked thoroughly. The *old* ditch is not from the recent removal of the dikes in this area but from the removal of earlier dikes, most likely the ones dug by hand.

The old ditch (dotted line superimposed on the picture) and the spoil islands (to the right) separating South Bay from Back Bay, viewed from Back Bay looking south.

In normal and high water Back Bay provides sheltered areas which may be your only choice on windy days. It is reasonably easy wading (sort of). Once schools of reds enter Back Bay they tend to spread out a little. This makes for excellent fishing at times. By all means stay low. You will find fish in nine inches of water, and less… and it will be great sport! Obviously there is no such thing as blind casting in Back Bay other than in the old ditch and in the white spot at the southern entrance from South Bay.

The storms and other factors influence the growing of the grass in Back Bay. At times a healthy growth provides a good environment for redfish. In other years the grass disappears and the area is just black mud, but the grass will likely come back.

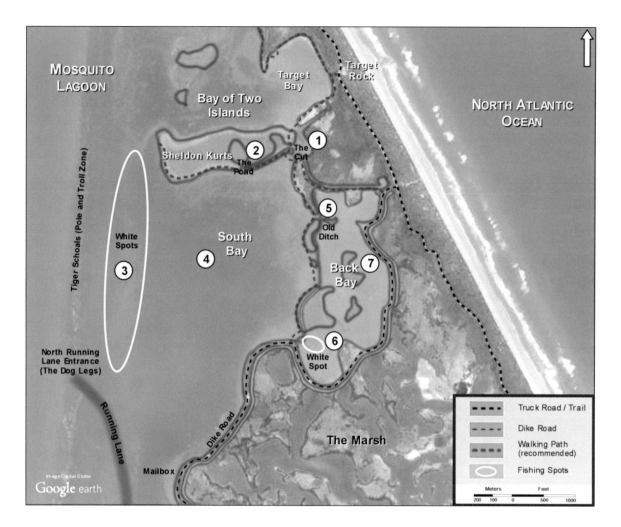

Reference to Map

1. The Cut to Target Bay: reds only; easy wade across the large shallow cut along the shore of Target Bay; easy crossing of old ditch to South Bay (two to three feet only) but follow dotted red line on map; deeper areas inside the cut and behind the island sometimes hold reds that may be blind cast in any water levels.

2. The Pond: reds only; muddy and deep in the old ditch, difficult access and wade; blind cast reds which may hold in ditch; watch for tailing and bait busting in shallow; seasonal.

3. White spots in the middle of South Bay: mostly reds, occasional trout; easy wading but access long and difficult (grass over soft bottom); can be blind cast; good in normal water level; can be very good in low water; too deep in high water.

4. South Bay (all of it): reds only, singles and schools; grass over soft bottom, difficult wade; always good but a vast expanse to find fish.

5. Old ditch behind spoil islands (Back Bay): reds and trout; cross ditch carefully (up to three feet in normal water level, north deeper than south), muddy and soft bottom; deep enough for blind casting; can be good in all water levels; low-water fish refuge at times.

6. White spot at southern entrance to Back Bay: mostly reds, occasional trout (big ones); muddy and soft bottom; blind cast white spot and deep spots around island; can be good in all water levels; low-water fish refuge at times.

7. Back Bay (all of it): reds only, singles; very shallow water over thin mud and sparse grass, *wadeable*; sight fishing only; normal and high water only (too shallow for low water); seasonal.

Starting from the truck road access to Back Bay and extending south to Glory Hole the dike has not been removed. The impoundment is noted as The Marsh on the Top Spot map. It is the northern part of Hunt Area 3 of the Refuge, thus the name *Area 3* sometimes used. Authorities used to maintain the level of water constantly higher than in the lagoon with gates at the culverts.

The Marsh viewed from the dike at one of the new culverts.

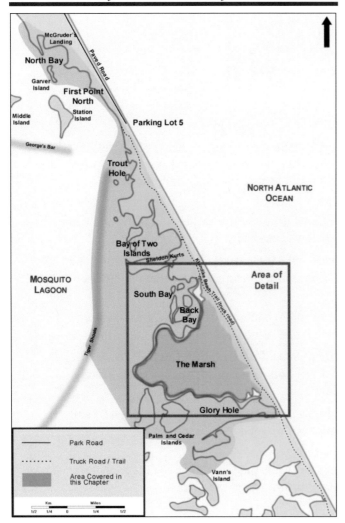

Consequently, there was no flow and no access for lagoon fish. There was also no egress for those fish living inside the marsh. And there were quite a few, as duck hunters were telling me. This has all changed.

In 2010 several new culverts were put in place. These culverts are gated. However, during most of the year they will be left wide open, thus allowing for the circulation of water and fish between the impoundment and the lagoon. At times of fluctuating water levels these culverts are points of current. For the fish inside the dike water flowing to the impoundment is dinner bell. In addition, the deep ditch inside the dike could become a natural refuge during periods of low and cold water of the winter.

Since it was separated from the lagoon The Marsh was of little interest for waders until now. It is far from Parking Lot 5 and it obviously harbored just a few fish that were hard to find. The access was not good and there were better and easier places to go. The new culverts open a vast marsh and a deep-water ditch to the fish of the lagoon… and to the wade fly-fishers.

The dike road has been cleared by the machinery and is walkable again. The new culverts are changing the environment for the better and they are changing the accesses. While the banks of the ditch remain covered with tall brush, which makes it unpractical to fish from the dike, the areas next to the new culverts have been cleared and they provide prime fly-fishing points to the deep water of the ditch.

The natural features of the lagoon such as the jagged shoreline, bays and flats, are on the marsh side of the impoundment and inaccessible from the dike. Access could be tricky. Do not try crossing the ditch that runs all along the dike at times of high water. It is then too deep to wade across anywhere. The only practical access to the bays and flats in high waters is from the truck road / Klondike Beach Trail, assuming it is open to the public. At the Back Bay "exit", instead of taking the dike road keep walking south on the truck road / trail in the direction of Glory Hole. At several points the road comes close to the marsh and you can walk to the water.

When the water is low you may attempt to cross the ditch from the dike at a few points near the culverts. This is limit, but it can be done. You may have to make several attempts. It is impossible to tell from the dike how deep the ditch is, but you can make an educated guess as to the location of the shallower areas. The dike is uniformly wide and level, and all material to build it originally came from the ditch. At the bends the amount of material needed to build the dike is spread over a longer or shorter length of the ditch depending upon the direction of the bend; therefore, the ditch will likely be a little shallower along the outer bends and deeper along the inner bends. A few inches will make the difference between wading across or not. While this is not exactly solid bottom there is some footing under the loose sediments at the bottom of the ditch. A little scary maybe, uncomfortable certainly, but doable. This is not for everybody and only for this section of dikes where alligators are not present. Once you find one crossing point that works for you, note it for all future crossings. But remember that it will work only in low water.

The Marsh is a new, promising area that will need to be explored thoroughly. As the area has only recently been open year round to the fish of the lagoon it will take some time for patterns to develop. But some spectacular fishing may await the venturing wade fly-fisher. Since there is no access for boats you will likely be alone in your world and you will find good shelter from the wind. It may be just a matter of time for this fishery to develop.

You should also keep your eyes open for juvenile Tarpon. The severe cold snap of the 2010 winter killed most resident Tarpon; however, they have come back in most areas. With a depth of three to five feet the ditch along the dike has the potential to hold juvenile Tarpon and may be deep enough for their survival during the cold snaps of our winters.

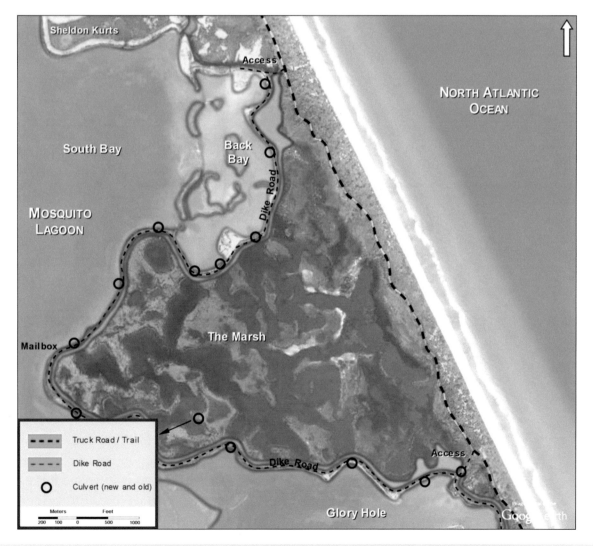

Glory Hole

According to some sources the name was given by one angler after an especially good fishing day at this spot. This is much better than other possible explanations for the origin of the name.

You will notice on the maps that the pre-diked lagoon and the ocean come dangerously

The author with a 24-inch Black Drum in Glory Hole.

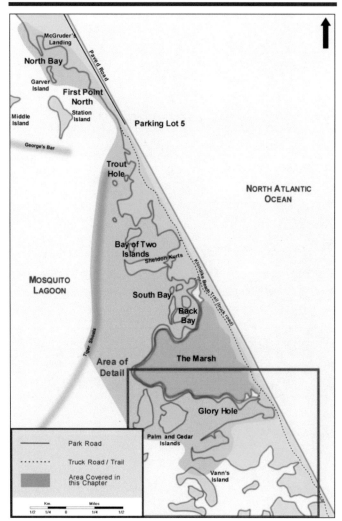

close at Glory Hole. This may be the location of one of the temporary inlets in ancient times. It may also become an inlet in the future with the rise in sea level.

Glory Hole is the practical limit of the wading territory if you access it on foot from Parking Lot 5. It is a three-mile, one-hour walk on the truck road / Klondike Beach Trail, assuming it is open to the public. The "exit" to Glory Hole is the only one after the Back Bay "exit". You cannot miss it. It will take you on the dike road between The Marsh and the north shore of Glory Hole and you can conveniently enter the water at the first culvert. This will put you close to the best fishing spot of this large area (see large-scale detailed map next).

You can also reach Glory Hole by walking on the dike around The Marsh from the Back Bay "exit". It is a longer walk and it may be mandatory if the truck road is closed to the public. It may be worth it to check what is going on in The Marsh. If for your own reasons you decide to walk along the shoreline of the lagoon or worse, try shortcuts, be aware that there are some dangerous soft spots in this area. Do not venture in the narrows between the dike and Palm and Cedar Islands.

Many anglers reach Glory Hole with carry-on crafts launched from WSEG Boat Ramp (see page 127). It is a shorter paddle than from Parking Lot 5. However, you may have trouble aiming directly at the entrance to Glory Hole early in the morning with a mist over the lagoon. In low water you may have to drag the craft over the shoals at the limit of the Poll and Troll Zone. If you come by boat you must enter at the pilings marking the south running lane and then take the north-south running lane to Bird Island. (The east running lane to Cat Hammock may seem shorter on the map but it is not practical in low water.) From Bird Island it is a long pole to Glory Hole and it may be a difficult one in low water.

Anglers reaching Glory Hole in a carry-on craft or light boat should be aware that the return trip may not be as pleasant as the morning paddle. Indeed, you may be facing the dominant afternoon northwest wind in the open water of the lagoon. While Glory Hole is reasonably sheltered from the wind you will face the full brunt of the waves on the return trip.

You will find in Glory Hole the replica of South Bay: skinny water above thick grass. The northeast end of the bay (close to the truck road) is very shallow and muddy. This is no place where you want to be unless the water is high enough for fish to be in this mud bowl. As you work your way to the open water most of Glory Hole is covered in thick grass and is relatively shallow. There are very few white spots big enough to warrant fishing them; therefore, fishing is restricted to sight fishing when redfish come up on the flats and tail. However, there is one large area that is both deep and relatively free of grass. This is what will take you to Glory Hole and it is worth the ride. Indeed, not only will you find reds, including schools, and large trout in this area you will also find Black Drum, quite a few of them and they are the perfect size for taking flies. As a bonus this spot is large enough to accommodate a few fishing partners. Being close to the north shoreline it is very easily accessed on foot and it has some protection against the north wind. It is marked as "White Spots" on the large-scale detailed map next.

Given the distance of Glory Hole to Parking Lot 5 you will likely be the only wader, but you may not be the only angler. The place is well known and you may be surprised to find that you are not alone in your world. Anglers come to Glory Hole in power boats. It is inside the Pole and Troll Zone and there are no direct running lanes to it. The place is not easily accessible by

---

VANN'S ISLAND

Vann's Island (spelled *Vanns* on topographical maps) is named after John Darling Vann and his family. Born in 1832 in north Georgia from a mother who was an Indian princess of the Cherokee tribe and from a father who was a Dutch trader, John Darling Vann came to Allenhurst, Florida in 1863 and got a job helping haul boats on the Old Haulover Canal with mules and oxen. Later he became a Coast Watcher for the government and walked the beach from Shiloh to Titusville looking for ships and people in trouble on the beach. While doing this he found enough lumber on the beach to build a fine house of mahogany and other lumber from shipwrecks and moved to Vann's Island in 1872.

This island of approximately 10 acres was the only high shell island in the area of mangrove islands around. Vann's Slough was the access to Vann's Island.

The Vann's family farmed the island, growing vegetables and onions that they sold in large quantities to the boat travelers on the waterways. John also fished and sold eggs and cured hams to travelers heading down to Haulover and in the Shiloh area. He and his wife lived and raised two children on the island until she died in 1896. He continued to live there with his son, John Daniel and daughter, Mabel, until his son left and moved to Oak Hill.

John Darling and his wife were very prominent people and had many friends from all over Florida, Georgia, and the Carolinas. People would come down for the winter and stay on the island. There were not many safe places for them to stay on the mainland. Vann's Island was listed on all the sailing charts as a haven for travelers. The people who came would stay with them, sometimes forty or fifty people. According to son John Daniel the Vanns held parties and dances that would start on Friday and last until the middle of the next week. During the Prohibition bootleggers smuggled whiskey and spirits right through the heart of Mosquito Lagoon in an attempt to evade the law. Vann's Island was one of the better place to "drink a few", and the family hosted parties on the island that still resonate today.

Preacher's Island is situated a short distance south of Vann's Island and is the southerly limit of Tiger Shoals and the Poll and Troll Zone. It was named for a travelling preacher who refused to stay at Vann's Island and instead camped for the night on the next highest island.

Sources: Volusia.com;
and personal research.

power boat in normal conditions and even less so in low water. And it is somewhat hidden from view. Unfortunately, you may witness boats coming or leaving under full power. Take a picture of the offender, enlarge the boat tag, and send it to the chief ranger of the Park.

There is one last fishing spot that I have hesitated before including it in this book as a destination that can be reached on foot. Vann's Slough is technically within the general area of Glory Hole and it is indeed accessible on foot. It is a walk… But you have already walked a lot to get to Glory Hole, so why not go all the way?

At the Glory Hole "exit" instead of taking the dike road north as you would to fish Glory Hole take the dike road to the *south*. Go around the mouth of the bay, walk the entire south shore of Glory Hole, and keep going until you reach the farthest point. Vann's Island is facing you. You may have to pick your way to the water a few hundred feet before you reach the point. There is some potential soft area at the point. Vann's Slough is a small area of deep water between the southern point of Glory Hole and Vann's Island. It is shown on the large-scale detailed map below. The slough has surprising geography, including a very deep trough that you cannot wade across, and shallow spots in the middle that look very much like submerged spoil islands from the digging of moorings. This matches the history of Vann's Island (see text box). Vann's Slough has "fish home" written all over it and indeed it is, in all water levels. The wading is on soft ground, but not as bad as it looks, as long as you stay off the deep and away from some black areas around the shore.

If you are coming by boat in low water the most convenient running lane is the north one. If you take the east running lane you will have to pole a length of very shallow water before reaching Vann's Slough.

North End of the Park

Even with the best planning one day it will happen: Parking Lot 5 is full and there are already cars in line waiting to park. You can only park in designated areas. The day is ruined. Well, not quite. I would not travel just to do this, but since you are already in the North District of Canaveral National Seashore, you could consider one of the alternatives in the north end of the Park. Turn around and drive back toward the entrance of the Park.

There are no accesses to the lagoon from Parking Lot 4. The first access to the lagoon on your way back is Parking Lot 3 and Castle Windy Trail. This is the only spot in the north end of the Park where you can wade and fly-fish for redfish with some probability of success. The other spots further north are almost exclusively a trout fishery, with a diversity of fish at Turtle Mound, including Bluefish. These fishing areas offer a river-like environment with a firm shell bottom and access to the deep water of the old navigation channel of Mosquito Lagoon.

The fishing areas and their accesses shown on the map next are covered in detail in this section, from south to north (as you return from Parking Lot 5): Castle Windy off Parking Lot 3; the Eldora Loop; Raggety Gap; and Turtle Mound. Aside from Parking Lot 3, which is rarely full, none of the parking areas give access to the beach. Your chances of finding a parking spot are excellent, even at the busiest times.

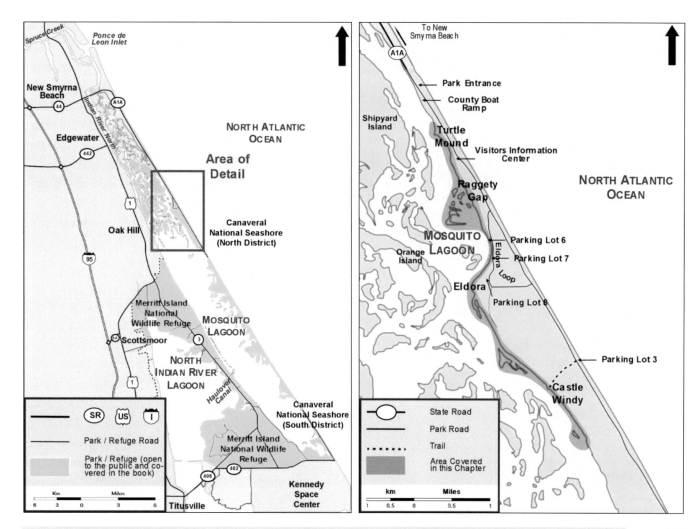

Castle Windy

From Parking Lot 3 take Castle Windy Trail to the lagoon. This is just a seven- or eight-minute walk, but bring the bug repellent. At the lagoon, you will observe that the principal characteristic of this area is its proximity to the channel. This is the old channel, the one that was used for transportation before the construction of the Intracoastal Waterway. Boats (and fish) use it as a travel lane today. This is one place where you can fish the transition zone between deep and shallow over a large area and there will be significant differences in the type and quantity of fish, depending upon the season and water level. You have the choice of three destinations.

Your first choice is to fish right there at the foot of the trail on and around the sand bar. This is going to be trout only, mostly small and mid-sized *schoolies*, although I have seen schools of slot-size fish at times. The trout will be in the deep water around the sand bar. You may have to look for them a little but you will eventually find them and it will be non-stop action on a weighed fly that you will let fall to the bottom and "trout-strip". The bottom is firm and this is very easy wading. The major difficulty will be to find a comfortable position where you have enough room for a back cast without being too deep in the water.

From the point off Castle Windy, looking north. A typical river environment.

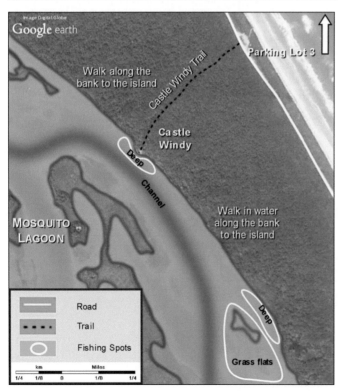

A second choice is to go south. This is much more serious in terms of fish, but also in terms of difficulty. Walk along the shore for approximately 30 minutes. Because the vegetation along the shore is overgrown, you have to walk in the water. The bottom is a little soft, but this is doable. It is easier in low water. I would not recommend it when the water level is above 0.60 on the height gauge at Haulover Canal. Near the end of your 30-minute walk you will encounter a small island surrounded by flats of mud and grass where reds are usually present. Trout will also be found in this area: some big ones swimming with the reds and the mullet closer to the island and smaller ones, much more numerous, in the deeper water closer to shore.

A final choice is to go north. This is a much shorter and easier walk. Usually you will be able to walk on shore or very near it, in good terrain. You will reach a group of islands separated from shore and from the channel by shallow mud and oyster flats. Depending upon the season and water level trout and redfish may be present on these flats. This is not my first choice and this spot has never been very generous for me, except for the memorable catch of a nice Crevalle Jack in the spring. You may have a different experience.

Eldora Loop

Next on your way back from Parking Lot 5 and proceeding toward the north is the Eldora Loop. It has two parking lots directly on the lagoon (6 and 7) and one giving foot access to Eldora State House and a fishing dock (8). There is also a fishing dock close to Parking Lot 7. There is a launch for carry-on crafts at both Parking Lots 6 and 7; however, the one at Parking Lot 7 is much more convenient. The shoreline between Parking Lot 6 and Eldora State House is a good wading area, and all three parking lots provide a practical access to the lagoon. This is a river environment and because the deep channel runs right along the shore you will be limited to wading along the shore and casting to deep water. As previously mentioned this is the old navigation channel of Mosquito Lagoon prior to the Intracoastal Waterway. The shoreline is mostly hard pack shells and easy to wade. Generally you will find adequate room for a back cast. Between Parking Lot 7 and the Eldora fishing dock groups of old pilings provide some structure in an otherwise regular and featureless shoreline. Big trout may be caught early in the morning among those pilings.

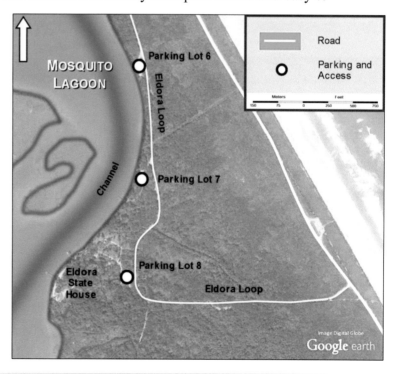

During the coldest days of the winter, when the water temperature falls into the 50s and low 60s, you may find a bunch of big trout in the deep channel off the old pilings. This is potentially one winter thermal refuge for trout if you can find them along the channel. Indeed, this is not a well-defined spot. If regrouped in the deep-water channel the concentration of big fish can be anywhere and will not be visible from the surface.

HISTORY OF ELDORA

The name Eldora may come from a shortened version of *Eldorado*, a common Spanish term for treasure and would refer to rumors of a buried treasure that would have attracted the early settlers from Missouri and Georgia to this area. More down to earth, the name could be a combination of early settlers Ellen and Dora Pitzer.

The land was granted in the 1880s. According to survey records it consisted of orange trees, a clearing along the shoreline, and a wagon road from the ocean to the wharf on the lagoon near the shell mound. The location of the settlement had everything to do with the natural channel of Mosquito Lagoon, a navigable waterway that was to become the engineered Intracoastal Waterway with the pending opening of the new Haulover Canal in 1888. Local residents, who numbered anywhere from 100 to 200 in the late 1800s, fished, crabbed, clammed, and grew citrus. Those products were loaded on passing sail and steamships bound for northern markets. This commerce created a bustling economy. Eventually the community had its own post office and school. But there was more to it than those industrious activities. Early in the twentieth century, Eldora also became a place where people from the north would come for the winter. Today's Eldora House was in fact Eldora Hotel. Most guests came to New Smyrna first by train; then, headed south along the barrier island via Riverside Trail, Turtle Mound and the beach. Eldora had become one of the snowbirds' destination that, according to The Florida Star, was "one of the most healthy spots on earth where many invalids from the North are to be found in great numbers ..."

The Roaring Twenties brought subdivision plans, development projects, and the promise of wealth to the community. These hopes were flattened by a perfect storm of events. Between 1924 and 1934 the Intracoastal Waterway was relocated on the other side of Mosquito Lagoon, bypassing Eldora, which became isolated. Mother Nature dealt the second blow. Hard freezes struck the area destroying much of the citrus crops. The economic depression in Florida preceded the more notorious 1929 nationwide and worldwide depressions by three years. Finally, any possibility of recovery of the real-estate market and of Florida's economy was destroyed by the September, 1926 hurricane. Like numerous other small communities Eldora never came back. Fishing camps operated in the vicinity for several years before the entire area from Turtle Mound to the House of Refuge was taken over by Canaveral National Seashore in 1975.

Eldora House is the only original structure still standing. It has been renovated and turned into a museum by the Park and it is open to the public and free.

Sources: Susan Parker. 2008. *Canaveral National Seashore, Historic Resource Study*. Edited by Robert W. Blythe. National Park Service. Atlanta. www.nps.gov/history/history/online_books/cana/cana_hrs.pdf (as of this writing);
Jimmy Jacob. 2010. *Eldora: A Florida East Coast Ghost Town*. Atlanta Outdoor Examiner, Examiner.com. Atlanta;
and personal research.

Eldora State House at Christmas. Recently restored, it is now a museum and is well worth a visit.

Old pilings and shoreline at the Eldora Loop. Big trout may hang around early in the morning.

In the worst of the winter you will notice that the place is wide open and can be badly beaten by the northwest winds.

Other than the elusive winter thermal refuge in the channel the shoreline offers the same type of fishing that you can do on the sand point at Castle Windy. Early in the morning you may hit some big trout in the shallow. Later in the day you will likely find schools of small trout in the deeper water. Cast them a weighed fly and catch one every second cast. You will not likely find redfish in this environment.

This area will be definitely better when the water level is normal or high and the water temperature mild. In the cold and low water of the coldest winter days the place may be barren.

Raggety Gap

Raggety Gap is the area along the east shore of Mosquito lagoon situated between Eldora and Turtle Mound. The name appears on topographic maps. It is also locally called "The Leases" as it is an oyster-growing area. It is accessible by parking at the Visitors Center and walking along the shore toward the south or by parking at Parking Lot 6 of the Eldora Loop and walking along the shore toward the north. You can also launch a carry-on craft from both accesses.

Contrary to the adjacent areas Raggety Gap offers some geography and shelter from the wind, thanks to the bunch of small islands. The basic geomorphology of the place is comparable with what you have north of Castle Windy, but the area between the main channel and the shore is wider. It remains a river-like environment with firm bottom. There are oyster bars, tidal current in secondary channels, and some deep spots.

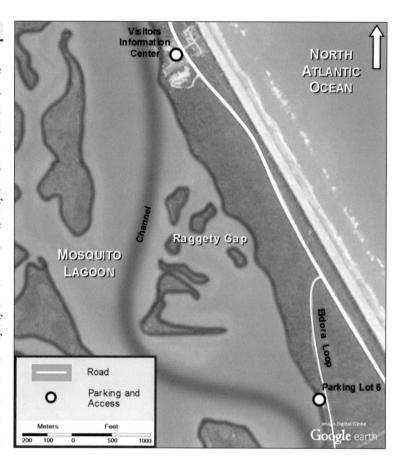

The place looks good on the map. Indeed, it may be at certain times of the year and in certain conditions. In my visits I found mostly small Spotted Seatrout. You may have a different experience with this spot. For me, it has been a waste of time.

Turtle Mound

Turtle Mound is an environment similar to the other spots along the north end of the Park as far as the ease to wade and the relative absence of redfish. However, at Turtle Mound you will regularly find Weakfish and Bluefish. I recommend a visit to Turtle Mound to anglers new to wade fly-fishing or to fly-fishing in salt water. This is the ideal setup to get a sure footing, practice your casts, your stripping and hook sets. To access this spot park along the paved road in the designated spaces at Turtle Mound, just a few hundred feet past the Park admission booth and the County

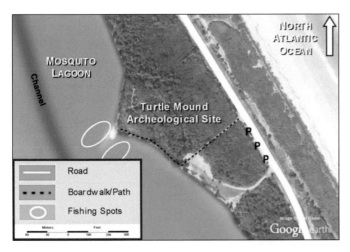

Boat Ramp. Take the path that leads to the mound (this is the boardwalk north of the parking). Leave the boardwalk near the shoreline and walk north along the shore (to your right) for approximately 400 feet until you come to the point. You will clearly see that the point extends quite far in the water as a sandbar with one or two feet of water on top, depending on the general water level and on the tide. Wade on the sandbar and fish the deep holes on either side, depending on the direction of the current. Small trout will likely be mixed with Weakfish and Bluefish and the occasional Ladyfish and Crevalle Jack in season. Use a weighed fly, anything will do, and a heavy shock tippet or steel wire if blues are present.

This area is the most affected by tide in the entire territory covered in this book. The presence of Bluefish will likely be conditioned by the tide, as these fish seem to come and go in schools with the tide. I and others fishing this spot could not figure out which tide brings the fish, if there is one. But you will likely notice a change, for the good or otherwise, with every change in the tide.

I have heard from reliable sources that the deep holes on either sides of the sand bar can be a winter thermal refuge for large trout under certain circumstances. As is the case for the Eldora Loop, Turtle Mound can be badly beaten by a bad northwest wind in the winter.

You can wade surprisingly far out on the sand bar at Turtle Mound.

TURTLE MOUND

Turtle Mound is the highest shell midden in the nation. It was built mostly from oyster shell by the prehistoric Timucuan Indians who visited the site repeatedly over centuries. This two-acre site contains over 35,000 cubic yards of oyster shell, extends more than 600 feet along the Indian River / Mosquito Lagoon shoreline, and stands about 50 feet tall. In prehistoric times it was at least 75 feet high. Visible for miles offshore the mound has been used as a navigational landmark since the early days of Spanish exploration. In 1605 Spanish explorer Alvaro Mexia visited the site, called Surruque for the Indian tribe that lived in the area during the 16th and 17th centuries, and reported natives launching their dugout canoes at the mound's base. Besides Surruque the place has also been named Mount Belvedere, The Rock, Mount Tucker, and Turtle *Mount*. Over the years, this huge feature began to take the shape of a turtle—hence its current name. Contrary to most others the Turtle Mound shell midden has been largely preserved. The top of the mound offers a commanding view of the ocean and of Mosquito Lagoon. To prevent the degradation associated with the climbing a boardwalk allows an easy access to the top. On September 29, 1970 Turtle Mound was added to the U.S. National Register of Historic Places.

Sources: Volusia County Heritage, a partnership between the Volusia County Historic Preservation Board and the Volusia County Government;
Susan Parker. 2008. *Canaveral National Seashore, Historic Resource Study*. Edited by Robert W. Blythe. National Park Service. Atlanta. www.nps.gov/history/history/online_books/cana/cana_hrs.pdf (as of this writing); and personal research.

2 – SOUTHEAST MOSQUITO LAGOON IN THE PARK

The South District of Canaveral National Seashore is off Titusville on State Road 402. Without being an exact replica, it is generally comparable with the North District in that most of the visiting traffic is oriented toward the ocean-side beach, named Playalinda Beach in this area. And like the North District the South District opens up to Mosquito Lagoon at a few locations. These are the access points covered in this book, from south to north as you travel from Titusville or from points north on Kennedy Parkway.

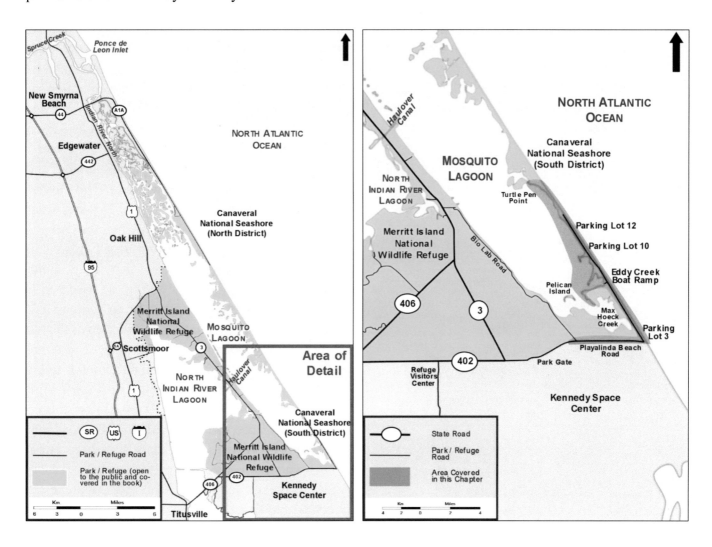

But before Playalinda Beach Road reaches the beach and veers north along it you will be travelling due east in the vast marsh south of Mosquito Lagoon. To the trained eye of Tarpon hunters this marsh holds some fly-fishing potential.

Playalinda Beach Road

The Park admission gate to the South District of Canaveral National Seashore is just off Kennedy Parkway on State Road 402, or Playalinda Beach Road. The 3.5-mile drive to the beach is a boring 35-mph hiatus for most people. The road crosses the marsh south of Mosquito Lagoon and is paradise for bird watchers. This is a salt marsh with water flowing in and out of Mosquito Lagoon in high water. The main inlet is Max Hoeck Back Creek. At the dike on Mosquito Lagoon the culvert is controlled to let lagoon water flow in during periods of high water and to prevent marsh water from flowing out during periods of low water. This is done for the purpose of mosquito control; therefore, the salt marsh does not dry out when the water level falls in the lagoon. The deeper holes of the salt marsh are typical nursery for baby and juvenile Tarpon. They presumably enter Max Hoeck Back Creek as babies through the culvert at Mosquito Lagoon in high water. As they grow they must seek the deeper water spots that will shield them from the drops in the water temperature typical of our winters. This is where the dredged holes and ditches come in handy. Indeed, while Max Hoeck Back Creek and the other ponds of the marsh have few natural areas that are deep enough for survival of juvenile Tarpon in our climate the dredged holes and roadside ditches do. Therefore, as unlikely as it may appear, Playalinda Beach Road is a juvenile Tarpon fishing spot.

Tarpon can be anywhere in these ditches and you should look for them everywhere. The mouths of culverts can be fish-holding spots. Flowing water means dinner of course, but even when the culverts are not flowing previous scouring usually results in slightly deeper water where fish may hold. Playalinda Beach Road is new. But the road bed is not. This was the old railroad, later moved one-half of a mile to the south. For the construction of the old railroad a few borrow pit were dug. These are difficult to distinguish from the natural ponds today except for their regular shape. One such borrow pit is next to Max Hoeck Back Creek to the east. It is no longer easily accessible on foot from the road and the overgrown vegetation prevents fly-fishing. But it is deep enough to be a refuge for juvenile Tarpon. Areas in the vicinity of this borrow pit are more likely to hold fish.

More recently for the construction of Playalinda Beach Road (on the old railroad bed), ditches were dug on both sides of the road. These ditches are just deep enough for Tarpon to survive in them. Since there is an extensive network of culverts the fish can find their areas of comfort and will sometimes be found right along the road.

One potential determinant for the location of juvenile Tarpon along the road is Max Hoeck Back Creek. This creek is the main route from the lagoon to the marsh. While it is hard to see in high water the geomorphology of the area suggests that the little channel west of the main creek was the main streambed—or important among other streambeds—when the level of the ocean was much lower in prehistorical times. This was then and is probably now the highway for the circulation of fish.

Roadside ditch along the north side of Playalinda Beach Road. This section is a little wider and is the most likely place for juvenile Tarpon.

The roadside-ditch spot shown on the map and in the picture is between the two branches of the creek and is near the borrow pit above-mentioned. It has a few good openings from the side of the road for a back cast. Since the water depth is limit juvenile Tarpon may have to find refuge somewhere else during the cold winter months; therefore, you may not find them at this location all the time.

This is inside the Park. Parking is restricted to the designated spots. There are several, strategically located. Walking along the road is your best bet. However, you can drop a carry-on craft from some of the designated parking areas and explore the ditch and connected marsh on the north side of the road. The ditch on the south side of the road can be fished from the road side but you cannot drop a craft in it, because it is in the security area of NASA. You can drop a light boat

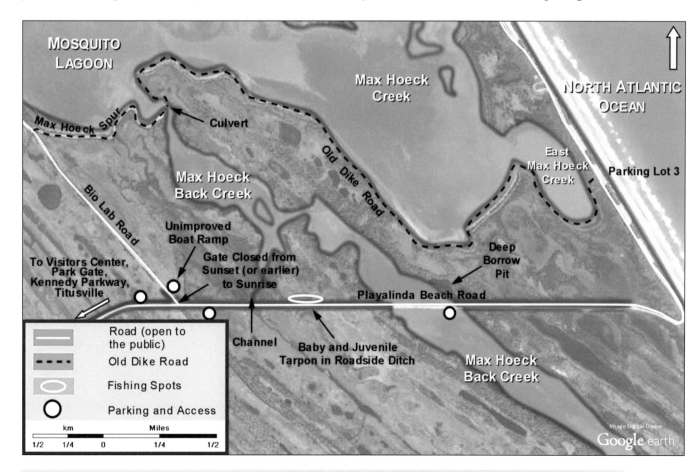

Odd couple taking the sun and watching fly-fisher (glad to be in a boat) near Playalinda Beach Road.

from a trailer (with a vehicle that has good traction) from an unimproved ramp at Bio Lab Road. Duck hunters use this ramp. You may find the ditch quite narrow at a few locations. Nevertheless, you have access everywhere on the north side of the road.

Blind casting from the best openings in the bushes is not the way on these or on any other Tarpon. These fish will most likely be grouped in just one or two spots and will likely move with the seasons and the fluctuating water levels. You must see fish rolling and make a positive Tarpon identification. Then, and only then, you will figure out a way to put a fly to them. This is ditch fishing, with obstacles and potential tangles everywhere. Finesse in not on the menu. Use a strong leader and winch the fish out of there as fast as you can. They should all be babies or young juveniles. While the Tarpon will likely be small the alligators are not. This is home for them and they are both abundant and big. Stay high and dry and keep an eye around all the time.

Playalinda Beach

Aside from Eddy Creek Boat Ramp giving access to Mosquito Lagoon and covered next the South District of Canaveral National Seashore is entirely focused on the beach on the North Atlantic Ocean, called Playalinda Beach. For the wade fly-fishers a few parking lots of Playalinda Beach provide little-known but convenient accesses to southeast Mosquito Lagoon.

The wading access points are, from south to north: Eddy Creek Boat Ramp; Parking Lot 10; and Parking Lot 12. The truck road / Klondike Beach Trail that runs north the entire length of the Park is off limits to the public. The old dike road that goes around Max Hoeck Creek and links the southeast and southwest shores of Mosquito Lagoon can be walked from Parking Lot 3 and gives access to fishing spots in the south end of Mosquito Lagoon. The trail is overgrown with tall grass. A better access to these fishing spots is from Bio Lab Road in the Refuge and this is covered in the next chapter on page 146.

The entire three-mile wading territory of southeast Mosquito Lagoon between Eddy Creek and Turtle Pen Point is a shallow grass flat interspersed with white (sand) spots. This is typical redfish tailing territory in normal water levels and can provide very exciting fishing early in the morning when the fish are actively feeding in calm water. Once this period is over the fish will tend to gather in white spots or deeper areas of their choice. This can also provide good fly-fishing opportunities; however, finding these fishing spots wading is not easy. Other than for the specific fishing spots shown on the next pages drifting in a kayak or a boat is the best way to fish this general territory.

Eddy Creek

Eddy Creek was most likely an inlet in a distant past. It has serious geography, with a deep channel in the south half of the creek, islands at the point that almost block access to the open water, and a very nice grass flat in the north half of the creek. Eddy Creek is also the only boat ramp in the South District of Canaveral National Seashore. It is an unimproved ramp minimally maintained but adequate for light boats and vehicles with adequate traction. The open water past Eddy Point can be a little shallow in low water. At the busiest times of the year you may want to get there early because there are very few parking stalls for trailers. Same applies if you carry a kayak or canoe on car tops or in pick-up beds: the regular parking spots are not numerous either and are shared with dock anglers, people fishing along the shores of Eddy Creek, and by beach goers.

The fishing dock at Eddy Creek. The deep water is along the south half of the creek (left on the picture).

On top of being the closest boating access to the south end of Mosquito Lagoon Eddy Creek itself is a good fishing spot. The area close to the dock is the deepest; however, the entire south half of the creek is a deep channel and is one of the winter thermal refuges of the lagoons. During cold snaps trout will congregate by the thousands in the deep areas of Eddy Creek, earning the place the unequivocal surname of the "Trout Hole". You can wade anywhere from the south shore of the creek. It is firm and this gives you access to the deep water right along the shore all the way from the dock to the point and around it. In the coldest periods of the winter this will likely be your best bet.

The north half of the creek can also be waded at will. You can access it by walking on the recently leveled and filled area of the old dike. There is a well-beaten path from the loop of the dock and boat ramp (see map). This is not a sign of high foot traffic to the entire creek but the path made by bait casters to the shore of the creek at the right of the dock. You will most likely have the entire north half of the creek to yourself; indeed, it is a little soft. Access it directly from the bait casters opening north of the dock or from a very small opening in the bushes near the first point (marked on the large-scale detailed map next). One enticing opening at a ditch would put you in very soft terrain; trying to cut through the shoreline shrubs would tear your waders. Follow the indications on the map.

The entire north half of the creek is a good grass flat. You may wade it to cast to the deep section of the creek and this can be useful in the winter when the wind is blowing from the wrong

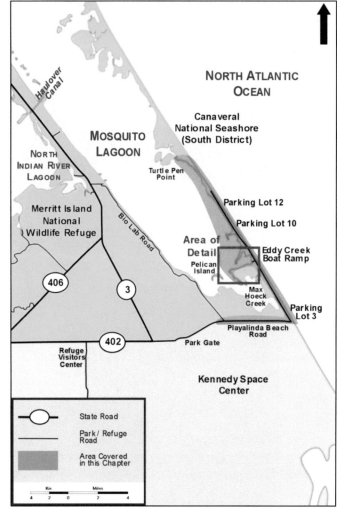

direction. But you will mostly fish the flat itself for redfish tailing in the grass, and the good white spots marked on the map. Several areas along the shoreline are slightly deeper and are particularly favorable for tailing fish as well as for shore cruisers and bait busters. You can wade everywhere on a reasonably good bottom, for a grass flat, that is. The only spot where you should not go is an enticing opening inside the creek near the tip of Eddy Point. It is marked on the map.

The south shore of Eddy Creek can be walked at will and, if you are up to it, will give you access to the entrance of Max Hoeck Creek. You will find a good spot of deep water very accessible between the east island and the shore. It is marked by white PVC pipes. Trout in all sizes are often present in this deep-water area, more so in low water. As you progress south the sand-bottomed deep water becomes a grass flat. This transition zone, marked as "Last Point" on the map, is a favorable environment for larger trout and for redfish.

It is a 1.2-mile walk from the ramp to the Last Point. For most waders this is the limit of a comfortable walk. It is also the limit of the comfortable wading terrain. Plenty of fish await you in Max Hoeck Creek, in fact not a creek at all but a large bay with a mixture of grass and white spots in knee-deep water: perfect tailing ground for redfish and also a place where you will find schools at times in the winter. These large flats are better fished from a carry-on craft or light boat since you will likely have to cover a large territory to find fish. Early in the morning you may spot tailing fish accessible on foot.

You will likely prefer to work Max Hoeck Creek from the opposite shoreline and this is a long wade from Eddy Creek. And there is the *other* wildlife. While you may feel that this is really too close to the ocean for alligators there is a diked marsh between the paved road and Max Hoeck

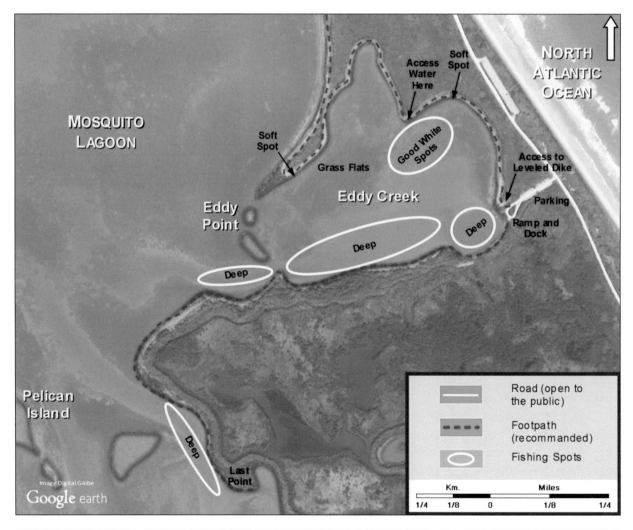

Creek. Alligators live in this marsh and will routinely show up in the salt water of the lagoon. Bio Lab Road in the Refuge provides an easier access on foot (see page 144). But this is also a long walk.

Parking Lots 10 to 12

North of Eddy Creek we are leaving the south marsh and we are back on the narrow barrier island in a setup that is comparable with the one found at Parking Lot 5 of the North District of Canaveral National Seashore. In theory this area is free of alligators.

Galliniper Point and Basin are the next significant geographical features to the north. There is an area of slightly deeper water and good white

Looking at NASA installations from the Last Point *south of Eddy Creek. Mosquito Lagoon wade fly-fishing with a view.*

spots north of Galliniper Point that can be easily accessed from Parking Lots 10 or 11. Walk on the road half-way between the two parking lots to the sign "PARK IN DESIGNATED AREAS ONLY", find a beaten path through the shrubs to the water or pick your way; it is a very short distance. The best path to the water is a short distance south of a white PVC pipe in the lagoon near the shore.

The good area of white spots is a few hundred feet from the access point, around two white PVC pipes. It is marked on the map. It harbors redfish and trout in normal and normal-high water levels. In my experience, this is the best spot in the entire area.

You can walk all around Galliniper Point to reach the middle of Galliniper Basin, where additional white spots in deeper water may also harbor fish in normal or high water levels. The deeper area is between the point and the first of the two white PVC pipes. Walking around the point is not bad. However, getting to the white spots from the point involves walking on thick grass over soft bottom and is not for everybody. The presence of fish in this area is seasonal.

Away from shore and a little south of Galliniper Point there is a sand bar that goes half-way to the Whale Tail. If you are up to it you may reach the sand bar on foot in low and medium-low water levels and follow it half-way to Whale Tail Shoal. Along the sand bar and south of it lies a long channel of deeper water. The area of deeper water may harbor fish at any time, mostly trout in the winter. Also the transition zone between the sand-bottomed deep water and the shallow grass can be a winning combination for redfish, again mostly in the low water of the winter.

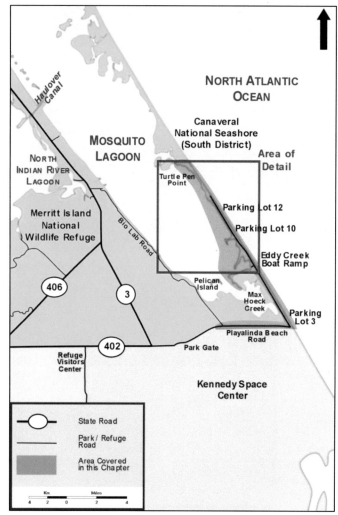

The last access to the beach is Parking Lot 13. The area north of it is closed to the public and the Backcountry permit is for the beach only. While you are not allowed to walk on land (except on the beach, with a Backcountry permit) you are allowed to wade the shoreline; the lagoon is never closed. Parking Lot 13 can be used to access the lagoon because access is no longer blocked by a ditch; however, it involves walking through the bushes. Parking Lot 12 is not the northernmost but it is the most convenient access to the open waters of Southeast Mosquito Lagoon at this location.

Anglers have beaten a convenient path to the water from the north end of Parking Lot 12. You can drag a carry-on craft on this path but there will be some suffering. Access to the lagoon is muddy, but not dangerous if you go straight out toward open water. Do not attempt to cut to the right along the shore. This will get you into a soft area and serious trouble. Given the rough path and muddy bank many anglers prefer to launch their carry-on craft at the Eddy Creek Boat Ramp 1.9 miles south. Waders do not have this choice.

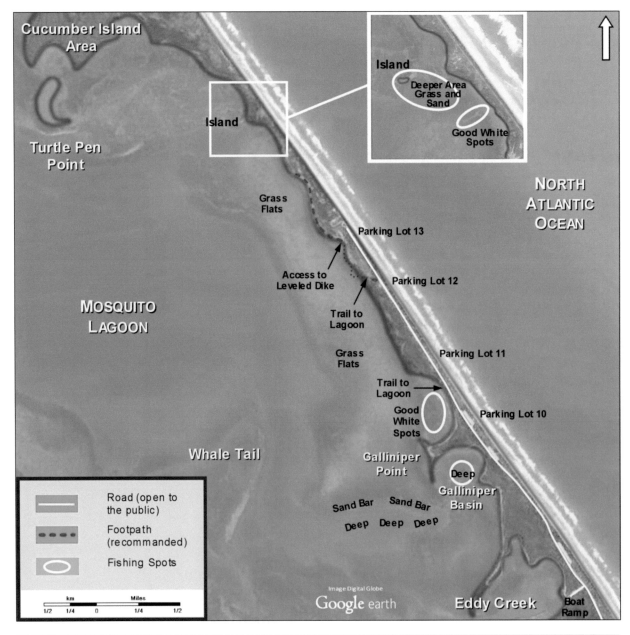

This is not as bad as it looks. Indeed, the muddy access point from Parking Lot 12 is the exception along this shoreline. Wade straight out to the open water, make a wide swing and come back either north or south to a reasonably packed shoreline that you can walk.

Going south is not very easy but doable. You may have to alternate between open water and shoreline. This is easier in low water; however, the grass flat is not very deep and will likely become devoid of fish in very low water. The shallow grass flats typical of the area are interspersed with some white spots. You will find redfish tailing in the grass in the morning and lying in the white spots during the day.

The white spots north of Galliniper Point viewed from the open water. One of the good spots in this area.

Going north is much easier. Indeed, a long section of dike has recently been leveled and provides a very easy path for the wader (although this may be stretching the legality of walking along the shoreline). This easy section starts close to the access point and goes north for half-a-mile, well on your way to *The Island*. The bushes have begun to grow on this barren area and at some point in the future it may become more difficult to walk. However, as of writing this is the closest thing to walking on a road. All along your walk you may see fish tailing in the grass flats along the shore and there are a few nice white spots that you can fish. However, the best spots that I have found in this vast area are around the small island that lies 175 yards from shore one mile north of Parking Lot 12.

Three hundred yards before reaching the island there is a line of white spots in a slightly deeper area. This line of white spots has been very productive for me. It is marked on the inset of the map as "Good White Spots".

All around the island—except toward the shore, where there is a shallow sand bar—you will find slightly deeper water and a mix of grass and sand. This is one easy-wade spot that is deep enough to be blind cast in normal water level.

Further to the north Turtle Pen Point and Cucumber Island area are significant geographic land features. The geography extends in the water, with sand bars, sloughs, grass flats and deeper areas. According to Captain John Kumiski, a renowned guide of the lagoons (www. Spottedtail.com as of this writing) this area is one of the best of the lagoon, regularly harboring reds in the 20-pound class. However, there are no accesses allowed from land and I consider the walk along the shore beyond the reach of wading. If you want to reach this area with a boat or carry-on craft you have the alternative of launching at Bio Lab Boat Ramp and crossing the open water of the lagoon.

The small island north of Parking Lot 12. This is the practical northern limit of the wading territory from the south.

3 – SOUTHWEST MOSQUITO LAGOON IN THE REFUGE

South of Oak Hill the southwest shore of Mosquito Lagoon is in Merritt Island National Wildlife Refuge (the Refuge). This is a park-like environment without the same level of infrastructure, without the restrictions on parking, and with more flexible hours than in the Park. You need a Refuge Fishing Permit to fish in the Refuge, free and self-procured on the Internet. Go to www.fws.gov/merrittisland/ and look for *Fishing Regulations* (as of this writing). You may take advantage of the longer hours. Contrary to the Canaveral National Seashore you can enter as early as you want and you do not have to rush out to make it at the gate before 6:00 PM. There are no gates. The Refuge closes at sunset. In Refuge language, *closes* means that you cannot be fishing from shore after sunset, and this includes wading. However, you can certainly fish until sunset and drive out in the dark.

There used to be fishing camps north of Haulover Canal: Swift's Camp is shown on a map of 1880; Shiloh Camp and Beacon Camp are shown on more recent maps. The old side roads giving access to these camps are closed to the public and all installations have been removed. Two boat ramps currently provide the only public accesses to Mosquito Lagoon: WSEG and Beacon 42 Boat Ramps. Both are accessed by a short side road off Kennedy Parkway. The accesses to

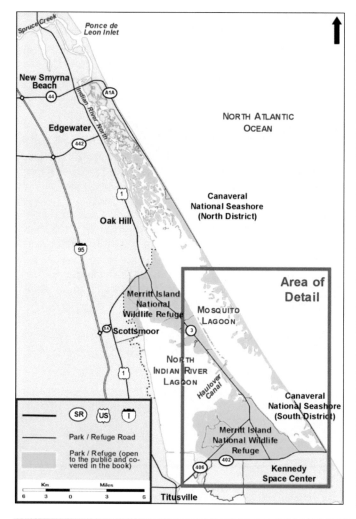

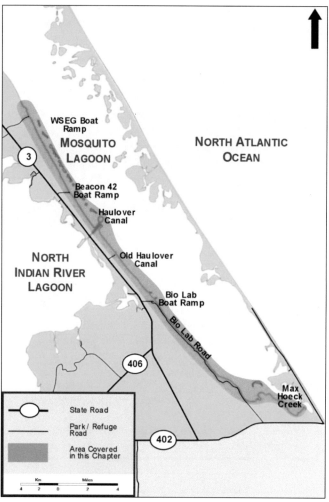

Mosquito Lagoon at, and south of, Haulover Canal are much more numerous and are covered in the next sections.

Generally, the topography of the west shore of Mosquito Lagoon is comparable to the one of the barrier island along the ocean: relatively straight and featureless. This was the beach in prehistoric times when the sea level was higher. However, it offers multiple fish habitat and wade fly-fishing opportunities because it was significantly modified by men before the takeover by NASA and the establishment of the Refuge. North of Haulover the Intracoastal Waterway has changed the landscape forever. South of Haulover several small service canals have been dredged inland and the south end of the lagoon has been diked for mosquito impoundments.

This chapter is divided into four sections, from north to south: North of Haulover Canal; Haulover Canal Area; South of Haulover Canal; and South End of Mosquito Lagoon. Within each of these four sections, the subsections correspond with the different accesses to Mosquito Lagoon on foot.

North of Haulover Canal

Wading opportunities along the west shore of Mosquito Lagoon north of Haulover are limited by both the lack of accesses[33] and the nature of the terrain. The old village of Shiloh, straddling the county line, and WSEG Boat Ramp are the northern limit of the pre-NASA modern development in this area. The vast area north of it was either occupied by a section of Elliott Plantation (Ross Hammock) in the early days of Florida or left in a wild state. The shoreline is straight and featureless in this section of the lagoon, a reminder of the ocean beach in prehistoric times, and

---

HISTORY OF SHILOH

The village of Shiloh was settled in January 1883 on the narrow strip of land between the west shore of Mosquito Lagoon and the east shore of North Indian River Lagoon, astride today's Brevard and Volusia Counties. It was originally settled by Mr. John Kuhl from Illinois. When the Kuhls came to Florida, there were no wagon roads anywhere in this section, only trails through the scrub and timber. Oak Hill and Eldora existed as well as the settlement of Clifton, north of Haulover Canal. The next village was Titusville. The population of Shiloh was 35 in 1886.

Shiloh was a trade center for the Indian River, being on the main channel of Mosquito Lagoon (from Eldora across the lagoon) and near Haulover Canal. Shiloh also had a thriving citrus growing industry that was pioneered by names that we now find on our fishing maps: Manning Griffis (for Griffis Bay), George Kuhl (for Georges Flats), J.E. Patillo (for Patillo Creek), James A. Taylor (for Taylor Road / WSEG Boat Ramp), etc. The population of Shiloh peaked at 181 residents in 1925. In 1945 it was down to 97. Like many small villages of the area whose economy was based on the citrus trade killer frosts dealt a fatal blow to an economy that had already been weakened by the Great Depression and changes in the axis of development. NASA took over the territory in the late fifties.

Very little remains from this settlement today. Driving Kennedy Parkway and WSEG Boat Ramp the only hints of the previous existence of the village of Shiloh is the name "Shiloh Radar" and a few concrete slabs where buildings once stood at the intersection of the road leading to WSEG Boat Ramp.

Sources: Susan Parker. 2008. *Canaveral National Seashore, Historic Resource Study.* Edited by Robert W. Blythe. National Park Service. Atlanta. www.nps.gov/history/history/online_books/cana/cana_hrs.pdf (as of this writing);
Brevard County History, Indian River Journal;
and personal research.

---

[33] Most of the side roads shown on some maps are closed to the public.

there is very little fresh water. Consequently, the area is not normally frequented by alligators but there may be exceptions, and one should always be cautious nevertheless. This is not the best area for wading.

There are only two accesses to Mosquito Lagoon open to the public north of Haulover Canal: WSEG Boat Ramp and Beacon 42 Boat Ramp. Both offer limited wading opportunities. WSEG is the northerly one and the first one that you will encounter as you travel south on Kennedy Parkway. The intersection of WSEG Boat Ramp and Kennedy Parkway is the approximate location of the county line and of the old village of Shiloh.

WSEG Boat Ramp

The name is from the call letters of a radio station that broadcast this area from a tower located here before NASA. The dirt road leading to WSEG Boat Ramp bears the name Taylor Road on some maps. See text box next. The intersection of this dirt road with Kennedy Parkway is where the village of Shiloh was located and a few old foundations are a reminder that this place was once busy.

The parking of the boat ramp is unimproved—in fact you squeeze between trees under the canopy—and the boat ramp is minimally improved with open concrete pavers. The basin and the canal are very narrow. When the water is low, launching a sizeable boat there could be challenging. Of course the ramp is adequate for canoes, kayaks and light boats. Because it is considered *unimproved*—it is indeed a little muddy, parking is what you can find, and the road may be rough—public use of this ramp remains free. If you have the benefit of a light boat or carry-on craft you will find a good environment north of the ramp. In this area, the Intracoastal Waterway is some distance from the shoreline and the spoil

---

HISTORY OF J.A. TAYLOR

In August 1884, Mr. James A. Taylor, a young man of 19, came to Florida in a spirit of adventure and to visit an aunt, Mrs. Jane Dixon, at City Point. Mrs. Dixon had come to Florida in 1870. Returning to Kentucky in 1885, Mr. Taylor became Florida-sick and, now married, landed at Shiloh with a wife, three children, provisions for one year, and 35 dollars—11 of these dollars due on freight.

Mr. Taylor set out a grove of five acres. During the winter of 1894-95 two freezes came; the first ruined the fruits; the second froze the trees to the ground. Mr. Taylor moved to Eldora and secured work. By successful management he was able to replant the groves. At one time he owned about 1,500 acres. Mr. Taylor was President of the Shiloh Packing Company, as well as one of its directors. He was Supervisor of the Shiloh School for many years and, with his neighbors, met many of its expenses. He had a large modern home lighted by a Delco Plant, which also lit the Taylor Store.

Sources: Susan Parker. 2008. *Canaveral National Seashore, Historic Resource Study*. Edited by Robert W. Blythe. National Park Service. Atlanta. www.nps.gov/history/history/online_books/cana/cana_hrs.pdf (as of this writing);
Brevard County History, Indian River Journal;
and personal research.

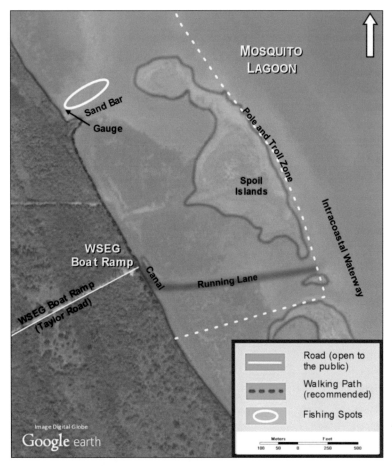

MOSQUITO LAGOON

Sand Bar

Gauge

Pole and Troll Zone

Spoil Islands

Intracoastal Waterway

WSEG Boat Ramp

Canal

Running Lane

WSEG Boat Ramp (Taylor Road)

Image Digital Globe

Google earth

	Road (open to the public)
	Walking Path (recommended)
	Fishing Spots

Meters   Feet
100 50 0   250   500

islands are on the shore side of the waterway. This has created an interesting geography of shallow bays and deeper passages between the spoil islands. There is good grass on the flats and nice white spots in the passages. A large section north of the ramp is a Pole and Troll Zone. There is also some shelter from the dominant west wind. The fish seem to move easily from the deep water of the Intracoastal Waterway to the shallow grass flats.

The boat ramp is the only foot access to the lagoon. The access is a bit tricky because of the very soft shoreline along the canal in front of the ramp. Do not attempt to wade along this canal. However, once you make it out of the boat ramp area the shoreline and the flats can be waded.

To reach the *wadeable* stretch of shoreline from the boat ramp follow loosely defined footpaths to the shoreline on either side of the parking area. Under the thin layer of dead grass you will find a nice shoreline of hard sand—it was the ocean beach several thousand years ago—that can be waded once you get far enough from the ramp. Typically, the flats are a little soft but manageable. At times of normal and normal-high water levels the flats will yield reds tailing or schooled up and single reds and trout in the white spots. The areas surrounding the spoil islands are generally firm. Unfortunately, the best fishing areas are a little far and you need a boat or carry-on craft for a practical access to them.

There is one welcome exception. Less than one-quarter of a mile north of the ramp there is a sharp point and a very shallow sand bar. On the north side of the point, there is a gauge (see picture). The much deeper water north of the sand bar is a magnet for fish. Since it does not have a black-mud bottom, the place does not seem to be a regular winter thermal refuge. But you will often find fish in this large deep spot in all conditions, including in the cold water of the winter. The spot can be fished from any side in any water level. In extreme high water you may still be able to fish it from the sand bar, but the walk along the shore will not be as easy.

When boat traffic is light you may also find fish holding in and around the running lane to the boat ramp. Again, stay away from the shoreline around the ramp when wading out to the running lane. You should be able to cross this shallow running lane at will in low water.

The gauge north of WSEG Boat Ramp. The deep water in front is a good spot in all water levels.

Beacon 42 Boat Ramp

This is also a ramp that has been minimally improved; however, the parking area is clear, level, and much larger and the area is not free (see picture and text below). The ramp basin and the access canal are deeper than at WSEG and typical flats boats can be launched there in all water levels. For the same reasons as at WSEG the wading access is tricky and may be impossible other than in very low water. I do not recommend this boat ramp for wading. If you insist and find your way to the open water, you will find an environment comparable to the one described at WSEG Boat Ramp (preceding subsection), albeit a little poorer in my opinion. The deep ditch that runs along the shoreline south of the ramp almost to Haulover Canal is one spot that you may wish to work. It is much easier to access it on foot from Haulover Canal (see next).

Three improved boat ramps of the Refuge (Beacon 42, Bairs Cove and Bio Lab) and Black Point Wildlife Drive are fee areas. Users of the fee areas have the option to purchase a $5.00 daily pass on site from a self-serve fee station (cash or checks), or a $15.00 annual pass good for all Refuge fee areas, or the $35.00 annual pass for Canaveral National Seashore (good for the two Park districts and all Refuge fee areas) available at the admission gates of the Park and at the Refuge Visitors Center. When buying the annual Park pass ask for the mirror-hang tag. (All fees are as of this writing.)

Haulover Canal Area

The part of the Haulover Canal Area covered in this chapter is the east part, on Mosquito Lagoon. Coverage of the fishing territory north of the canal begins next. The fishing territory south of the canal is covered in the following subsection. The west part of the Haulover Canal Area, on North Indian River Lagoon, is covered in the next chapter on pages 159 and following.

Haulover Canal Area North

There is only one good access to Mosquito Lagoon immediately north of Haulover Canal. The area accessible is not terribly exciting for geography but there is a good spot that few people know: it is the deeper water along the shore that starts a few hundred yards north of Haulover Canal and extends half-way to Beacon 42 Boat Ramp. Reaching this spot involves walking on a footpath along Haulover Canal and then wading to the spot *away* from shore, not walking along the shore. This convoluted access, the low visibility, the difficult boat access in low water and the lack of parking close to the spot are likely good reasons for the very low traffic at this spot.

Park at the Manatee Observation Deck. Parking at this location may be a little safer than in more remote places of the Haulover Canal Area due to the constant traffic to the Manatee Observation Deck. You will see the remnants of an old road to the northeast that is blocked and is now seriously overtaken by vegetation. A well beaten footpath from this road will take you along Haulover Canal. You can fish the canal itself from at least one spot where there is just enough room for a back cast. Bait casters frequent this spot. Now is the time to use your sinking line and weighed flies. This is not my game, but you may hit it at the right time. The tide carries through the inlet and everything swimming in the lagoons either lives in or passes through Haulover Canal. It has the reputation of yielding big Red and Black drums.

At the end of the path you are at the southern limit of the large flat that lies between the shore and the spoil islands. The path ends at a narrow side channel that cuts the access to the big spoil island at the entrance of the canal. You may be able to wade across the side channel in very low water. However, the water is generally too deep. It will become shallower as you wade north and swing around it. You can then wade to the big spoil island in low and normal water levels and explore all areas at the entrance of the canal and around the spoil islands. This will yield fish at times, mostly schools of reds

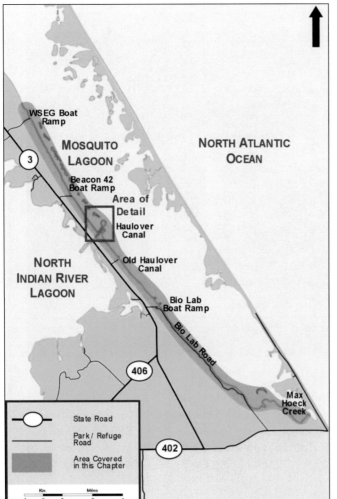

that move back and forth from the deep waters of the Intracoastal Waterway and Haulover Canal to the passages between the spoil islands and to the shallow flats inside.

The flats between the spoil islands and the shore are *wadeable* in all water levels except the highest. The bottom is variable, never very soft, never firm, a mixture of grass and sand where you will find reds in the right conditions. There is little geography in this vast flat and the fish will be anywhere when the water is warm enough. In the cold and low water of the winter I find the area to be nearly deserted.

One area in this vast, nondescript flat is of interest: the deep ditch along the shore. Starting at the first small point north of the canal this ditch may be a natural feature; however, it was most likely dredged to allow navigation and raise the bank. Indeed, the numerous remnants of docks, pilings, seawalls and other works along the shore suggest that the place was the site of fish camps at the times of the village of Allenhurst right up to the takeover by NASA.

To access this fishing spot from the end of the footpath just wade straight to it, aiming at the first point. Do not attempt to follow the shoreline to reach the point. There are serious soft spots in the stretch of shoreline close to the canal. Once you reach the first point make sure you are on the open-water side of the ditch. This long stretch of deep water will be best fished from the open-water side where the edge of the ditch is conveniently a little shallower than the surrounding flats. The ditch extends approximately 2,000 feet toward the north. You will find in it reds in season and trout all the time. Given the soft bottom and depth of the water, this is a thermal refuge for trout in the winter and permanent home for big trout all the time. Thanks to the mature forest

along the shoreline, the place offers a reasonable protection from the dominant west wind in the winter. It is also easy to cast in a south wind. Fish can be anywhere along this deep area. Since they tend to concentrate you may have to work the entire length of the ditch. It is generally worth it.

If you come by boat Bairs Cove Boat Ramp is just across Haulover Canal and Beacon 42 Boat Ramp is a short distance north. In low water the flats become very shallow and it may be difficult to navigate to the ditch. If you paddle or come with a light boat it is an easy journey from both ramps or from Rookery Island on North Indian River Lagoon, an unimproved ramp at the end of the road that parallels Haulover Canal. In all cases you will want to wade along the ditch and cast in it from the open water, not try fishing it off a boat or carry-on craft.

North of Haulover Canal on Mosquito Lagoon. Deeper water along the shore and remnants of docks suggest that the place was once busy.

The shoreline of Mosquito Lagoon at the mouth of Haulover Canal and immediately south of it is not very interesting. Access is easy: just walk on the old dirt road along the canal. The old road becomes a footpath near the point. The shoreline is generally white sand, although there are a few muddy areas. The water is relatively deep close to shore and it may be difficult to wade in high water. The bottom is a regular mix of sparse grass and sand and there is not much geography. From a boat, you may be able to spot fish in this vast expanse; from a wading point of view the only practical fly-fishing is sight fishing for redfish, either tailing singles or schools, if and when you can spot them.

For the wader the interest of this area lies a short distance to the south in the deep channel along the shore and the numerous canals, most likely the remnants of a subdivision that either failed or was stopped when NASA took over. The dirt roads are still there, more or less, and the connecting asphalt road is still drive-worthy. It is now closed to motor vehicles, but open to walking. Most of the canals are shallow and overtaken by vegetation. These canals harbor juvenile Tarpon. When there is enough dissolved oxygen in the water you may also find Snook in the canals. They can be fished, sort of, only in high water and only from a very light boat or a carry-on craft that you may have to drag from the lagoon over the shallow entrances. Finding a spot with enough room for a back cast will be a challenge and your nine-foot rod will seem ridiculously long. You can launch from Bairs Cove, Rookery Island, or the Old Haulover Canal (see next section, page 135). At times, when the water is high, Tarpon and Snook can even be found outside the canals in the deeper water along the shore. Moving around in schools, these fish are usually quite aggressive and perfect targets from the open water.

Wading this area is not easy. At times, it may not be practical, and it may even be dangerous. However, if you are up to it you will likely be rewarded in the spot where I am taking you.

On most maps the second canal from the north looks like the others. It is not. The second canal is a much bigger affair than the others and it looks as if it has been maintained in the years preceding NASA, much like the Old Haulover Canal (see next). There are old foundations, remnants of seawalls and of concrete boat ramps on each side of the canal. The two sites on the shore of the lagoon on either side of the canal were likely used right up to the NASA takeover.

As is the case for the other canals this one harbors juvenile Tarpon all the time. Snook will also likely be mixed with the Tarpon when the water is sufficiently oxygenated. These fish are everywhere in the canal. While the fish holding far into the canal are off limits to the wader those holding near the mouth are readily accessible. You may even find some outside the canal, in the deep water along the shore. You can get a decent cast at them from a few spots along the shore; however, this is not a comfortable bottom to wade.

As is the case for most Tarpon and Snook territories the terrain can be dangerous when the water is warm. You may think there is no fresh water around and therefore no alligators. Dead wrong, on both counts. To build the infrastructures of this area a few borrow pits were created. They appear on the map in the Old Haulover Canal section next. They are filled with fresh water… and with alligators.

In the cold water of the winter Tarpon and Snook are not what will take you there. Indeed, the main feature of this canal is being a winter thermal refuge: it holds trout and redfish during the coldest period of the winter. Fish move between the open water of the lagoon, the deep channel along the shore, and the canal itself. You may have to do some looking around but you will likely find them.

Access may seem convoluted but in fact it is as easy as it gets. Walk either one of the two old roads shown on the map and you will be on the shore of Mosquito Lagoon in just a few minutes.

(A third road between the two canals is not practical any more since it does not make it to the shore.) From the *north* road, you are directly on your destination, the second canal. You will work the channel at the mouth of the canal and the canal itself from the north side: both the channel along the shore and the canal are too deep to cross in most water levels. If you are right handed, this is the position that you want to cast in the channel along the shore, using the canal as room for a back cast. But casting in the canal will be more difficult.

From the *south* road, you will cross little canal no. 3 south of your destination (it is not deep at the mouth and the bottom is firm) and you will walk along the shoreline (or on land, the site is reasonably clear) to the destination second canal. Again both the channel along the shore and the canal itself are too deep to cross: you will fish from the south side of the canal. If you are right handed this is the position that you want to fish the canal, using the mouth of the canal in the lagoon as room for a back cast. Contrary to the northern access casting into the deep channel along the shore will be more difficult because of the limited space for a back cast along the shore.

From either side this is where you may need a little faith. To properly fish the channel at the mouth of the canal and the canal itself and get the room for a back cast you will likely have to make a few steps in the canal. Go ahead. You will sink, but it will stop: one foot of mud over firm bottom (more or less, both…). A little scary but doable.

You may be tempted to push deeper into the canal; indeed, there are good reasons to do this, especially when you see Tarpon rolling. (Typically, Tarpon tend to roll just a bit beyond my longest cast…) Careful. Again, while you may think this is salt water only and therefore relatively free of alligators it is not, as we will see in the next spot to the south.

Second canal from the north. This canal looks like it was maintained up to the NASA era; there are remnants of concrete boat ramps at the entrance on both sides of the canal.

South of Haulover Canal

In this section we are continuing the coverage of Southwest Mosquito Lagoon from Merritt Island National Wildlife Refuge, proceeding from north to south, with the Old Haulover Canal, Bio Lab Boat Ramp and finally Bio Lab Road, which will take us all the way to the south end of the lagoon.

The first four miles of shoreline south of Haulover Canal are generally regular and a featureless affair that was the ocean beach in prehistoric times when the water was higher. The vast flats along the shore are visited by fish of the lagoon but finding them on foot in this featureless area is not easy. The specific fishing spots will be mainly restricted to those created or modified by men. Fortunately, there is a significant number of these, mainly in the form of old canals, between the Old and the new Haulover Canal. There is also some interesting geography created by men at, and around Bio Lab Boat Ramp.

The lower four miles of shoreline are along a vast marsh. It would have interesting geography if it had been left alone but it has been diked for mosquito impoundments and most of Bio Lab Road is a dike road. There are few accesses to Mosquito Lagoon and the diked shoreline is of limited interest for the wader. This is where all the tourists in the world go to sightsee alligators from the safety of their running vehicles.

As one gets closer to the south end of the lagoon the flats become very shallow and the opportunities for wade fly-fishing are increasingly limited in the low water of the winter.

Coverage from north to south of the southwest shore of Mosquito Lagoon south of Haulover begins with the Old Haulover Canal.

Old Haulover Canal

The Old Haulover Canal is one mile south of the *new* Haulover Canal. Take the dirt road to the east (no road sign as of this writing) and drive approximately one-eighth of a mile. You will reach the entry basin of the old canal. There is some rudimentary parking there and an unimproved ramp that allows for the launch of carry-on crafts and light boats from a trailer, if you have the traction.

The interest of this spot lies mainly in the canal itself, the entry basin and the old channel in the lagoon. From the parking you have a foot access to the open water of the lagoon. Just follow a beaten footpath along the east shoreline of the entry basin. This will take you to the open water of the lagoon at an entry point that is manageable. You should be extra careful in this area because of the soft spots along the shore.

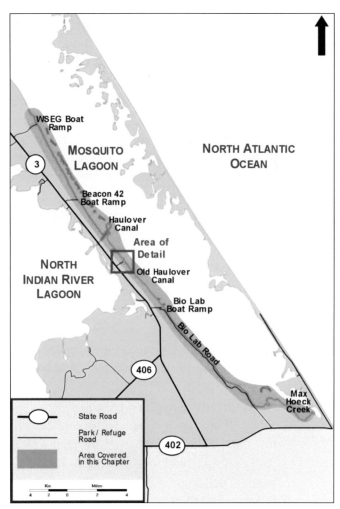

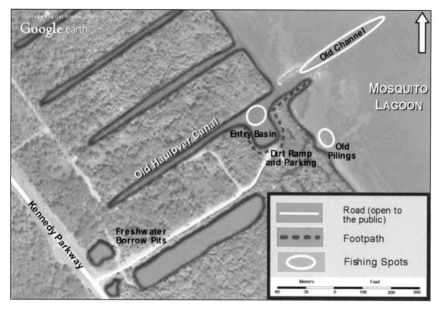

In the open water of the lagoon the old channel is the extension of the canal and is marked by old pilings. This is one spot of deeper water in the otherwise vast shallow flats that characterize this general area. You can cross the old channel in low water and choose the best side to work it. Fish hold in this slightly deeper water and you can work it far into the lagoon. In my opinion, there is little interest in the rest of the flats of this area of the lagoon except for tailing or schooling redfish, if and when you can spot them. Finding these fish is not an easy task on foot even if the bottom is not too bad.

The only other areas that may be worthy of the wading effort is the deeper water next to a group of old pilings near the shore a short distance south of the channel. The rest is a nondescript flat beaten by the wind and without geography. Fish will certainly be present at times, but this type of fishing involves covering lots of water to find fish and is better done from a boat. Raging Fish Camp was located south of the Old Haulover Canal before NASA and there may be some interesting geography around the site. However, it is not practically accessible on foot.

As mentioned above, the main interest of this spot lies in the old canal itself and in the entry basin. The westerly half of the Old Haulover Canal between Kennedy Parkway and Granny Cove on North Indian River Lagoon is almost completely destroyed and you cannot even see it unless you explore it on foot in the woods. Likewise, many of the old dredged canals to the north are being overtaken by vegetation. This is not the case for the easterly half of the Old Haulover Canal, east of Kennedy Parkway. It has been maintained, widened and dredged deeper. Although this part of history seems to have been lost, sportfishing is most likely the answer. Indeed, this area was occupied by renowned fishing camps before NASA takeover. A 1954 map shows a road to the Old Haulover Canal and Indian Lagoon Fish Camp north of it.

This canal is juvenile Tarpon habitat like most other canals along the shore south of Haulover. This one is easier to fish because it is wider and more easily accessible. When the water is clear and oxygenated enough it also harbors Snook. The canal itself can only be practically fished from a boat (and only a small one at that) or a carry-on craft. Aligning your back cast with the canal to avoid the intruding vegetation will be your primary concern. And your nine-foot rod will feel a little long. But it can also be fished on foot, at least the easterly part of it. Indeed, you can walk to a wading position at the southwest corner of the entry basin by following a footpath in the underbrush next to the shoreline (see red dotted line on the map). You will find just enough firm bottom to line up with the canal and to have the space for a back cast. Cast to juvenile Tarpon that may happen to be at this end of the canal, and to the occasional Snook that live in the canal when there is enough oxygen.

This is salt water. However, there is plenty of fresh water around. Indeed, the three borrow pits that you see on the map are freshwater and *Alligator Country* big time. Check your back.

While you will fish the old canal for Snook and juvenile Tarpon the interest in the entry basin is different. Aside from the fact that it may be visited by the Tarpon and Snook of the canal at times the entry basin is a winter thermal fish refuge that is very well protected against the dominant northwest winds. This makes it a good destination in the coldest and windiest days of the winter. Surprisingly, you can wade right into the entry basin from the ramp. Despite its spongy look and terrible feel right along the shoreline the bottom is not bad after a few steps. But there is an easier access at the mouth of the canal on the northeast corner of the entry basin. Bait fishermen have beaten a footpath to it from the parking area (see red dotted line on the map). From the mouth of the canal, you have plenty of room for a back cast and you can easily work the entire entry basin. In the middle of the winter expect trout in all sizes, including some big ones. On warmer days, if the water is well oxygenated, Snook will also show up in the entry basin.

As mentioned previously there are several smaller canals between the Old and the new Haulover Canals and they look promising on the maps if you have a canoe, kayak or very light boat. They harbor juvenile Tarpon permanently and Snook when the water is clear and oxygenated. However, their accesses to the open water of the lagoon are severely restricted or completely blocked in low water. You cannot wade the mud near some of these old canals. Therefore, the shoreline north of the Old Haulover Canal is more or less off limits to waders unless you want to swing way out in the open water, and then only when the water is low. I find it impractical and a lot of work. The only spot of interest for waders is the second canal from the north, and it is covered in the previous section on page 132.

OLD HAULOVER CANAL

Constructed in 1854 the canal served as a traditional crossover point for travel down the inland waterway. Until its construction cargo was carried across the land (thus the origin of the name "haul over") and then loaded on boats which continued southward. The canal was three feet deep and 10 to 14 feet wide and was constructed by the slaves of a local citrus grower. The Old Haulover Canal was abandoned in 1884 when the new Haulover Canal was constructed nearly a mile to the north.

Sources: Susan Parker. 2008. *Canaveral National Seashore, Historic Resource Study.* Edited by Robert W. Blythe. National Park Service. Atlanta. www.nps.gov/history/history/online_books/cana/cana_hrs.pdf (as of this writing);
Brevard County Historical Commission;
and personal research.

The Old Haulover Canal today is typical home for baby and juvenile Tarpon and Snook. Access is much easier with a small boat.

View of the Old Haulover Canal in 1891. Image courtesy of Brevard County Historical Commission.

Bio Lab Boat Ramp

Bio Lab Road gives access to the eponymous boat ramp on southwest Mosquito Lagoon. Take it off Kennedy Parkway approximately three miles south of Haulover Canal. A fee is required at this ramp (see page 129). From the parking lot of the Bio Lab Boat Ramp you have access to the large north ditch. But this is only half of the story. Go back on your tracks a few hundred feet, take Bio Lab Road to the south and park after the pump. You now have access to the smaller south ditch, to the ditch inside the dike and to Mosquito Lagoon, both south *and north* of the ramp (more on this later). If Red Drum, Spotted Seatrout, juvenile Tarpon and Snook, all in one day is on your bucket list the address is Bio Lab Boat Ramp.

The main attraction of this area is the deep and wide ditch north of the ramp. It is prime Snook and Tarpon habitat. Most of the entire south bank of the ditch is accessible and it can be fly-fished on foot. On top of having access to one of the best territories for juvenile Tarpon and Snook you can even park along the bank. This is one of the very few spots in the territory covered in this book where you can access a large Snook and Tarpon fishing spot from the bank in relative security and find room for a back cast. This is *Alligator Country* but they tend to keep to the other side of the ditch and the banks are high and cleared. Nevertheless, look over your shoulder and stay away from the deep water.

To access the south ditch and Mosquito Lagoon, both south *and north* of the ramp, park near the fenced pump area a few hundred yards south of the boat ramp. The south ditch is a much smaller affair than the north ditch. In fact, few people take notice of it, let alone fish it. It is not as deep and water quality is not nearly as good. This is a typical environment for baby Tarpon and it is thick with them. It is off-limit to boats but you can stand on the bank (or wade in a few steps) and cast to rolling baby Tarpon. This spot is limited in size and there are just a few places with adequate clearing and room for a back cast.

You may also see Tarpon rolling in the ditch on the marsh side of the culvert. There is an adequate opening from which you can cast to them. These Tarpon tend to disappear in cold water. Park near the fenced pump area, a few hundred yards south of the boat ramp.

As strange as it may sound, you have to enter the water *south* of the boat ramp to be able to wade the lagoon *north* of the boat ramp. Indeed, Bio Lab Boat Ramp is surrounded by three deep channels that are good for boaters but bad for waders. The old channels are generally too deep to wade across and you would not even think of trying the deep black mud at the mouth of the ditches along the shoreline. The shoreline itself is not good wading and, depending upon a number of factors, it can be strictly off-limit. Therefore, you will have to go around all of this by entering the water south of the mouth of the south canal and wading away from the shore in

WSEG Boat Ramp

MOSQUITO LAGOON

3

NORTH ATLANTIC OCEAN

Beacon 42 Boat Ramp

Haulover Canal

Old Haulover Canal

NORTH INDIAN RIVER LAGOON

Area of Detail

Bio Lab Boat Ramp

Bio Lab Road

406

Max Hoeck Creek

402

State Road

Park / Refuge Road

Area Covered in this Chapter

Km   Miles
4   2   0   2   4

The north ditch of the Bio Lab Boat Ramp harbors juvenile Tarpon and Snook and can be fished from shore.

The south ditch is a much smaller affair but it harbors a thick population of baby Tarpon.

the open water to avoid the deep boat channel (see the dotted yellow line on the large-scale detailed map next).

It is a long walk and it may get seriously uncomfortable in high water. Nevertheless, you will likely be rewarded by favorable geomorphology. Indeed, north of the boat ramp is part of the general location of Dummit Grove, before NASA and the establishment of the Refuge. Several ditches were dug inside the shoreline and some of them may harbor Snook and Tarpon; however,

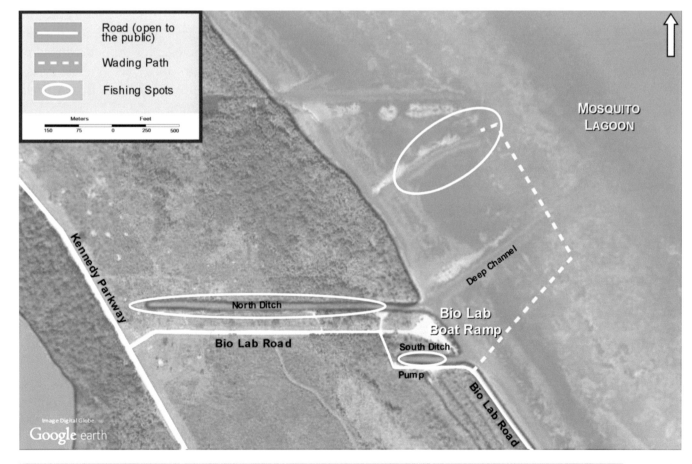

Old pilings, channel, spoil island, remnants of past commercial and sportfishing activities, north of Bio Lab Boat Ramp.

their access is nearly impossible. Channels were dredged in the lagoon, presumably for water transportation or for fish camps, and the pilings are still there.

This man-made geography provides deeper-water spots that harbor fish all the time, especially in periods of low and cold water. You can usually count on catching sizeable trout as well as reds in these sloughs and on the surrounding flats.

The drawback for the wading angler to this good fishing environment is the difficult access. All considered, this is not the ideal wading area. If you have a kayak, canoe, row boat or any other type of light vessel now is a good time to take it along and use it simply to cross the channels and make it safely away from the boat ramp area, especially in high water. You can then park the craft and do your regular and much more productive wading act.

Bio Lab Road

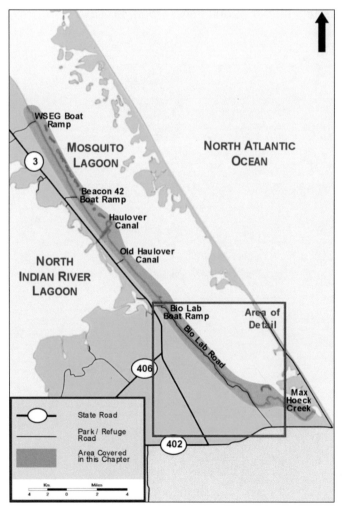

South of the boat ramp, Bio Lab Road gives access to a long stretch of Mosquito Lagoon. Past the pump this road follows the shoreline in the Refuge and it ends at Playalinda Beach Road inside the Park. The Park closes the gate at Playalinda Beach Road every day at 6:00 PM (sometimes a few minutes ahead of time…). You may have to come back on your tracks if you planned to leave by Playalinda Beach Road and you timed it a little tight.

As mentioned above, parking at the pump just south of the boat ramp will give you access to Mosquito Lagoon both north and south of the boat ramp. Contrary to the convoluted access to the area north of the ramp your access to the area south of the ramp is just a matter of wading out anywhere in normal and low water levels. The northernmost section of the road is right along the lagoon and you can park anywhere convenient and access the water. There is a pull off at the bend two-thirds of a mile from the boat ramp.

There is a large flat approximately 800 feet wide all along the shore where you will likely find redfish, both tailing and schooling. This flat is called West Flats on the Top Spot map. The bottom is sparse grass interspersed with sand patches and is reasonably firm. However, since the entire area has no geography at all, you may have to cover long distances (or patiently wait a long time) to see fish. Or you may get lucky and see tails or even a school in the winter. I would keep this for early mornings when reds are tailing and when you may have a better chance of seeing schools.

The middle section of the road is separated from the lagoon by a ditch and there is only one access to the lagoon. There is a sizeable pull off at a place that the locals have named The Two Palms. It is 2.6 miles south of the ramp. This is your closest access to the Whale Tail shoal with a carry-on craft. Whale Tail is a confirmed prime holding spot for big, spawning-size redfish. Unfortunately, you cannot wade to it from shore and wading the flats along the shore is not as good as further north. But you may hit it right at any time, more likely early in the morning.

At the southern end of Bio Lab Road when the road comes back along the shoreline of the lagoon you may again park anywhere convenient and access the lagoon. There are two pull offs in this section of the road. The locals have named the northernmost The Two Dead Trees. There is some slightly deeper water along the shore, but generally this spot is not much different than the rest of the area.

The second pull off is more interesting. This is the site of an old fishing or hunting camp named Bull Camp. You can still see the old pilings of the dock. All around these pilings you will find a large area of deeper water that holds fish regularly. This spot is frequented by bait and spin

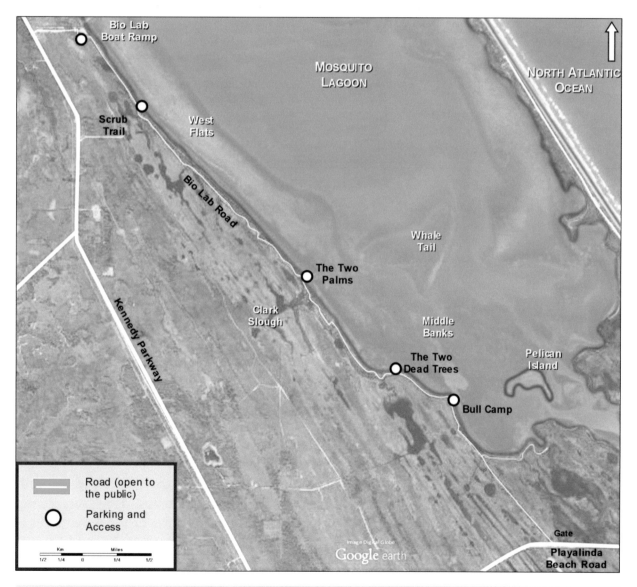

The Two Palms.

The Two Dead Trees.

Old pilings in Mosquito Lagoon at Bull Camp.

casters and is most likely the best spot along Bio Lab Road. The wading is reasonably easy. It may be a winter thermal refuge at times, but it is not a reliable one in my experience.

Unknown to most the *west* roadside ditch (on the marsh side) along Bio Lab Road sometimes harbors baby Tarpon. This is a narrow ditch with plenty of vegetation, which makes it an unlikely fly-fishing affair. Nevertheless, there are several clearings along the road and a few unimproved ramps for the hunters where you can get some room for a back cast and cast to Tarpon if they happen to be rolling in the area. The fish tend to be on the small side, will likely be closer to the north end of the road, and will likely disappear when the water temperature drops in the winter.

You will never be alone there and I suggest you stay on dry land all the time and watch around for the *other* wildlife. Whether you see them or not, you can be assured that the alligators are there.

Bio Lab Road leads to the *South* District of Canaveral National Seashore, *inside* the Park gate. You do not need to pay a fee or to have a Park pass to drive on Bio Lab Road from the north; however, you must turn *right* at Playalinda Beach Road and leave the Park. Report first to the Park admission gate if you intended to continue east toward the beach. And, as mentioned above, there is a gate on Bio Lab Road at Playalinda Beach Road that is closed after the regular Park hours.

All this area is *Gatorland*, big time. Alligators live in the fresh and brackish waters of Clark Slough and in the ditch along the road. Bio Lab Road is extensively travelled by visitors to sightsee alligators and they see them, plenty of them, and big ones, all the time. In theory alligators should stay in the ditch and marsh across the road where they have fresh water. That is in theory… Watch your back all the time. The lagoon should be relatively safe from alligators in the winter, when the water is low and when you can tell what is going on along the well-defined shoreline at all times. However, during periods of warm weather, when the water level is high and the shoreline is flooded, I would be very prudent and constantly keep an eye on the shoreline.

South End of Mosquito Lagoon

Contrary to the straight and rather featureless geography of the shore along Bio Lab Road the south end of Mosquito Lagoon is a diversified area that offers multiple fish habitats in all seasons and water levels. My biggest red comes from this area. There are two foot accesses to this general area. From the west you can walk on Max Hoeck Spur to the culvert of Max Hoeck Back Creek and beyond on the old dike road. From the east, you can walk the old dike road from Parking Lot 3 of the South District of Canaveral National Seashore.

At the parking area off Bio Lab Road before the chained Max Hoeck Spur you can launch a carry-on craft. You can also launch a light boat or carry-on craft from Eddy Creek Boat Ramp in Canaveral National Seashore. The use of a carry-on craft or light boat is the easiest and sometimes the only safe way to explore the entire south end of Mosquito Lagoon. However, in low water level navigating this area with any but the lightest boat is not practical.

The main foot access to the south end of Mosquito Lagoon is the dirt road named Max Hoeck Spur off the southern end of Bio Lab Road. This road is chained at Bio Lab Road and closed to motor traffic. You can park near the intersection with Bio Lab Road and walk. It is a short two-thirds-of-a-mile walk to the culvert of Max Hoeck *Back* Creek. From the culvert the old dike road goes all the way around Max Hoeck Creek and *East* Max Hoeck Creek to Parking Lot 3 of Canaveral National Seashore. This dike road was closed years ago, but the dike has not been removed and the old road on top of the dike can still be walked. The walk is easy close to the culvert of Max Hoeck *Back* Creek. It may become uneasy further away and you may choose to walk some stretches along the shoreline.

Bio Lab Road can be a painfully slow drive from the north, with large potholes everywhere (as of this writing) and slow-moving tourists sightseeing alligators. To avoid this you can access Bio Lab Road from the southern end, off Playalinda Beach Road. This is inside the Park and the entrance fee (or your annual Park pass) is required. Note that Bio Lab Road is gated at Playalinda Beach Road outside of Park hours.

The second foot access to the south end of Mosquito Lagoon is from Parking Lot 3 of the South District of Canaveral National Seashore. This is the easterly access to the old dike road that goes around the entire south end of Mosquito Lagoon to Max Hoeck Spur and Bio Lab Road. Despite the sign "Barricade" on the chain this road can legally be walked. However, the tall grass may make your walk rather uncomfortable. Park at Parking Lot 3.

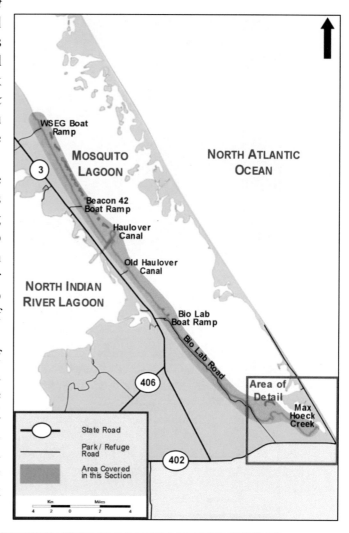

Max Hoeck Spur used to be open to the culvert at Max Hoeck Back Creek but is now chained at Bio Lab Road. You can park and walk. As mentioned above you can launch a carry-on craft at this location. It is not as clean as a boat ramp, but doable. The walk to the culvert—the end of the drivable portion of the dike road before it was closed—is two-thirds of a mile. Along the road you may find a few acceptable foot accesses to the lagoon by picking your way through the mangroves. There is a good opening close to Max Hoeck Back Creek.

Southwest Bay is very shallow south of Pelican Island. This is a typical grass flat that is good tailing grounds in high water. In low water the place is usually deserted. The bottom is a little soft but it can be waded at will. You may have to cover a large territory to find fish. A little more interesting is the slightly deeper area west of Pelican Island and north of it. Find loose groups of white spots among the grass that will likely hold fish. You can also fish the transitional zone between the grass and the sand a few hundred feet from the west shoreline. Generally, it is better to use a carry-on craft or light boat to cover the vast featureless expanses in this area. Carry-on crafts and light boats will reach this area in any water level. Flats boats will reach it but will have a hard time taking off in low water level. Big boats have no business there.

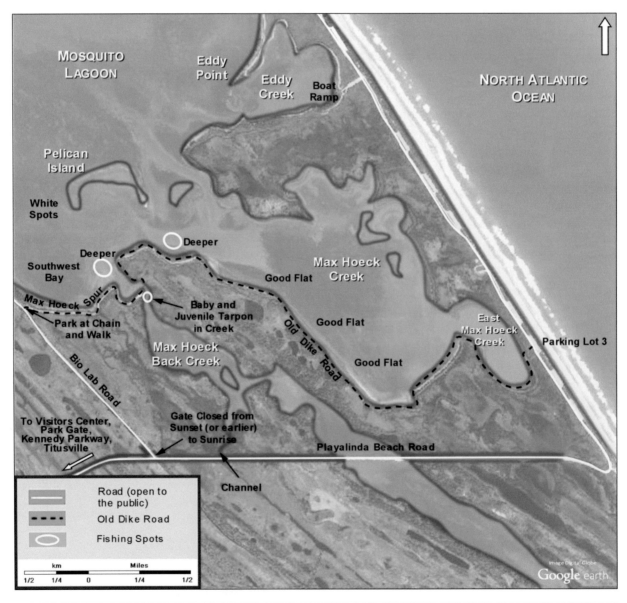

There are good flats and deeper spots north of Pelican Island, including the famous Whale Tail shoal. However, this is either too far for most waders or too deep to access from shore. If you insist look it up on the Top Spot map.

The areas around Pelican Island and the little island east of it are generally shallow and soft. You may find redfish cruising the shoreline when the water level is high. There is a lane of slightly deeper water between the two islands and another one between the small island and the east shore of Mosquito Lagoon. Boats use the latter as a running lane. It is a job to wade there from anywhere.

Max Hoeck Back Creek

The southwest end of Mosquito Lagoon becomes a vast expanse of nothing in the lowest water levels of the winter.

Max Hoeck *Back* Creek south of the culvert (inside the dike) is a vast marsh that is off limits to wading. It is home to juvenile Tarpon that you can target on foot from the culvert.

Max Hoeck *Back* Creek on the lagoon side (north of the culvert) is a shallow loose black mud affair and you have no business wading near it. However, at the mouth of the creek in the lagoon, off the point, the water deepens and the place becomes an excellent trout spot and a winter thermal refuge. This is where geology and the natural history of Florida become helpful. Back in prehistoric times when the level of the ocean was much lower than it is today the level of the lagoon was also lower. Max Hoeck Back Creek was likely a running creek draining toward the north. This creek carved a streambed that still exists today at its mouth in the lagoon. Of course we are talking here of an ancient channel approximately one foot deeper than the surrounding. But in today's lagoons one foot can make all the difference, especially if there is some black mud near it that can store some heat during periods of cold water; therefore, the transition zone at the mouth of the creek is a winter thermal refuge for trout and small reds. Away from the mouth of the creek and into the lagoon the bottom is firm and clean and the area is the equivalent of a large white spot, slightly deeper in the middle where the ancient streambed is. At times this spot can be *trout*

unlimited, with many fish being among the biggest trout of the lagoons. In my experience this is one of the most reliable trout spots in the southern end of Mosquito Lagoon.

The easiest foot access is from Max Hoeck Spur before or after the culvert. To access this spot directly from the west side—before the culvert— walk in the opening off the road at the point, a few hundred feet before the culvert, and wade to the spot from the west. To access it from the east side—after the culvert—walk one-third of a mile from the culvert on the dike road, get in the water at the point and wade to the spot from the east. It may be a little soft right along the shoreline at the point but this is not major. The deeper area tends to be closer to the point and easier to access from this side. But the direction of the wind will likely dictate your choice of access.

The deeper water off the point at the mouth of Max Hoeck Back Creek is arguably the best spot for trout in the southern end of Mosquito Lagoon.

Max Hoeck Back Creek inside the dike harbors juvenile Tarpon and can be fly-fished from the dike.

Max Hoeck *Back* Creek is the most significant connection with the salt marsh at the southern end of Mosquito Lagoon. The gated culvert lets salt water in the marsh in high water and keeps it inside the marsh in low water for mosquito control. This culvert is on the streambed of Max Hoeck Back Creek and is likely the main gateway for baby Tarpon swimming from Mosquito Lagoon to their typical nursery area inside the dike. While the creek itself has few natural areas that are deep enough for the survival of juvenile Tarpon during the cold snaps of our winters the ditches dredged to build the dike and road are deep enough in certain areas. Juvenile Tarpon live in those deeper holes. One of these is at the culvert of the dike at Mosquito Lagoon. At this location the natural streambed of the creek and the man-made ditch on the impoundment side combine to form a deep and large enough area to harbor Tarpon. Combining juvenile Tarpon fishing early in the morning at this spot with wading the lagoon later in the day for trout and red fills a fishing day nicely.

You can cast to Tarpon on foot from the culvert. If you want to attack these Tarpon with a carry-on craft—a good idea at any time for Tarpon—you must launch at the nearest spot on Bio Lab Road. Paddle the lagoon to the mouth of the creek and up to the culvert. Make sure you are on shore before getting off the craft: this black mud is nasty. Carry the craft across the road/dike and relaunch on the marsh side.

You can also reach this area from the south; indeed, Max Hoeck Back Creek goes all the way to Playalinda Beach Road (and beyond, through culverts under the road). You can launch a carry-on craft or a very light boat from a trailer (if you have the traction) at an unimproved boat ramp at the intersection of Bio Lab Road and Playalinda Beach Road. This is in the Refuge, just after the gate. Follow the ditch along Playalinda Beach Road one-third of a mile and take one very narrow opening to the north. This narrow opening will soon become the well-defined channel of Max Hoeck Back Creek (or one significant among multiple channels). Follow to the north in a lake-size opening in the marsh to the culvert. You may also find an alternative suitable launching spot from one of the designated parking areas along Playalinda Road. This is in the Park and you must stick to the designated parking areas and you must launch on the north side of the road. It is a nice and scenic paddle to the culvert following the ancient streambed. At certain times of the year you may find Tarpon anywhere the water is a little deeper. However, my experience with the Tarpon in Max Hoeck Back Creek is that they tend to be in the deep spot next to the culvert to Mosquito Lagoon.

Max Hoeck Creek

The next bay is Max Hoeck Creek (the previous one was Max Hoeck *Back* Creek). Max Hoeck Creek is the big bay and the main feature of the South End of Mosquito Lagoon. This vast bay will be better explored with a craft for practical reasons and, at times, for your security (more on that later). But you can access it on foot. From the culvert on Max Hoeck *Back* Creek continue on the old dike road toward the east. This is not the most comfortable walk at times because the road was closed a long time ago and some areas are taken over by the vegetation.

You can fish a deeper area in the first small bay. This is a short walk and the spot is shown on the large-scale detailed map on page 144. This deeper area harbors trout, mostly small but some bigger, in most water levels and can be quite good in low water.

You can pursue further southeast on the old dike road. When it becomes uncomfortable because of the tall grass and bushes you can switch to the shoreline, which is easy to walk in low and normal water levels. However, I strongly suggest the use of a vessel during the alligator-critical periods of the year. This is not only *Gator Country*; this is the factory... Do not think for one minute that they have "their" side (behind the dike) and be content with it. Salt water or not, these critters use the lagoon extensively. Nevertheless, you may decide to wade the south end of Mosquito Lagoon in the winter and I have met people who did it for years (and looked whole). Wade only after a good reconnaissance of the place, stay away from the shore, and do not wade during the critical alligator mating and nesting periods in late spring and early summer. And consider again the use of a light boat or carry-on craft that you can launch from Eddy Creek Boat Ramp.

Whether you walk or paddle, the west shore of Max Hoeck Creek is the place to go, based upon my own fishing experience, conversations with regulars, and judging from most of the traffic that I have seen in this area. It is also the only area that is accessible to boats in low water levels. The west shore provides a mixture of deeper water, grass flats, good white spots and these always productive transition zones between grass and sand. If you go on foot (despite my warnings concerning alligators) the easiest access is to walk from Bio Lab Road. However, walking from Parking Lot 3 of the South District of Canaveral National Seashore is an alternative. If this sounds to you like an expedition, it is. It is so much easier to launch a light boat or carry-on craft from Eddy Creek Boat Ramp.

Last on your long walk toward the east on the old dike road if you made it that far—or first if you are parked at Parking Lot 3—*East* Max Hoeck Creek is a shallow muddy affair that is devoid of fish in low water level. The same goes for most of the east shore of Max Hoeck Creek almost up to Eddy Creek, where it is nearly impossible to wade, where there is no road on the old dike allowing for an easy access, and where alligators are also very much present despite the apparent lack of fresh water.

MAX HOECK

Max Hoeck Creek (and Max Hoeck *Back* Creek, and *East* Max Hoeck Creek) were named for a German immigrant who tried to homestead the area. Unofficial history refers to a colorful character who brought in Germans to work for him and had ways of making these immigrants work for free.

One of the oldest historical sites of the Timucuan Native era in Canaveral National Seashore is a 4,000-year-old shell midden named the Max Hoeck Midden, located near Playalinda Beach. The site dates from the Late Archaic period (or stage). The Archaic stage is the second period of human occupation in the Americas, when people exploited wetland resources, creating large shell middens, before sedentary farming. It is from around 8000 to 2000 BC. The Late Archaic stage is from 5000 to 3000 years ago and precedes the Woodland stage, when ceramics became widespread.

The burial mound is approximately seven feet high and 45 feet in diameter at its base. It is composed of earth and covered with mature vegetation.

Archeological research was taking place as of this writing. The site is identified as East Max Hoeck Midden / CANA 78; BR00909. There are indications of previous looting and the exact location is currently kept secret for security reasons.

Sources: Susan Parker. 2008. *Canaveral National Seashore, Historic Resource Study.* Edited by Robert W. Blythe. National Park Service. Atlanta. www.nps.gov/history/history/online_books/cana/cana_hrs.pdf (as of this writing);
and personal research.

4 – NORTH INDIAN RIVER LAGOON IN THE REFUGE

This chapter covers the east shore of *North* Indian River Lagoon that I define as being north of State Road 406 and the railroad. Merritt Island National Wildlife Refuge (the Refuge) is the public access to the entire east shore of North Indian River Lagoon.

Since this is all within the Refuge remember that you need a Refuge Fishing Permit, free and self-procured on the Internet at www.fws.gov/merrittisland/ and look for *Fishing Regulations* (as of this writing). The Refuge is not gated and you can access it as early in the morning as you choose. It closes at sunset, which means that you can fish until sunset and drive out in the dark.

Kennedy Parkway from Oak Hill and State Road 406 from Titusville are the two access roads. They are paved and open all the time. Since the end of the space shuttle program the Park and the Refuge no longer routinely close areas for the launches at Cape Canaveral. Most of the dike roads that used to be open to motor traffic in the past are now closed and open to foot and bicycle traffic only. The remaining side and access roads open to motor traffic are unpaved and subject to periodical damage from storms. Check the web site of the Refuge at www.fws.gov/merrittisland/ (as of this writing) and look for the *Current Events and Closures* link on the home page.

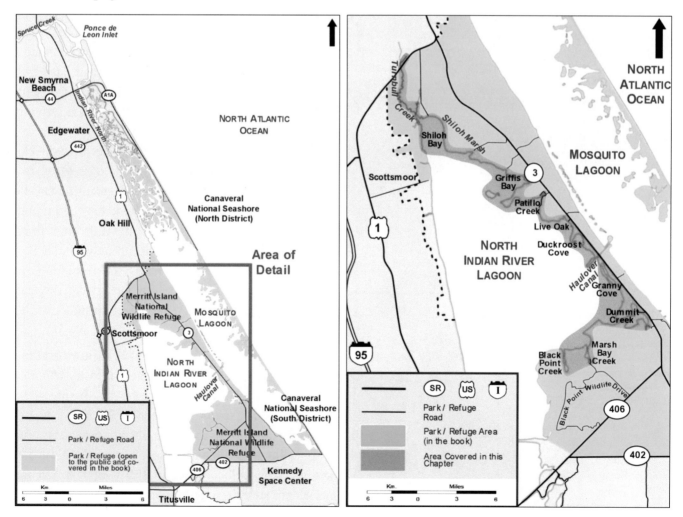

Coverage of the wade fly-fishing territory accessible on foot is from south to north, starting with the areas accessible from L Pond Road off Black Point Wildlife Drive. Next are Dummit Creek, the Haulover Canal area, Live Oak and Patillo Creek. A long section follows, accessible by Shiloh Marsh Road (now closed to motor traffic) that extends all the way north to Shiloh Bay and Turnbull Creek. Coverage of the area and of the book ends with Turnbull Creek, from the lagoon to US 1.

L Pond Road

L Pond Road (also called L Dike Road) is the dike road that winds around the southeast end of North Indian River Lagoon. L Pond Road was closed to motor traffic in 2009 and is chained at both ends. You can walk or bike it by parking at either end.

This part of the North Indian River Lagoon has geography and L Pond Road gives foot access to diverse and very good spots for wade fly-fishing. The northeast end of L Pond Road is exactly three miles south of Haulover Canal, a few hundred feet past Sendler Education Center and only a few feet past Bio Lab Road. There is a dirt parking area at the dike and you can park and walk to the best spots of Dummit Creek. These spots are covered in the next section.

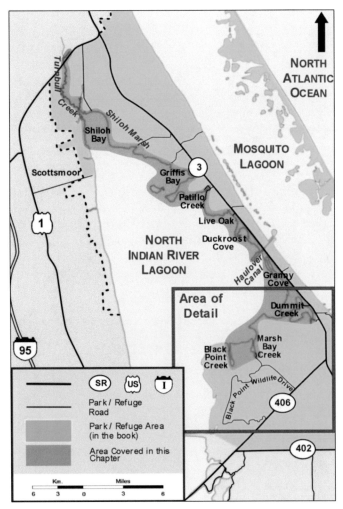

The southwest end of L Pond Road connects with Black Point Wildlife Drive near its end, approximately one mile before the junction with State Road 406. Since Black Point Wildlife Drive is one way you have to enter it from the southwest and drive it all the way at low speed before you can access L Pond Road. Black Point Wildlife Drive is a fee area (see page 138). L Pond Road itself can be driven a short distance and is chained at the lagoon. You can park near the chain and walk on L Pond Road to Marsh Bay Creek and around Marsh Bay Point. Walking the entire length of L Pond Road takes a little less than one hour, one way. You can also use L Pond Road to reach Black Point Creek, as we will see next.

The impoundment behind L Pond Road (and behind Cruickshank Trail to the west) is *Alligator Country*, big time. They live on the marsh-side of the dike and will usually stay there. *Usually*. I do not recommend wading anywhere near shore in this area when alligators are active and I generally limit my visits to the coldest days of the winter, when the beasts are sound asleep.

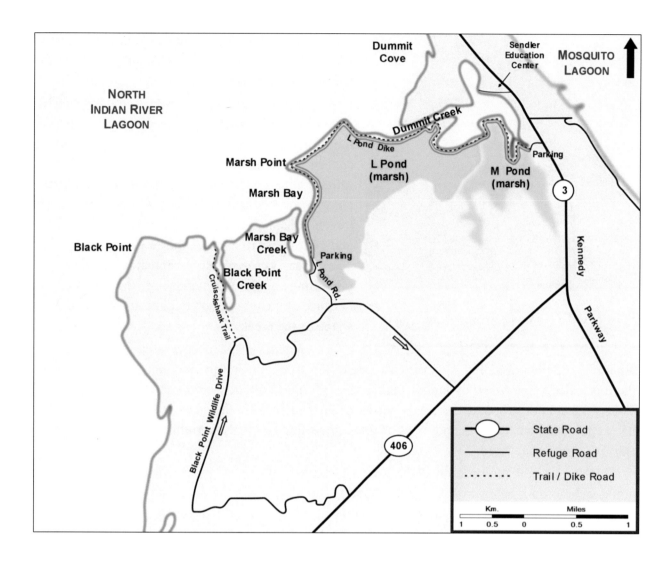

Black Point Creek

Black Point Creek is the most remote fishing spot accessible from the southern end of L Pond Road. I will admit that it is a stretch. Indeed, after reaching Marsh Bay Creek on foot you must walk one additional mile along the shore of North Indian River Lagoon. This is not a problem in low water level, which is usually the case in the coldest days of the winter. In high water level the walk along the shore may be more difficult and, as higher water usually coincides with higher temperature, the area can become dangerous. Again, this is *Alligator Country*. I would recommend that you launch a light boat at Sendler Education Center or at Haulover—or a carry-on craft at the south end of L Pond Road—to fish it safely at any other time than the winter. Note that you will not fish inside Black Point Creek from any sizeable boat in low water level because it is unlikely that you will be able to get through the very shallow mouth.

Speaking about access, there is another one, so much easier. However, it is forbidden. The Refuge regulations are:

"You may not crab or fish from Black Point Wildlife Drive or <u>any side road connected to Black Point Wildlife Drive</u> (except L Pond Road). You may not launch boats, canoes, kayaks from Black Point Wildlife Drive <u>or any side road connected to Black Point Wildlife Drive</u>, (except L Pond Road)."

Black Point Creek viewed from inside. Cruickshank Trail is on the left.

According to the rangers simply walking to Black Point Creek on Cruickshank Trail in full fishing attire is forbidden.

Black Point Creek may be a slug to reach but it is well worth the effort. Indeed, the place may be the ultimate shallow-flat-thick-grass-redfish-tailing spot in North Indian River Lagoon. You will know it the minute you wade in and it will only get better as you proceed inside the creek. The bottom is never treacherous; however, it is never comfortable either and your legs will confirm this at the end of the day. The area is generally protected against the prevailing northwest winds of the winter, not because of the orientation but because of the narrow shape of the creek.

Generally, the deeper area is closer to the dike/trail and the grassy flat is on the east side of the creek. Approximately half-way up the creek there is a deep spot (*deep* by lagoon standard) with mud bottom where you can catch big trout. This is the only deep spot and the only permanent trout habitat in the creek in low water level. The back end of the creek is a round bowl of thick grass that has just the right depth for tailing reds. Big fish congregate there.

You are not allowed to walk back to the mouth of the creek on Cruickshank Trail. Should you decide to do it be aware that a small, muddy ditch separates the dike from the creek near the mouth and you cannot wade this, trust me. You can safely re-access the creek and the open water of North Indian River Lagoon at the culvert a short distance from the mouth of the creek.

Marsh Bay Creek

Marsh Bay Creek is at the southwest end of L Pond Road, where the road is chained. Marsh Bay Creek and Marsh Bay constitute a diversified area that can be fished successfully in all water levels. However, what will most likely take you there is that Marsh Bay Creek is a winter thermal refuge for fish, a very important one.

Access is on foot from L Pond Road, open from Black Point Wildlife Drive and chained at the dike, allowing boat access to the marsh for hunting and foot access to the old dike road for fishing. Park at the chain and walk on the old dike road. You can launch a carry-on craft on the lagoon side at this location. If L Pond Road is closed at Black Point Wildlife Drive and foot access denied—a rare situation that I have encountered once in the past—you can always reach Marsh Bay Creek with a carry-on craft or light boat that you can launch on Dummit Creek at Sendler Education Center. You can also walk from the northeast end of L Pond Road. This is nearly a one-hour walk.

Not wanting to sound like an old mother, but I have to stress again that this is *Alligator Country,* big time. I strongly suggest that you save wading this area for the coldest winter months.

The first fishing spot that you will encounter on L Pond Road is a little grassy pond at the southwest end of the creek, across the first narrows. From a distance the place looks like nothing and nobody fishes it. You can walk to it by crossing the first narrows and walking along the south shore of the large, round bay. The little grassy pond offers a prime territory for tailing reds. An old ditch at the entrance provides a safe passage for the fish to and from the lagoon, the little grassy pond and the ditch relict behind the old dike. This ditch relict provides a deep-water spot that redfish frequent. (See picture next.) Kneeling on the point next to the ditch is an excellent way to ambush the fish. In these areas, as you may expect, the bottom is soft and there are a few very uncomfortable spots.

As you proceed inside Marsh Bay Creek there is a large round bay that is a shallow flat with good grass, especially in the southwest corner. You will frequently see big reds tailing and cruising the southwest shoreline. I cannot remember one single time when I did not find reds in

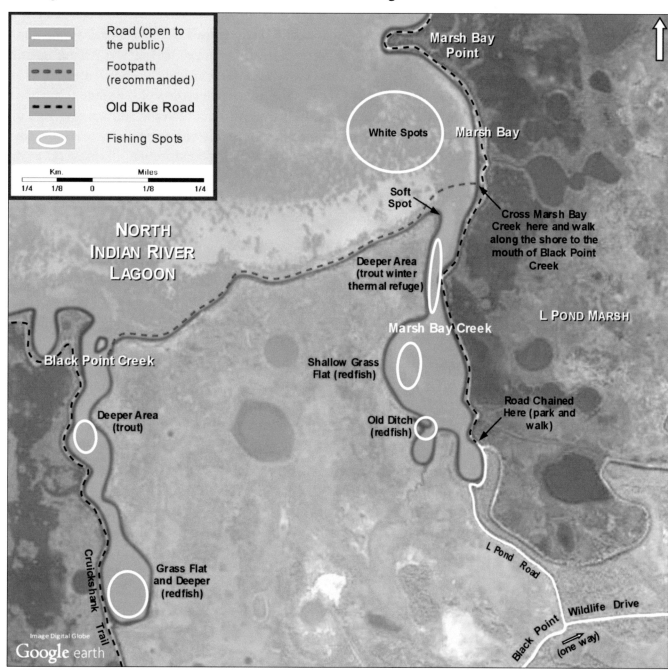

The ditch relict behind the old dike and the entrance to the small pond. Deep water heavily traveled by redfish.

this spot. Catching them in this very shallow water is another story. Indeed, this spot is always difficult to wade due to the sticky bottom and is very difficult to fish in very low water. In the cold winter days, I usually save it for the end of the afternoon when the water warms up on the shallow flats and redfish become active again.

It is a very short walk from the chain on L Pond Road to the narrows and main section of Marsh Bay Creek, and this is one of my favorite destinations when it gets really cold and rough in the middle of the winter. At the narrows the water is deeper and the bottom is muddy. It is a little soft right along the shore. However, it gets better as you move away from shore but it will always remain a little sticky. The black mud and deeper water are most likely the key to the very good productivity of this spot in the coldest days of the winter. The black mud and deeper water capture and retain more heat from the sun than the surrounding shallow sand flats. The water will be slightly warmer in the morning and it will warm up more rapidly than the surrounding flats on a sunny day. This makes it a winter thermal refuge like several in the lagoons, and Marsh Bay Creek is arguably one of the best. Consequently, trout in all sizes, including *mothers*, and reds in small- to mid-sizes congregate in this spot during the coldest periods of the winter.

Most of the time on cold, windy winter days the comfortable casting position will be from the west side of the creek. In low water, which is generally the case in the winter, you can wade right across. In higher water make a detour away from the narrow spot of deep water and you will find shallower water to cross to the other side. There will be limited shelter from the wind when it is from true north. However, most cold winter winds are from the northwest and this section is reasonably sheltered. Strangely, even during periods of continuous cold weather fish seem to move in and out of there. I have had countless experiences of finding loads of fish in Marsh Bay Creek on miserable windy, cold, and cloudy days. And the next day, on a glorious blue-bird winter day, most of the fish are gone.

Marsh Bay Creek looking north: the point (right) and the narrows are viewed from the entrance to the large round bay.

The last fishing area in a northeast direction is Marsh Bay. It is the area outside of the creek itself and it is open on the lagoon. The bottom is a mixture of grass, where you will frequently see tailing reds, and white spots, where you will cast to holding reds and big trout. The bottom is comfortable. In the middle of the winter, when the water gets cold and very low, this area will be largely devoid of fish and only occasionally harbor a small school of reds. In normal water level the place is worth the trip.

Dummit Creek

Dummit Creek is the easternmost point of North Indian River Lagoon. Since it does not drain much of an area it is a bay as much as a creek. You can choose your access to Dummit Creek. The first access is off Kennedy Parkway. Take the second of the two one-lane dirt roads just after the sign "Sendler Education Outpost" and the historical marker "Douglas Dummett – Dummett Grove"[34], approximately 2.5 miles south of Haulover Canal. This will get you on the north shore, approximately at the midpoint of the creek. There is a good unimproved ramp at this location and you could use it to launch a light boat. Dummit Creek is too shallow for navigation with any other than the lightest boats during most of the winter. You can wade most of the creek. Since the channel next to the shore in this area is too deep to wade across you must continue and park at the point to wade to the open water of the lagoon or across the creek to reach the Big Bay (marked on the large-scale detailed map next) and other fishing spots along L Pond Road. The wading is not bad but never comfortable, and you must be up to it.

The second access is L Pond Road, approximately half-a-mile further east on Kennedy Parkway. You can park in a parking area where the road is chained and walk. It is a long walk to the best fishing spots shown on the map and I prefer to use the Sendler Education Center access at the point and just wade across.

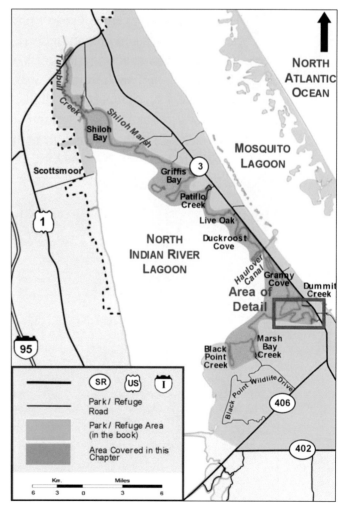

There is a third access, a marginal one. A little over one-eighth of a mile southbound on Kennedy Parkway past the entrance to Sendler Education Center there is an old drive that almost disappears in the woods. In fact, it is just two tracks and barely wide enough for a car. This was most likely the old drive to a fishing camp on Dummit Creek. It will take you at the east end of the deep channel that runs along the shore. There are some old pilings next to the shore that suggest an old dock, and this is a good fishing spot. Bait casters sometimes fish at this location. However, fly casting to the deep water from the shore is not practical. Wading out to your left from this point you should be able to swing around the deep water and work back to the channel from the open water in the direction of the lagoon. This is not the most practical access to Dummit Creek and it has been posted in the past.

The head of the creek is well protected against any wind; however, because of the soft-mud

---

[34] A bad case of twisted spelling, the original Dummett (for Capt. Douglas Dummett) becomes Dummit (in Dummit Creek and Grove on all maps) and can also be Dummitt, or even Dunnit (on an old census map…).

bottom, the water will tend to turn muddy and it becomes very shallow in the winter; therefore, it is not the destination that it appears to be on the map. This is also *Alligator Country*, and while they should stay on the other side of the dike *in theory* you may not wish to test the theory at any other times than in the coldest days of the winter. And by then the place is usually too shallow and devoid of fish.

As you reach midway in the creek, patches of grass appear, the water is clearer and you have a serious chance for tailing reds when the water level is adequate in the grass flat shown on the large-scale detailed map. Note that you can cross the creek in this general area in any normal water level.

As previously mentioned a deep channel runs along the shore from the point of Sendler Education Center (*Alternative Access* on the map) half-way into the creek to the old pilings (the third access previously mentioned, also marked as *Alternative Access* on the map). Part of this channel was most likely dredged in the boat ramp area. The southeast part is either natural or was dredged a very long time ago. This deep channel will harbor fish all the time, mostly trout, and is a winter thermal fish refuge. It is sheltered against the north wind. In the coldest and lowest waters of the winter this spot should be on your to-do list when the wind comes from the north (a west, or even northwest wind may muddy the water).

The west half of the channel, where the boat ramp is located, tends to harbor school-size trout. This section can even be fished from the shore if the wind allows. You will find this a very easy wade on sand-packed bottom. Indeed, this is one spot that is accessible to waders who cannot tackle the ordinary mud and spongy grass of most other fishing grounds described in this book. Of course it may also be fished from the open water, and this is the best choice. To get to the open-water side of the deep channel you will likely have to go around from the point (*Alternative Access* on the map) or cross at a shallow section at the point east of the boat ramp, as shown on the map.

The east side of the channel, from the crossing point east of the boat ramp to the old pilings, is where the fun is. It must be fished from the open water. You can cross at the point in low water,

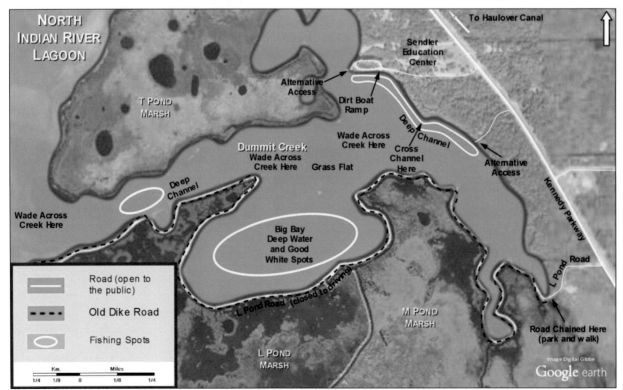

as shown on the map. From this point fish the channel going east by wading in the shallow water on the lagoon-side of the channel (this is not bad wading in mud and grass) and casting back into the channel as close to the mangroves as you can. And brace. This is not an area where you will catch many fish, but the size of them… I have caught some of my largest trout ever at this location in one of the coldest and windiest winter day. At the old pilings you will notice that the channel widens and there are more but smaller fish. Past the old pilings the channel disappears. Go back on your tracks. Again, this is for a north wind, as a west wind may muddy the water.

The eastern part of the deep channel along the north shore harbors big trout.

The Big Bay shown on the large-scale detailed map is an excellent fishing spot in all water levels, including the very low levels of the winter when fish will tend to concentrate in this deeper water, and when most big boats have no access to it due to the shallow entrance. It has areas of relatively deep water with several good white spots, mostly in the west end. It harbors reds, mid-sized and large trout, and Black Drum. The Black Drum that I regularly see there in the winter tend to be on the small side and are usually from the middle to the south shore of the bay. In the summer big Black Drum will sometimes show up at this spot. In my experience this is the best area of the entire creek. However, it is not well protected against the north wind and the bottom is a little soft.

Progressing toward the mouth of the creek in the lagoon the channel deepens. This deeper area is a winter thermal fish refuge and it may yield significant quantities of fish in the coldest days of the winter. They will be mostly school-size trout and under-slot reds. The deep water is closer to the south shore, toward the dike road. Along the north bank there is a grass flat where you may find redfish tailing. The channel is too deep to cross in high water. Cross before the deep water, near the Big Bay, or past the deep-water area, well into the open water of North Indian River Lagoon.

At the mouth of the creek, as you enter North Indian River Lagoon and Dummit *Cove* (that many people confound with Dummit *Creek*), the water becomes shallower and the bottom turns to sand with very sparse grass. This area is very easy to wade; however, it is exposed and there is little underwater topography for permanent fish habitat. During the winter schools of reds roam this area. Finding them wading can be a challenge. A boat is better suited to find these fish. However, once you have found the general area that the schools roam wading is the best way to chase these very wary fish in such an open terrain.

Fred Althouse with a typical red caught in the Big Bay of Dummit Creek in February 2007.

HISTORY OF DUMMETT GROVE

Colonel Thomas Henry Dummett and his son Douglas operated a large sugar plantation in the Barbados Islands in the 1820s. They had to leave with their slaves after the passing of the British Abolition Act. On their way to a stop-over for supplies at New Smyrna legend has it that they sailed past the Cape Canaveral area and smelled the fragrance of wild orange blossoms. Young Douglas Dummett resolved that he would someday return and cultivate these wild oranges. They established a sugar mill in Bulow but eventually went to New Haven, Connecticut where Douglas got an education at Yale College.

Front and aerial views of Dummitt Castle. Images courtesy of Brevard County Historical Commission.

Douglas Dummett later returned to establish a grove at a location south of the old Haulover Canal about the year 1830. He got his first budwood from a Mr. Jones who lived between New Smyrna and Port Orange, and budded some old wild sour orange trees. This was the beginning of the Indian River variety of orange, considered the best in Florida.

Dummett earned the title of Captain as a senior officer of the Florida Central Militia, also called the *Mosquito Roarers* in battling the Seminole Indians. The Indians later returned the favor by burning his large log home twice. The original Dummitt Grove trees survived the frost of 1835 while most other sweet oranges on the East Coast were killed. In 1869 Dummett Grove was the largest orange grove in the nation with 1,350 bearing trees. The famous Indian River oranges were shipped all over the East Coast with the help of slaves. However, just before the Civil War Dummett had to sell all his slaves at an auction in Deland and the grove became unattended and declined. Dummett had an unhappy relationship with his first wife and later married one of his black slaves and moved to New Smyrna.

In 1872 an Italian nobleman from the New York's high society and his wealthy wife, Duke and Duchess of Castelluccia, bought the grove and constructed a mansion. They had guests from all over the world who came to fish, hunt, ride, play and eat the famous oranges. Following the death of the Duke of Castelluccia the structure was sold to Judge John S. Cochran from Ohio and converted into a hunting lodge. The grove received only minimal caretaking. During the winter of 1894-95, the grove was severely damaged by a big freeze and was severely pruned back. The property was sold to Eugene James Drennen in 1895 who operated it and shipped the prized fruits to Florida East Coast Railway dining cars and Flagler Hotel chain until his death in 1916. The property remained unattended for several years; however, as of 1926 there were still about 2,000 trees of different ages in the grove. The property was later taken over by Marguerite Drennen, daughter of Eugene, who revived and operated the grove and remodeled the mansion and the coffee house down by Dummett Bay. Marguerite Drennen owned the property for 30 years. She was an author, planned to write a novel about the history of the grove, and was instrumental in nudging the authorities to recognize the historical value of the site.

The property became part of Kennedy Space Center in 1963. A few trees from the old grove, the old stone chimney, and a coquina well remain on the site and there is an historical marker at Sendler Education Center. Preservationists under the supervision of the Brevard County Historical Society had the mansion, called Dummitt Castle, moved to Parrish Park in Titusville in 1964. The mansion unfortunately burned down in December of 1967.

Source: C.A. Bass. *Historical Sketch of the D.D. Dummit Grove at Allenhurst, which is Supposed to be the Oldest Grove in Florida.* 1926. Historical Paper No. 14. Florida State Horticultural Society. Deland, Fla.;
War, Romance, Scandal in Dummett Grove Past. 1958. interview of Margarite Drennen, author and past owner of the property. Daytona Beach Sunday News-Journal;
Jason Parker, Florida Citrus Hall of Fame;
Brevard County Historical Commission;
Titusville, Florida Centennial — 1867-1967;
and personal research.

Haulover Canal Area

The Haulover Canal Recreation Area is a vast and diverse territory that you may explore at your own rhythm. This is the site of the former village of Allenhurst, a thriving sport-fishing community that was expropriated when NASA took control of the area. All buildings were demolished. You can see a few remaining foundations on the shore of Granny Cove. In this section we cover the west part of the area, on North Indian River Lagoon. The east part of the area on Mosquito Lagoon, is covered on pages 130 and following.

The shoreline of North Indian River Lagoon around Haulover Canal is accessible by foot and it has geography. Since it is not diked and there is no fresh water in sight there should not be any alligators around. In theory. I have been told otherwise; therefore, check your back.

Haulover Canal splits the area in two and there is obviously no wading across. You must choose your side. Access to the shoreline south of the canal is from the parking area at the Bairs Cove Boat Ramp, which is a fee area (see page 129), and from the old roads south of the access road to the ramp, where parking is unregulated. Dummit Cove is the southernmost area that you can reach from the Haulover Canal Area; Granny Cove is sheltered by the peninsula and easily accessible; Bairs Cove is next to the eponymous boat ramp.

Access to the shoreline north of the canal is from Birds Island Road that runs parallel with the canal up to the point called Rookery Island. There is an unimproved boat ramp at the point and it is free. You can walk along the shore of the lagoon from the point. You can also cut across the narrow peninsula on sand roads that may be a bit rough at times to reach the shore of the lagoon and work your way to the north.

Granny Cove

Granny Cove is the official name of the cove lying between the peninsula and the barrier island where the old subdivision and fishing camps were situated. A canal cuts through the peninsula and gives deep-water access from the lagoon. The cove, the peninsula and the canal are most likely part of a subdivision that either failed or was stopped when NASA took over. A 1954 map shows fish camps in this area. It is a complex environment. The interest in this area stems from its sheltering from the dominant winter wind and the winter thermal fish refuge in the deep ditch that surrounds the peninsula.

Access by boat is from the Bairs Cove Boat Ramp and is convoluted. Follow the Intracoastal Waterway (ICW) far enough into the open waters of North Indian River Lagoon to reach water that is deep enough to navigate outside the ICW. Line up with the canal in the distance and follow a narrow, deep-water channel to the canal leading to Granny Cove. Access by carry-on craft or light boat is easier. From the same boat ramp departure point cut through an opening in the south bank of Haulover Canal and follow the deep-water ditch all around Bairs Cove to the canal leading to Granny Cove.

Access by foot is also a bit tricky. You have the choice of fishing from the peninsula, which gives you access to the deep ditch that surrounds the peninsula. Alternatively, you can access the rest of the cove from the east shoreline, including the canal itself, the deep ditch inside along the peninsula (from wading to the middle of the cove) and all areas south of the canal. But you must make up your mind ahead of time. From the peninsula, you cannot go anywhere else because the surrounding ditch is too deep. If you are off the peninsula you cannot work any area north of the canal on the open-water side.

Foot access to the peninsula is off the service road (the old road) along Kennedy Parkway. Driving southbound on Kennedy Parkway turn right approximately one quarter of a mile south of the bridge following the directions to Bairs Cove Boat Ramp. Instead of turning right again at the service road towards the boat ramp turn left (south on the old road) and park at the first dirt road a few hundred feet to the south. This dirt road is in fact one of the streets of the old subdivision. It is blocked with a pile of dirt and a ditch. From this point walk on the old street to the peninsula and

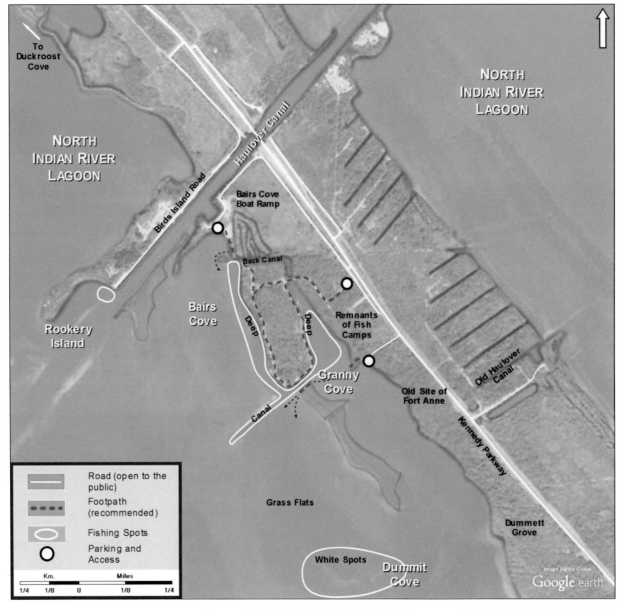

to all points along the shoreline around the peninsula. The shoreline is all easily *wadeable* and in several spots the openings in the trees allow for a full back cast. Fish are everywhere in this deep ditch. You can also fish part of the canal and the ditch along the west shoreline (on the open-water side) all the way to the north-side Back Canal. This is very comfortable fishing. Indeed, this is one spot accessible to waders who cannot tackle the mud and spongy grass. However, you are prisoner of the peninsula because the ditch surrounding it and the canal are too deep to wade across. In some areas you may struggle to find space for a back cast. And during weekends you may have to share the space with bait casters.

The canal to Granny Cove, viewed from inside the cove.

The second (and my favored) access is from a small unnamed dirt road[35] off Kennedy Parkway approximately three-quarters of a mile south of Haulover Canal. There is room to park two cars at the end of this road at the lagoon. You can easily launch canoes and kayaks. Anything on a trailer would be a challenge (including turning the trailer around). This access puts you on the water and Granny Cove can be waded directly from there. You can walk on a footpath to the point and cross the cove at this point much more easily, even in high water level. In all cases this gives you access to the entire area of Granny Cove from the east and from the south up to the canal and up to the deep ditch surrounding the peninsula. You will be able to cast into the canal and into the deep ditch surrounding the peninsula in low water by wading right in to the middle of the surprisingly shallow cove. However, you will not be able to access the peninsula itself. You can easily access the flats south and west of Granny Cove, including Dummit Cove.

Granny Cove itself may be of interest at times, but not always. Although there are some areas of slightly deeper and promising water the bottom is uniformly covered by a thin layer of black mud and is generally devoid of grass. It is *wadeable,* never very comfortable, and the shoreline can be a little soft at some places. The cove is well protected against the wind; however, the water will turn to mud quickly if it is stirred, either by wind, mullet, or waders. The deep spots are next to the east shore. You can tell that areas along the numerous old pilings have been dredged. These deeper spots and the natural refuge of the old pilings can yield big trout if you cast to them from the open water.

Some of the characteristics of Granny Cove mentioned above may make the place less appealing at certain times of year, notably in high and warm water. However, in the coldest of the winter Granny Cove is one of the thermal refuges of the lagoons. It has the required features: easy fish access to the open water of the lagoon even in the lowest water levels, deep water, black mud (for heat retention), and protection against the northwest wind. You will find

The northern end of Granny Cove on a cold windy day. While the open waters of the lagoon were not welcoming, all was nice and quiet here. Catching trout in all sizes was a bonus.

---

[35] The name appears as Circle Road on Google earth (and on some GPS-based devices); however, there are no other indications of such a name anywhere.

The old pilings at the point near the access road to Granny Cove are a testimony that the place was once busy.

trout in all sizes in the deep water during the cold winter days. Granny Cove is one excellent destination on the cold, windy days of the winter.

The canal acts as a highway for fish in and out of the cove. It is also permanent residence for school-size trout and it is part of the winter thermal fish refuge. The eastern part of the canal can be fished from the peninsula. The entire canal can be fished all the way into the lagoon from the south side by crossing the cove at the point (as shown on the map). This also allows you to wade the flats off the island and Dummit Cove.

Schools of reds frequent the flats of Dummit Cove to the south and you can easily wade to them. Expect to see tailing fish as well. The bottom is a little soft but all *wadeable*. It is made of good grass and some white spots: perfect environment for redfish and big trout. You just have to find them in this big sprawl. In the low waters of the winter I have had better luck way out around the markers.

Bairs Cove

Bairs Cove is shallow and grassy and may be a good tailing area for redfish in certain water levels; however, the main interest of this area lies in the numerous canals that come back around the boat ramp area, the deep ditch along the shoreline, and the Back Canal between the peninsula and the boat ramp. These were presumably dug for the construction of the boat ramp, but some work may be mosquito control while other may predate the Refuge and go back to the subdivision or the fishing camps. The Back Canal, shown on the large-scale detailed map, does not exist on old maps.

Access by boat in low water is the same convoluted affair as to reach Granny Cove. You have to go quite far out in the Intracoastal, veer south where the water is deep enough, line up with the main canal to Granny Cove, follow the canal to the peninsula, and then turn north and follow the deep water along the shoreline of the peninsula. Doable but not practical. Please no motor.

The deep-water area along the west shoreline of the peninsula, looking south toward the canal.

Kayaks and light boats will find their way much more easily by cutting south just after the ramp and following the ditch along the shoreline around Bairs Cove where the water is a little deeper.

There is a good foot access. From the southwest corner (the closest to open water) of the parking lot of Bairs Cove Boat Ramp simply follow a beaten path headed south one hundred feet away from the shoreline. The path crosses a field of tall grass and then winds around the palm trees to the point. At the point you have a small side canal at your left, the entrance of a big canal (shown as the Back Canal on the map) at your quarter left, the peninsula in front, and the open waters of Bairs Cove to your right. There is a very small spoil island to your quarter right. The ditch along the shoreline is deep but manageable at this location. Cross this ditch toward the open waters of Bairs Cove *north* of (before) the little spoil island, where it is not very deep and relatively firm. You should be able to do this in all water levels except very high.

The fish-holding spot begins at the little spoil island, includes the mouth of the Back Canal in front, and extends south along the peninsula all the way to the canal to Granny Cove. It consists of a deep ditch along the shore of the peninsula and a nicely gradual slope toward the shallow flat of Bairs Cove. The deep-water area is very wide in some places and quite narrow in others. Follow the contour and cast toward the deep water. Proceed cautiously so as not to stumble on the submerged remnants of old pilings in the northern part of the area. The fish will be anywhere in this territory. They are mainly trout in all sizes, but also reds, mostly mid-sized ones (just under slot size). This is a winter thermal refuge along

Back Canal viewed from the bend inside.

with the Back Canal between the peninsula and the boat ramp, and the fish move back and forth. You can work the entire area up to the main canal of Granny Cove, the main canal itself going to the open water, and the entire shallow flat of Bairs Cove (when the water level is high enough).

This is not an area sheltered from a northwest wind; however, having the wind at your back you should be able to work the place well even on a windy day. The mature trees on the peninsula will buffer an east wind. In theory you have no access to Granny Cove and to any point south of the canal to Granny Cove. In theory. If you are really serious about it you can cross the canal when the water level is below 0.00 on the height gauge at Haulover Canal: http://waterdata.usgs.gov/fl/nwis/uv?02248380 (as of this writing).

Also, if you are up to it and suspect that fish are holding in the Back Canal north of the peninsula, you can wade it in low water level. From the point (where the footpath ends) cross the first small side canal to your left; it is not deep. Keep fishing from this side of the Back Canal, progressing toward the east and crossing all the shallow side canals until you get to the bend. From the bend access becomes uneasy, problematic, or clearly impossible, depending on your physical abilities and your tolerance to hard work and risk. Although this is all salt water I would be worried about alligators in this sector. This area has the right attributes to hold Snook and juvenile Tarpon at times; however, I never saw any. But you may. It is sheltered against most winds. But the wading is a slog.

North of Haulover Canal

The north side of Haulover Canal on North Indian River Lagoon is open to the public by an access road that you can take approximately one eighth of a mile north of the bridge. This dirt road (identified as Birds Island Road on some maps) parallels the canal from the remnants of the old bridge to the lagoon. You will find some spots with enough room for a back cast and you can work the canal with a sinking line and weighed fly. You will certainly find all the room that you need, plus a firm ground, at the western point, called Rookery Island. I never had much success there but you may. The western point is also the perfect place to launch a carry-on craft. If you have a vehicle with good traction, you may be able to launch a light boat from a trailer.

From points approximately midway on this road you can connect with a few shoreline points to the north. However, the access can be rough at times. The shoreline is not diked in this area but it is not very interesting and I do not see much interest up to Duckroost Cove, which is covered next. You can walk to Duckroost Cove along the shoreline and this is easier in low water.

Duckroost Cove

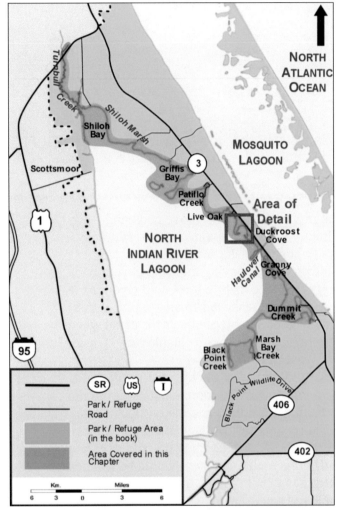

Duckroost Point (left) and Cove, viewed from the open water. There are good spots at the entrance.

Duckroost Cove is three-quarters of a mile north of Haulover Canal. It used to be accessible from the north service road of the Haulover Canal Recreation Area. This road, which becomes the dike, is now closed and it is posted near Kennedy Parkway. You can park on the road that runs along Haulover Canal, shown as Birds Island Road on some maps, and walk to the shore of the lagoon and then to Duckroost Cove along the shoreline in low water. I prefer the access from the north, on the old dike road. The little dirt road off Kennedy Parkway is a few hundred feet south of Live Oak. There is a small cemetery near the intersection. This road, which continues as the old dike road, is now closed at the lagoon. You can park where the road is blocked and walk on it to Duckroost Cove.

But before you go you may have a look at the area of the lagoon in front of the turn around and parking area. This is covered in the next section (Live Oak, page 166).

The walk on the old dike road to Duckroost Cove takes less than half-an-hour. Along Duckroost Cove the dike is lined with mangroves and there is some mud along the shore. Access to the water is limited. Follow the indications for access on the large-scale detailed map next.

Duckroost Cove is a big bowl with minimum topography. There is some slightly deeper water along the north shore and it is a little soft. Redfish will mill around in this deeper area and will work the shoreline at times. However, you have to hit them at the right time and this will be in normal-high water level and when mullet are not stirring the mud.

The limited interest of the cove lies in the winter in the large area of slightly deeper water in the middle of the cove, as shown on the map. The bottom is brown mud and a little sticky but nevertheless easy to wade. If you hit the place in moderately low and cold water you will notice that schools of mullet spend the winter in this area. Big trout and some small reds swim with them and the place is a thermal refuge during the winter for these fish. Despite its promising contour this area offers only a limited protection against the wind. Therefore, this is not for the worst days of the winter. It is not for warm weather either, since the brown mud at the bottom gets churned by mullet when the water is warm. You have to hit it at the right time. If you do you will likely catch several trout of decent size—and better—as well as some reds, mostly small.

The open water off Duckroost *Point* is a high-quality grass flat perfectly suited for tailing reds and you are most likely to find them there in normal and high water levels. There are some good white spots and slightly deeper water at the entrance of the cove and this should be blind cast routinely. In all this general area the bottom is nice and surprisingly firm for a grass flat; therefore, the return walk in low water could be partly along the shoreline, watching for signs of reds feeding on the flats a few hundred yards out.

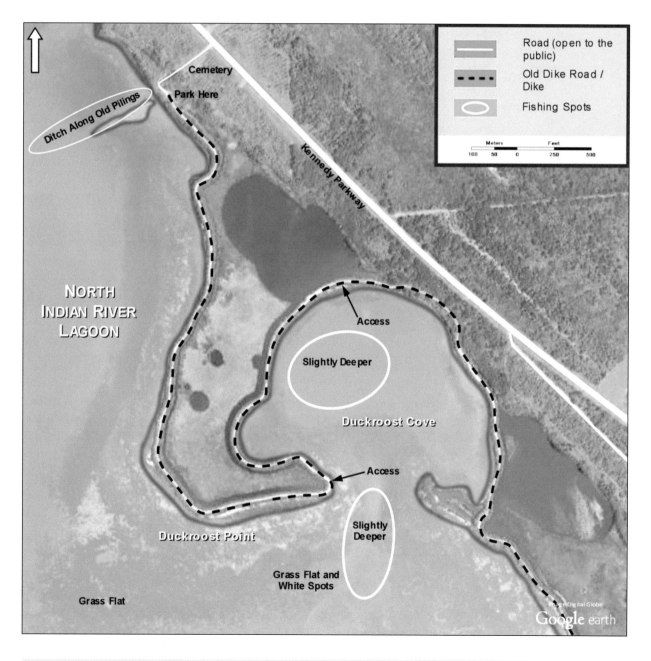

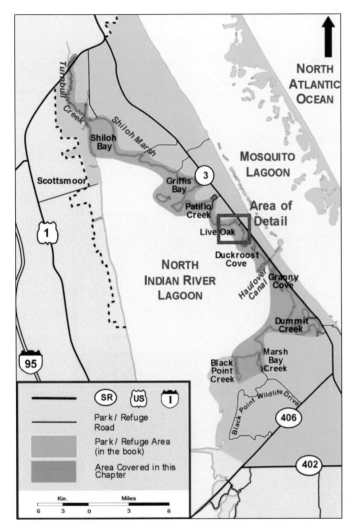

Live Oak Road is approximately one quarter-mile south of the white-domed radar and three miles north of Haulover Canal. This is the south end of Shiloh Marsh Road, now permanently closed to motor traffic. You can park and walk or bike the road.

Live Oak is higher ground than the surrounding marshes and the area was occupied before NASA and the establishment of the Merritt Island National Wildlife Refuge. You can still distinguish the aligned citrus trees of the former groves. Two small cemeteries and one historical marker dot the area, which was the location of the community of Clifton (see text box, page 168). Along the shore you will immediately notice that the place was once busy. The old pilings suggest a dock or a pier with a deep-water basin. Live Oak is a place from which you will easily launch a carry-on craft. If you have a vehicle with adequate traction you may be able to launch a light boat from a trailer at the unimproved ramp, depending on the water level and the conditions of the shoreline.

Live Oak is the only section of the shore in this area that is not diked. There is a square basin of deep water and soft bottom right along the shore that was likely dredged for moorings. This deep spot harbors fish most of the times and is a winter thermal refuge for trout. The best way to fish it is to enter the water north or south of the deep area and cast into it from the open water. Unfortunately, this spot is not protected from the winter winds and as such may not be a recommended destination in the windy and cold winter days.

A few hundred yards south of Live Oak lies a spot that you should not miss. It can be accessed by walking along the shoreline, or walking on the flats away from the shoreline, or by driving the small, unnamed one-lane road that gives access to the dike south of Live Oak. The old pilings and a small spoil island are unmistakable signs of an old dock. Indeed, there is a deep channel running along the south side of the old pilings. The combination of the old pilings and deep water next to them has big fish written all

The old pilings south of Live Oak suggest the place was once busy. The deep water along the pilings harbors fish at all times.

over it. As a premium, you can use the hard ground of the spoil island to get to the place and fish it. It does not get any better.

To get to the spoil island from the shore just walk right to it aiming at the middle of the island. This is a little deep, but the bottom at this precise location is firm sand—it is much softer on either side of this spot—and you should easily make it in low and normal water levels. You will likely hit trout and reds in this channel every time you fish it. Just hope for fish small enough that you can winch them out of there quickly, because those old pilings will cut your leader before you know it.

A few hundred yards north of Live Oak, there is a deep bay ending with a culvert. This is behind the white-domed radar (pictured). Fish will

First bay north of Live Oak. The radar in the white dome is a dominant feature of both lagoons.

sometimes be found in this slightly deeper area, which also offers some protection against a north wind. This spot works in normal water levels and is better when the water is cold; in warm water schools of mullet tend to churn the mud.

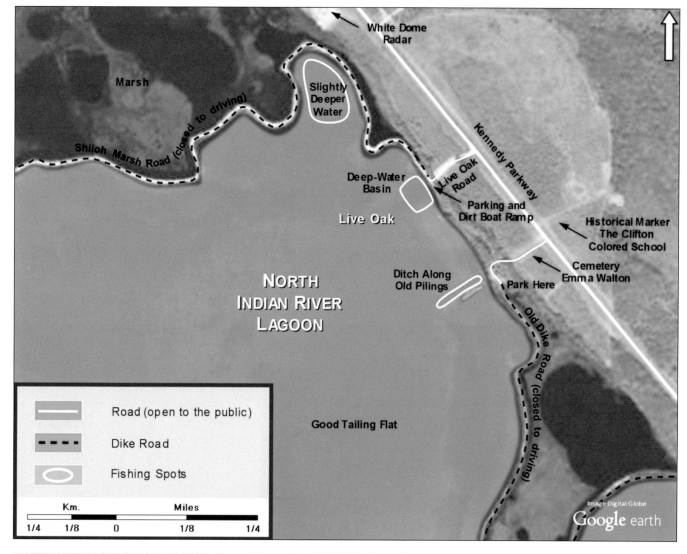

Away from the shore in this entire area the water is shallower and the bottom becomes relatively firm, a mixture of sand and patches of grass. These flats are perfectly suited for tailing reds and you are most likely to find them there in normal and high water levels. Given the large featureless area, this is not practical for wading, unless you can spot the fish by walking on the road. Roaming those large flats is mostly something that you want to do from a boat and when the water level is either normal or slightly higher (above 0.60 on the height gauge at Haulover Canal).

HISTORY OF CLIFTON

View of Clifton School, around 1890. Image courtesy of Brevard County Historical Commission.

In 1872, Butler Campbell, a former slave, moved from South Carolina and established an African American community several miles north of the Old Haulover Canal on the edge of Mosquito Lagoon, between Shiloh and Allenhurst (today's new Haulover Canal). Campbell initially named his homestead Laughing Waters but it soon took the name of Haulover. The community changed its name to Clifton in 1889. The post office was situated as part of a boat house on Mosquito Lagoon and a trail linked the mainland road (Kings Highway) and the Old Haulover Canal.

There were two well established communities on the strip of land between the two lagoons: Shiloh to the north (at the county line) and Clifton half-way to Haulover. Allenhurst (at today's new Haulover Canal) was not established as a post office until much later.

These communities did not increase much after the initial settlement in the 1880s. Shiloh had 50 residents in 1907 while Clifton also had 50 residents—one half the population that it had twenty years earlier. Contrary to the other villages and settlements in the area, Clifton had a significant percentage of African Americans, many of whom were employed in the citrus groves or as domestics for white families.

Between 1890 and 1891 a one-room schoolhouse was built for the black children of the Clifton community. A neighbor of Campbell, Wade Holmes, donated a one-acre lot adjacent to the Campbell property for the building site. Holmes, neighbor Andrew Jackson, and Campbell built a one room, 12 by 16 structure of heart pine lumber. The creation of the school illustrated the importance that these early settlers placed on education as a means for improving the lives of their children. Nine students initially attended the school. Classes were held during the summer months so the students could help with the citrus groves and other crops during the winter months. Professor Mahaffey, also African American, was the teacher. The school was reported as one of the best in the country and certainly contributed to the surrounding community and made a difference in the lives of its students.

When NASA took over the area in the 1960s all buildings of Clifton were demolished but the old school building was forgotten. The old school building was rediscovered recently by a group of historians led by John Stiner of Canaveral National Seashore. It was taken down and preserved to be restored and eventually reconstructed at a proposed Heritage Village in Titusville. On site, two cemeteries and one historical marker remain as testimony of the Clifton community and its black school.

Sources: U.S. Fish & Wildlife Service;
Susan Parker. 2008. *Canaveral National Seashore, Historic Resource Study.* Edited by Robert W. Blythe. National Park Service. Atlanta. www.nps.gov/history/history/online_books/cana/cana_hrs.pdf (as of this writing);
and personal research.

For a complete history of Brevard County consult: Jerrel H. Shofner. *History of Brevard County.* Three-volume collection available from Brevard County Historical Commission.

Patillo Creek

Patillo Creek is a very peculiar environment heavily modified by man. The open water of North Indian River Lagoon at this location is a very shallow flat of sand and sparse patches of grass. It is relatively easy to wade and is certainly visited by schools of reds and by trout at times. However, the featureless topography offers little in terms of shelter for fish. The estuarine areas of Patillo Creek are another story. The two main canals, the inside creek, and the network of ditches are permanent or seasonal home for just about anything that swims in the lagoon. Due to the diversity in topography Patillo Creek usually offers some areas sheltered from the wind. Unfortunately, the dredged canals are not easily waded, because the banks are very steep and lined with tall vegetation. Patillo Creek is one of the areas for juvenile Tarpon and Snook in the territory covered in this book; however, to get to them you will generally need a boat. Nevertheless, there are some limited opportunities to hunt these fish on foot.

The Main Canal (the one that opens on North Indian River Lagoon and leads to the inside creek) is the most frequented. It is very deep and essentially the domain of bait casters. To reach it from Patillo Creek Road, turn left at Shiloh Marsh Road and follow along the inside creek until you reach a fork. Keeping to your left at the fork leads to the entrance to the Main Canal and to the open water of North Indian River Lagoon. By entering the water at the point where it is shallow you can wade back toward the canal and fish the entrance from knee-deep water. Big trout hold at this spot (shown on the large-scale detailed map next) during the winter.

By turning right at the fork you are driving back along the Main Canal toward the northern end. There are several openings. You can launch canoes, kayaks (and even light boats from a trailer if you have adequate traction) from these openings along the main canal and from a few other places. For bigger boats, use the public ramps at Scottsmoor Landing (but not in low water – see footnote 36 on page 184 for directions) or Bairs Cove at Haulover Canal. The Main Canal is

---

TEMPORARY CLOSING OF PATILLO CREEK

In 2012 Patillo Creek Road was chained at the junction with Shiloh Marsh Road for the first time. Warning signs had been posted for years concerning littering. It would seem that the authorities have finally put the threat to execution. You may wish to check with the Visitors Center of the Refuge or the web site at www.fws.gov/merrittisland/ (as of this writing) before going. If the road is chained you can park in a rough parking area and walk to access any place you want on foot. This is a short and easy walk. You can also haul a carry-on craft a short distance and launch it in the inside creek at the culvert, thus gaining access to all areas from the water. This is a rough launch. Check it ahead of time. The unimproved ramp at the dike road is for hunters. You can launch a light boat from a trailer (only with a vehicle with good traction and when conditions are good) and access the marsh and ditch inside the dike, but not the open water.

uniformly deep to the end and right up to the banks. Wading is very limited. If you spot Tarpon rolling within casting range, you may find a few areas where there is enough room for a back cast.

Typically, Tarpon will congregate at the northern end of the canal, against the dike, where there is a culvert to the marsh. Fishing these Tarpon is mostly a boat job. Nevertheless, there are some limited opportunities to cast to the northern end of the canal from the dike. The foot access to this spot is a convoluted affair. From Patillo Creek Road, you have to turn right at Shiloh Marsh Road and drive this dike road all around the inside creek to the culvert at the end of the Main Canal. There are some limited possibilities to cast from the dike at the culvert. You should also have a look at the ditch on the marsh side. The culverts of this dike are blocked by horizontal wood planks on the marsh side to maintain a higher water level in the marsh. In very high water and during storms fish may get through. The ditch along the dike road may not be deep enough for the long-term survival of Tarpon. Nevertheless, you may find some rolling inside the dike. There are some openings in the vegetation allowing for a back cast from the dike road. In this marsh environment you will be very careful of alligators: this is *their* side.

The West Canal—*West* to differentiate it from the Main Canal—offers a better fly-fishing opportunity. From the dike road take the second drive, park there, and access the water at the cut between the Main Canal and the West Canal. (See insert on the map.) There is a large area of

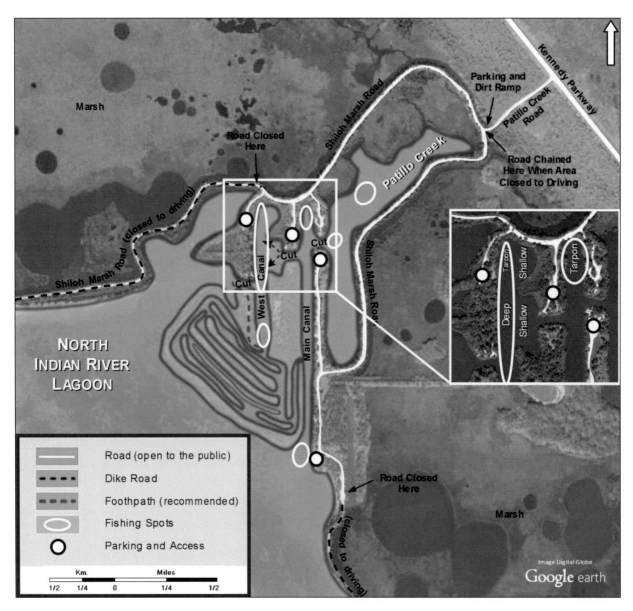

shallow water—a sector that has not been dredged—between the point, the cut, and the West Canal that can be waded up to the edge of the West Canal. This shallow area is hard bottom and can be easily waded except in high water. There is plenty of room for a back cast. From this position at the edge of the dredged area you can work the entire northern end of the West Canal, casting to the deeper water of the canal where fish hold. This is your best choice in a south wind. Be careful as you reach the line of dredging. There is some loose rubble near the edge and the drop is sudden. You should be able to work all the northern end of the canal in normal and low water.

You may find some limited accesses to the west shore of this canal from the next drive. There are a few openings that bait casters routinely use and that have some clearance for a back cast. You can reach the cut by walking through the bushes on a well-beaten path. Indeed, you may have to share this well-known spot. There is very little room for a back cast anywhere on the west shore except at the end of the foot path. In a north wind this is your best choice; however, you may get some dirty looks from bait casters.

A cut to the open water of the lagoon blocks the access to the southern part of this canal. In low water you can wade across the cut by swinging very wide toward the open water of the bay. The southern part of the canal is wild. There are no paths so you must find your way. There is practically no room for a back cast except at the very end of the canal, where it joins the network of ditches. This is the spot that you want to work, since it is the transition between the very deep water of the canal and the much shallower network of ditches. The entire southern end of the canal sees very little fishing traffic. However, you will have to share the spot with alligators... Be very careful. This is serious.

Main Canal viewed from the dike road. Typically, Tarpon will be at the northern end, near the dike road, where there is some limited room at the culvert for fly casting.

West Canal viewed from the dike road. Wade the shallow area and cast to the deep.

The West Canal is a winter thermal refuge for fish. From a wade-fly-fishing point of view the spot is not ideal in a typical winter northwest wind. From the best wading spot you have a head wind. On the other hand, I have worked the place in a raging south wind and it was just the perfect setting. This is one place that you should put on your list when a strong south or east wind keeps everybody home. Expect trout in all sizes, including some very small: this is a spawning and nursery area. Of course mother trout will also be around. Redfish, mostly under-slot size, also live with the trout, together with everything that swims in the lagoon. This includes Tarpon and Snook. You may find some at the northern end of the West Canal and if you do these fish can be wade fly-fished from the shallow area along the east side of the canal. However, remember that while they should stay on *their* side, the alligators that live in the marsh across the dike may not know all the rules. Since you will likely be wading in relatively deep water be very careful. While the place is relatively safe in the coldest days of the winter when the water warms up enough for Tarpon and Snook to become active it may become dangerous.

The marsh and the ditch along the dike road. If Tarpon are rolling in the ditch, they can be fly-fished from the dike road.

Patillo Creek is more like a pond. View of the inside creek from the cut to the Main Canal.

The network of ditches starting at the southern end of the West Canal is a unique environment. The depth is a uniform two to three feet, depending on the general water level of the lagoon, and the banks are lined with mangroves and shrubs that in theory provide the perfect environment for Snook and baby Tarpon. In the right conditions, high and warm but well oxygenated water, the ditches may provide good fishing for Snook and Tarpon. I have yet to hit it right. And you need a light boat or carry-on craft.

Finally, the creek (as in Patillo *Creek*) is a very different environment from the canals and ditches: it has been left to its natural state, except for the dike road around it. It is called Patillo *Creek*; however, this is more like a bay or a pond, albeit a long and narrow one. Again, access is a little convoluted. If you find a reason to do it you may access the creek at the culvert, right off Patillo Creek Road. This is not a friendly wading area. Along the dike road toward the north you are always within a few feet of the water and you may find one or two accesses that are semi-acceptable. The only comfortable access is to go north and all around the creek on the dike road; turn right next to, and go back along the Main Canal. The road dead ends at the cut between the Main Canal and the inside creek. Access the water at the cut or walk over the dune and the creek opens up in front of you. It is not a very large area, mostly hard packed, and you will find fish swimming with mullet in two feet of water. Thanks to the geography the area is well sheltered against a moderate wind from any direction. Two areas of the creek should be worked in the winter: the deep water next to the cut and the area just north of the shallow oyster bar. They are marked on the large-scale detailed map. Again, alligators live in the marsh across Shiloh Marsh Road and will occasionally venture on the lagoon side. I wade it during the winter months. I do not think I would venture into the creek during late spring and summer, and certainly not when darkness is falling.

HISTORY OF J.E. PATILLO

Mr. J.E. Patillo with his wife and three children, Herbert, Edna, and Ada, came from North Georgia to Florida in December, 1885 to their new home at Osteen. In 1889 Mr. Patillo moved to Shiloh in a house of one room, 16 by 20 feet. They started a grove of 25 acres the next spring. This grove froze in the winter of 1895, but Mr. Patillo went to work at once to start another of 150 acres of the Patillo Groves. Besides citrus fruits they had more than a thousand banana plants. They had a beautiful, modern home and many tenant houses and tenants on their 300-acre estate. A Delco Plant furnished electricity to light this home; the home of a son, Crawford Patillo; the several machine shops and garages. It also ran a refrigerator in each of the Patillo homes.

Source: *Brevard County History*, Indian River Journal.

Shiloh Marsh Road

Shiloh Marsh Road is the dike road that defines the east shore of most of North Indian River Lagoon from Shiloh Bay at the mouth of Turnbull Creek to Live Oak. Shiloh Marsh Road used to be open to motor traffic. Like most other dike roads it is now closed to driving. It is open to the public for walking and biking and these are excellent ways for waders to access the area. While driving on the dike road in the past provided an easy access it also brought traffic to the fishing spots. The restricted access has thinned the crowd significantly, thus potentially enhancing the experience for the wade fly-fisher.

Shiloh Marsh is a designated duck hunting area and several unimproved ramps inside the dike are used by hunters. These unimproved ramps can be used to launch kayaks and very light boats inside the dike. The deep ditch on the marsh side of the dike provides a handy highway to the fishing spots of the lagoon. You can paddle, row or even motor your way in the ditch along the dike to your favorite fishing spot and park the craft and go wade fly-fish the open water of the lagoon. You can also drag a kayak over the dike at some key locations to access the open water of the lagoon. Finally, you can launch a light boat from a trailer (with a vehicle with adequate traction) on the open water of North Indian River Lagoon from unimproved ramps at Live Oak and Patillo Creek to reach the fishing spots all along Shiloh Marsh Road to the north. The nearest improved boat ramps are Bairs Cove (Haulover Canal, page 162) and Scottsmoor Landing (footnote 36 on page 184). While the fishing areas of Live Oak and Patillo Creek can be reached from Kennedy Parkway and have already been covered in the preceding pages, Grassy Point and Griffis Bay are quality fishing areas that can be reached on foot by Shiloh Marsh Road. You may also find some fishing spots further north along the dike road, both inside the dike and in the lagoon; however, this is limited. Finally, you can drive to Shiloh Bay and the lower reaches of Turnbull Creek on the extension of Shiloh Marsh Road off US 1 south of Oak Hill. Because of the configuration of the area you will generally be able to find a spot reasonably sheltered from the wind.

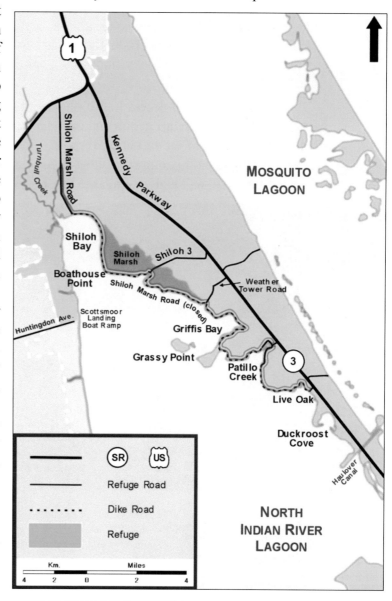

There are fish in the ditch and ponds of Shiloh Marsh inside the dike. The best spots, by far, are at the culverts, and the best times are when rising lagoon water flows into the culverts. You may find juvenile

Tarpon rolling in the deeper areas of the ditch anywhere along the road. Several areas of the dike road are clear of bushes and allow for very comfortable fly casting of the ditch and marsh. There are also alligators. Fishing the ditch and marsh, you are in their territory. Generally alligators do not frequent the open water of the North Indian River Lagoon. Generally…

Live Oak Road is the access to the southern end of Shiloh Marsh Road, now closed to motor traffic. The main access to Shiloh Marsh Road from the south is now Patillo Creek Road. From Kennedy Parkway turn west on Patillo Creek Road approximately three-quarters of a mile north of the white-domed radar and you will be at the dike road almost immediately. Turn right on the dike road, go around the inside creek, and park at the chain to reach on foot the fishing areas north of Patillo Creek toward Shiloh Bay. Two side roads allow access to Shiloh Marsh Road from Kennedy Parkway: Weather Tower Road and Shiloh 3. Note that these roads may be closed without any mention on the Refuge web site. If they are open at Kennedy Parkway both roads are nevertheless permanently chained at the marsh. You can park at the chain and walk to the dike road. You can launch a carry-on craft or a light boat from a trailer (with a vehicle with proper traction) from unimproved boat ramps and connect with the ditch along the dike road. In both cases a culvert at the junction of the access road with the dike road may funnel some current from one area of the marsh to the next. These outflows are dinner bells for the fish trapped inside the marsh. Weather Tower Road takes you just north of the Griffis Bay area. Shiloh 3 takes you to the creek south of Boathouse Point. This latter area is not covered in detail in this book because I cannot pinpoint any good consistent productive spots between Griffis Bay and Shiloh Bay. However, the area can be waded and you may find such a spot. I would keep it for periods of normal or high water.

The northernmost access to Shiloh Marsh Road is at Shiloh Bay. The access route to this part of North Indian River Lagoon and the Merritt Island National Wildlife Refuge is a small dirt road off US 1 north of the railroad overpass. Since US 1 is a divided highway at this location if you are traveling south you must make a U-turn after the overpass and come back over it. Go 1.8 miles and this road will end with a large crushed-stone parking area. You are now on the lagoon, and Shiloh Marsh Road becomes the dike road at this point. It is chained just after the parking lot. A few feet past the chain is the foot access to the mouth and lower section of Turnbull Creek. Launching a carry-on craft to the lagoon at this location require some hauling. As for all the other access roads to Shiloh Marsh there is an unimproved ramp used by duck hunters and you can launch a carry-on craft or a light boat from a trailer (with a vehicle with proper traction) in the ditch inside the marsh.

Shiloh Marsh is a designated duck hunting area and is heavily used by hunters during the duck hunting season, which generally falls between November 15 and February 15. Keep your distance from them and assume that a bunch of birds sitting strangely quiet on the water early in the morning are most likely decoys.

This beautiful redfish carving by Tom Burke proudly sits in the author's office as the winning prize of the Fly Fisherman's 2007 tournament. Tom Burke is a wood-carving artist based in Cocoa specialized in life-like wildlife. Visit the web site of Tom Burke Art at tomburkeart.com (as of this writing).

With Grassy Point and Griffis Bay the irregular shoreline typical of the east shore of both lagoons continues. Grassy Point and the smaller islands around this area are among the very few natural islands in North Indian River Lagoon. The shoreline will become more regular north of Griffis Bay. However, this is not nature but the work of man. Indeed, the vast Shiloh Marsh that begins north of Griffis Bay has been entirely diked for mosquito impoundment. Therefore, the regular and relatively featureless shoreline north of Griffis Bay is artificial. Grassy Point and Griffis Bay are the last diverse fishing areas as one progresses north along the east shore of North Indian River Lagoon.

Both Grassy Point and Griffis Bay used to be easily accessible by driving Shiloh Marsh Road, now permanently closed to motor vehicles. Foot access to this area is now by walking on Shiloh Marsh Road, either from Patillo Creek or from Weather Tower Road, if it is open. The nearest access with a carry-on craft is from Patillo Creek. In the best of cases this is a substantial walk or paddle and you will likely have the entire area to yourself. Better, you may be on fish that have not seen a fly or a lure in some time. This is a dramatic departure from the paranoid redfish that are being pounded almost daily in some areas of Mosquito Lagoon. Of course boats can and will visit this area at times, but I have yet to see substantial traffic. The nearest boat ramps are Bairs Cove at Haulover Canal and Scottsmoor Landing which is across the lagoon. The lack of traffic has to do with access, not with the quality of fishing. In my experience it is worth the walk.

While the Grassy Point area is generally shallow and typical tailing and schooling area for redfish Griffis Bay is a slightly deeper area than all the surroundings and as such it is a permanent holding area for redfish and trout in all sizes and at all times.

You should not enter the water anywhere from the dike road in this general area because there are very soft spots right along the shore. I have identified on the large-scale detailed map next a few safe spots where you can enter the open water with relative ease and gain access to the area. As a rule the immediate area along the shore may be a little soft—with some small patches *very* soft—but it will generally become nice and solid after just a few steps. As is the case everywhere in the lagoons once you are out in the open water it is always a relatively easy wade.

The first fishing area to the north is Georges Flats, and this is an official name and spelling that appears on topographical maps. No different from the surrounding flats to the untrained eye, Georges Flats is thick with sea grass and thus a magnet for the redfish that you will often see tailing. There is a large, round bay that ends with a culvert at the dike.

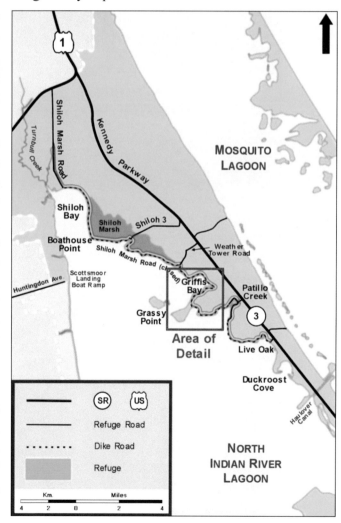

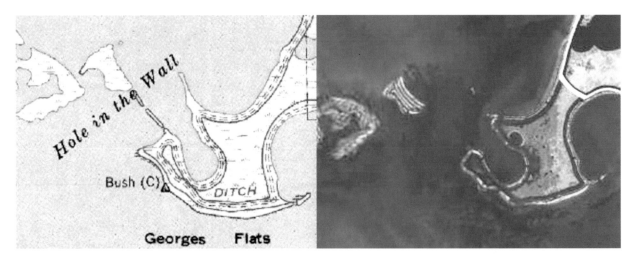

Old maps (left picture) show a causeway to Grassy Point (it is not called an island *on the old maps) and a channel punched in the middle, which may be the* Hole in the Wall. *This was all removed years ago. The dike used to go all around the point. The road was straightened a few years ago (right picture) and the dike was recently removed.*

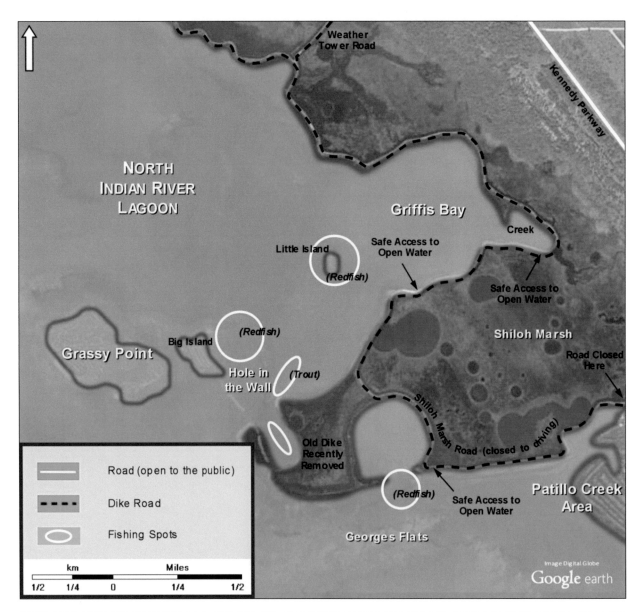

This was obviously a creek in prehistoric times; indeed, it is a little deeper at the culvert. The water is also a little deeper in the middle of this bowl and the bottom is brown mud, not threatening, but a little sticky. It is wadeable and should at times harbor big trout. Schools of mullet congregate in the deeper area in the middle of the bay and they tend to churn the mud. This is an area that resembles Duckroost Cove (see page 164) and it should be a winter thermal refuge. I never had much luck in this bay and I can't tell why. However, I had some memorable experiences catching redfish at the culvert when the water of the marsh was flowing into the lagoon. If you hit this situation remember that you can only catch these fish by wading from the open water and casting to the culvert, not the other way around.

Progressing north from Georges Flats you will notice that the area around the point was recently modified. The dike used to go all around the point. The dike was removed and the road straightened a few years ago. The area is now open to the lagoon. The removal work has created a number of deep and very muddy spots. So much the better, since these deep-water spots sometimes hold redfish and may be a thermal refuge in the coldest periods of the winter. Moreover, because of the configuration of the area there is always a spot sheltered from the wind. This is one area where you should check your back for alligators. It may be technically outside the marsh *now*. However, it used to be inside the dike and the terrain has *Alligator Country* written all over it. I keep it for the cold winter months.

The next area of interest toward the north is the "Hole in the Wall" and the point just south of it. According to old maps, there once was some kind of causeway linking the point with Grassy Point (it is not called an *Island* on the old maps) with a channel punched in the middle, which may be the *Hole in the Wall*. This was all removed a long time ago. You will notice that the general area is very shallow and may even prevent boats from motoring in Griffis Bay in low water unless they line up perfectly with the channel. I have consistently found a concentration of trout in all sizes just north of the Hole in the Wall, in the slightly deeper water between the small island and the point. This spot is shown on the detailed large-scale map.

Recent removal of the dike across Grassy Point.

Islands remnants of the Hole in the Wall, viewed from the water entering Griffis Bay.

Creek of Griffis Bay viewed from the dike road.

Grassy Point is (now) an island that you can wade all around. In normal water level redfish will often cruise along the shore busting bait and showing their backs, thus revealing their presence and direction. Ambushing these fish by hiding in the open water and casting a bug on their cruising path right along the shore is always a memorable hunt. The island next to Grassy Point is marked *Big Island* on the map, to differentiate it from the *Little Island* in the middle of Griffis Bay. There is a good spot east of the Big Island where the slightly deeper water will harbor schools of redfish and some big trout. As the spot tapers off to the shallow areas of the Hole in the Wall the transition zone is a good grass flat where redfish are frequently seen tailing.

Griffis Bay is deeper than the surrounding area and the bottom is uniform, mostly devoid of grass, and a little sticky. In normal water level it can be waded at will but it is a little too deep to target anything. It is home to reds and trout, both reaching impressive size. However, blind casting this large area is not practical and the odds are not in your favor. But any movement in the water should be cast to, even if it is mullet. One may turn out to be something else.

The area around the Little Island is a shallow flat covered with thick grass, a nice change from the bare surroundings. In the right water level redfish of impressive size frequent this grass flat, which is the perfect depth for tailing in normal water levels.

Despite its alluring appeal the creek is shallow and muddy and is not a consistent fish-holding area in low water. At times schools of big reds will show up in the creek for no apparent reason. Unpredictable as it may be the creek is frequented by big trout. I regularly found redfish cruising the south shore against the fill of the dike road.

Shiloh Marsh Road from Griffis Bay to Shiloh Bay

This is a long stretch of dike that separates Shiloh Marsh from North Indian River Lagoon. The shoreline is the dike / Shiloh Marsh Road and is not very interesting. In theory access to the lagoon is easy everywhere right off the dike road. In practice watch for muddy areas along the shore. Once in the open water the entire area is a large, shallow flat that has little geography and not enough grass to be a good tailing area for redfish. Exploring and fishing this area is much better from a boat or carry-on craft.

Large schools of Black Drum are sometimes found in this area. If the fish are active you will find them easily, but this is rare. Most of the time you literally have to stumble on the school to find it and, if the water is deep enough, you may run right past the fish without ever seeing them.

You may find fish on the marsh side of the dike, mostly around the culverts at certain times of the year. Indeed, when the rising lagoon water is allowed to flow into the marsh a dinner bell rings for the fish that live inside the dike. While I had reports from people who succeeded in timing these events, I have not had this chance myself.

Access to this area on foot is a straightforward but long affair. It involves a significant walk from the blocked end of Shiloh Marsh Road, either at Shiloh Bay off US 1 or at Patillo Creek. If the two side roads Weather Tower and Shiloh 3 off Kennedy Parkway are open you can park at the dike where hunters launch their boat inside the marsh and walk just a short distance.

Shiloh Bay

Local guides call *Shiloh* the northernmost part of North Indian River Lagoon at the mouth of Turnbull Creek. While the marsh behind the dike at this location bears the name, "Shiloh" belongs to the small hamlet that existed between the two lagoons at the county line before NASA takeover. For the purpose of this book I will call this bay Shiloh Bay, thus using a name that the locals use.

Shiloh Bay is large and of rather uniform geomorphology: water depth varies between one and two feet depending upon the general water level of the lagoon and is very regular. You can wade one quarter of a mile out from the access near the parking area. The bottom is mostly mud, always a little sticky, never bad, but never good. The grass is very sparse. In the winter when the water is cold and the mullet are largely absent, the water will be clear but generally too low to harbor fish regularly. Schools of reds and blacks will visit the bay, but there is no telling where and when. In low water trout will leave the bay and take refuge in Turnbull Creek. When the water rises and warms up in the spring schools of mullet will invade the bay and will churn the water a uniform muddy color. And the bay is beaten by the wind. There are better places. Nevertheless, Shiloh Bay has some appeal. In the summer, after a rainy season, Turnbull Creek turns to fresh water and most of the fish leave it to migrate to the nearest salt water. Shiloh Bay can then provide some memorable fishing, particularly for juvenile Tarpon.

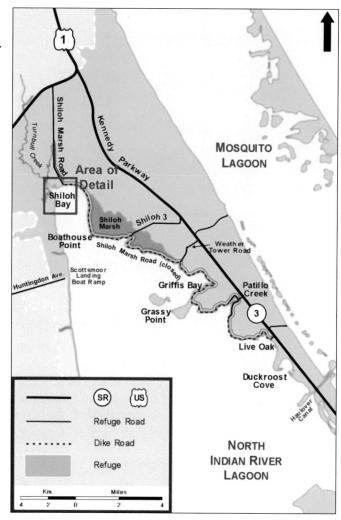

While the lagoon in this area has regular topography there is a hidden exception. You have to picture the place during the latest glaciation. Today you see the mouth of Turnbull Creek in the lagoon at sea level. When the level of the ocean was much lower the creek flowed into a slight

depression that is occupied by the head of the lagoon today and it had a well-defined streambed. This streambed still exists at the mouth and is a little deeper than the surrounding, which in this large flat area makes all the difference. At most times trout in all sizes can be caught in this old streambed. Reds and blacks will be rarer. However, since the old streambed is the highway for all the traffic in and out of Turnbull Creek you may be pleasantly surprised at any time. To access this deeper water simply walk along the shore and then straight out to the general area. Do not expect a sudden drop. When you begin sensing that there is a little more water, start blind casting systematically. The place is large enough to have fun all day. You can even share it with a friend. Talking about sharing the place, you may not be alone. From the access road to the county line on the west shore the shoreline of the lagoon is not diked.

The mouth of Turnbull Creek in Shiloh Bay; a well-hidden deeper spot along the ancient streambed.

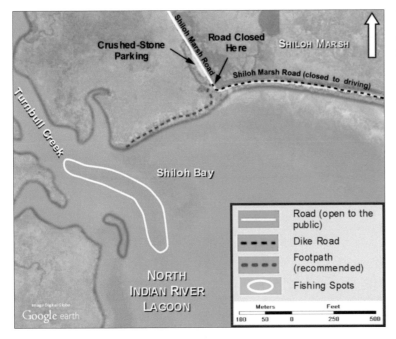

This includes the mouth of Turnbull Creek. All this is prime alligator habitat and the reptiles are notorious for venturing into the salt water of the lagoon. Watch your back in this area and do not, ever, consider wading with a fish in tow on the stringer.

You can reach the west shore of the lagoon by wading across upstream or downstream of the slightly deeper area at the mouth of Turnbull Creek. Contrary to the gradual taper along the north shore there are sections along the west shore—mostly close to the mouth of Turnbull Creek—where there is adequate water depth right up to the bushes lining the shore. This is one place where you can look for redfish cruising the shoreline and busting bait when the water level is favorable. As is the case when fishing for redfish along any shoreline, wade very quietly away from shore and cast right up against the bushes ahead of a cruising redfish or cast near fish busting bait if the water is deep enough.

South of the little island near the mouth of Turnbull Creek the general area along the west shore becomes less favorable and it is not on my bucket list. The next dike starts at the county line one-third of a mile south of the little island. A large school of Black Drum roam this end of the lagoon. Looking for them on foot is not practical.

Sunset over North Indian River Lagoon. This place can be beautiful.

Turnbull Creek

Turnbull Creek is located south of Oak Hill, at the northern end of North Indian River Lagoon. The name presumably comes from Dr. Andrew Turnbull's huge 1767 grant, which extended south past Haulover and north past New Smyrna. Turnbull was the founder of the first colony of New Smyrna, named after the town in Turkey where his wife was born. Old maps show Turnbull Creek as the North West Branch. In 1995 the Refuge began purchasing additional land in this area, and as a result Turnbull Creek as well as a significant part of the west shore of the lagoon are now within the Merritt Island National Wildlife Refuge or under the control of the U.S. Government. The accesses to Turnbull Creek are from US 1, either at the bridge or off Shiloh Marsh Road at the lagoon.

This is first-class fishing water. Indeed, Turnbull Creek is a true stream (contrary to most tidal inlets and narrow channels also called creeks) and it drains a small inland area at the Volusia-Brevard county line. Like many other rivers in Florida Turnbull Creek has tannin-stained water, the only one that you will find in the territory covered in this book. Those redfish and trout that are permanent residents of Turnbull Creek—mostly in the middle section and headwaters—will have a pale golden color while transient fish will have the silver bodies typical of Indian River Lagoon fish. This tannin-stained water is a blessing when you learn to work with it: the fish do not

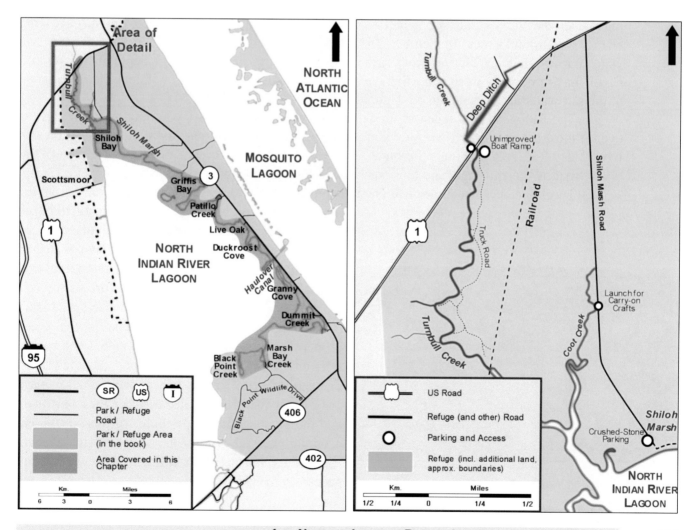

see you as easily. On the other hand you have to make sure that the fish has actually seen your fly, and several casts in the same general area may be necessary.

Turnbull Creek starts very small and fresh north of US 1. It soon becomes salt water and harbors Snook and juvenile Tarpon year round. From approximately midcourse to the mouth in North Indian River Lagoon, Turnbull Creek is visited by lagoon fish that are attracted by the deeper water and the food. In the winter trout use it extensively as a thermal refuge. I visit Turnbull Creek in all weather. However, it is during the coldest and windiest days of the winter that I appreciate one of its key attributes: sheltering from the wind. So next time a cold front collides with your plans to fly-fish the open waters of the lagoons head for Turnbull Creek. You will not be disappointed.

As you explore Turnbull Creek you will see signs that the stream had current in the past: sand bars, cut banks, and deep channels. Indeed, during the last glaciation when the sea level was much lower than it is today Turnbull Creek was a running stream. Since it has kept some of the geomorphology of its distant past Turnbull Creek is a perfect environment for all manners of swimming creatures. There are Snook in the entire creek when the water is warm enough; there may be juvenile Tarpon as well spread out in the creek when the water is high and warm enough. Black Drum are occasionally visitors. Reds tend to be found closer to the lagoon while trout are everywhere. And big ones. In the winter you are unlikely to encounter Tarpon or Snook in the lower part of the creek because of the cold water. On the other hand sometimes it is *trout unlimited*. I would wade Turnbull Creek very carefully, if at all, in late spring and summer. Indeed, you should be aware of the four-legged *other* wildlife. This is *Alligator Country*. I feel reasonably confident wading Turnbull Creek in late fall and in the winter when those beasts are sleeping. It may be another story in late spring and summer. Summer is also a season when you may see a big change in Turnbull Creek. Remember, this one is a true running stream and it drains upland storm water into the lagoon. During rainy summers, particularly in August and September, Turnbull Creek may turn totally fresh and will have a noticeable current. Most fish will leave it and migrate to the salt water at the mouth in the lagoon.

The Refuge closes at sunset. In Turnbull Creek *south* of US 1 you may be in the Refuge even if there are no signs. Therefore, you should leave at sunset or shortly after. You should also have a Refuge Fishing Permit, free and self-procured on the Internet at: www.fws.gov/merrittisland/ and look for *Fishing Regulations* (as of this writing).

Turnbull Creek has three different and connected environments. The lower creek, from the

Turnbull Creek in high water. The parking lot at US 1 may be under water.

mouth to the railroad bridge, is an extension of North Indian River Lagoon and provides food and deep water to the lagoon fish. It is navigable and accessible on foot from the crushed-stone parking area off Shiloh Marsh Road, just before the road is blocked and becomes the dike along North Indian River Lagoon. The middle section is the creek proper. From the railroad bridge to US 1 is a typical river environment that provides food and a few spots of deep water to lagoon fish as well as allowing a passage for fish and manatee between the headwaters and the lagoon. The deeper holes of this section are a winter thermal refuge. It is only navigable with light boats and carry-on crafts in low water. Foot access is from US 1 by walking on a rough truck road.

Finally, the headwaters upstream of US 1 are essentially the deep ditch along US 1, a small network of shallow secondary ditches, and the original creek itself, which continues north a short distance. The ditch along US 1 is one of the deepest spots in the lagoons (save for the Intracoastal Waterway) and it harbors a large population of Snook and juvenile Tarpon. It is accessible to light boats from a trailer from an unimproved ramp off US 1, but only in low water. When the water level is at, or above, 1.00 on the height gauge at Haulover Canal the parking lot and ramp are flooded (see picture). An alternative parking area and access on the northwest side of the bridge can be used to launch a carry-on craft when the water is high. Wading the deep ditch along US 1 is impractical and an encroachment on private property. Only one spot at the mouth of the ditch can be legally reached on foot and waded in relative security. But the access is marginal, at best.

Lower Creek

I define *lower* Turnbull Creek as that stretch that lies from the railroad bridge downstream to the mouth in North Indian River Lagoon. The wading access to *lower* Turnbull Creek is from a crushed-stone parking area near the lagoon. Take a small dirt road off US 1 immediately north of the railroad overpass. This is Shiloh Marsh Road (no road sign as of this writing). Since US 1 is a divided highway at this location, if you are traveling south you must make a U-turn after the

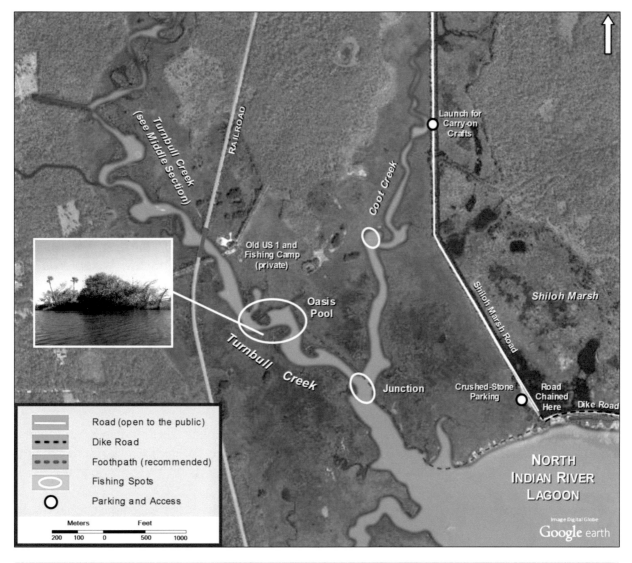

Turnbull Creek in low water. A boat ride anybody?

overpass and come back over it. Drive 1.8 miles on Shiloh Marsh Road to a crushed-stone parking area. You are now on North Indian River Lagoon and Shiloh Marsh Road turns left and becomes the dike road at this point. It is chained just after the parking area and closed to motor traffic. On the east side, duck hunters launch their boat in the ditch to access Shiloh Marsh. On the west side, anglers access the lagoon on a footpath that starts just past the chain. Kayaks can be launched at Coot Creek, up the road, when the water is high enough (see map). Kayaks and canoes can also be launched a little further down the dike road, at the first bend where the dike road comes close to the water, but you have to carry the craft some distance. Light boats can be launched at the unimproved ramp off US 1 if you are prepared to navigate it approximately three miles and through some uncomfortably shallow areas. You should not use gas motors. For any sizeable boat, the nearest ramp is Scottsmoor Landing.[36] Turnbull Creek should be navigated with a trolling motor (it is a manatee area) and is not navigable with a big boat upstream of the old US 1 and of the private fishing camp.

From the crushed-stone parking lot walk to the water and wade the shoreline to your right. The mouth of Turnbull Creek is a few hundred yards away and you cannot miss it. You can fish this bay, that the locals call "Shiloh" and that I call Shiloh Bay, and it may be quite good at times. As previously mentioned, when Turnbull Creek turns into fresh water during the summer rain season fish will take refuge in the nearest salt water and this is it. The bottom is firm. The extension of Turnbull Creek in the bay is a channel a little deeper than the surrounding and is a good spot. This area is described in the preceding section, on page 179.

As the shoreline turns you are entering Turnbull Creek. Keep walking along the northeast bank. The channel is sometimes too deep to cross in high water and you will likely have to stay on

Turnbull Creek at the railroad bridge, viewed from upstream.

the northeast bank for most of the lower portion of the creek, which is fine because this is the good wading side. If you decide otherwise, you may be able to cross the channel at the last wooden post inside the creek, and only in low water. You can cross Coot Creek at the mouth in Turnbull Creek in any water level and continue your progression upstream along the northeast bank, walking sometimes along the shore, sometimes in the grass near the bank. You may see a beaten path. You should stop within sight of the private fishing camp located on the east bank at the old US 1: this is private property.

From its mouth in North Indian River Lagoon to the railroad bridge Turnbull Creek runs a distance of 0.9 river-miles and is relatively wide and deep. It

[36] To access this ramp, continue on US 1 southbound approximately four miles and turn left on Huntington Avenue, cross the railroad and find the public boat ramp at the end of the road. Note that launching a big boat in low water at this ramp may be challenging.

is navigable and big boats will show up. They are a nuisance in such a small creek but you will have to put up with them. At the fishing camp the pilings of the old highway are just inches below the surface and will eat your prop if you attempt to navigate this far with a boat. You can launch a carry-on craft at Coot Creek, past the culvert, just before the bend on Shiloh Marsh Road. However, this is a little primitive and it does not work when the water level is below 0.20 on the height gauge at Haulover Canal. This is mostly for kayaks; most canoes would draw too much water for Coot Creek. If you have the stamina, you can paddle a carry-on craft from US 1.

John C. Gamble with a 25-inch trout in the Oasis Pool *of* Turnbull Creek *in December 2011.*

The junction of Coot Creek is a reliable fishing spot. Coot Creek itself can be good everywhere in high water. If you can muster the energy to wade to the first bend it is usually worth it. From the junction of Coot Creek to the straight section leading to the fishing camp you will likely find fish in Turnbull Creek at all times and in all water levels. The best spots are usually where the creek is a little deeper; however, do not hesitate to explore everywhere. One spot stands out in the lower creek: the *Oasis Pool*, a name that I have given it from the cluster of trees in the middle of the marsh (see picture inset on the map on page 183). It has special geomorphology, but you can hardly see it above water. Again, you have to picture the place a few thousand years ago, when the level of the ocean was much lower and Turnbull Creek was a running stream. The remnant of a small tributary is still visible today, entering the pool from the eastern bank. This tributary was flowing and it carved a streambed to the junction with the main streambed of Turnbull Creek along the west bank. Most unaware anglers miss the slightly deeper water of this ancient streambed, but the fish know it. Big trout hang there, swimming with schools of mullet. At times, groups of Snook visit the place. This is also one of the most likely spots for redfish and Black Drum.

Middle Creek

From the railroad bridge to US 1 lies the *middle* stretch of Turnbull Creek. It meanders over a distance of 1.6 river-miles. This section can be accessed on foot from the boat ramp off US 1. Walk on the truck road to access several good fishing spots from the east bank. This truck road is more a rough path than a road; however, it provides the guidance and visibility that you need to walk this environment in relative safety (and in the cold winter days only). You can cross the creek at several places in low water. Be aware of one hidden deep hole, marked as "Deep Spot" on the map. Again, this is for cold winter days only. You are now in the middle of *Gatorland*. At any other time, use a light boat, a canoe or a kayak that you will launch from the unimproved ramp off US 1 (in normal and low water levels) and navigate downstream to the good spots. Snook will be more numerous in this section than in the lower section. Trout will likely be found in good numbers, especially during the winter since Turnbull Creek is a winter thermal refuge. Red and Black drums will be occasional. Tarpon may be present at times, but not likely in the winter.

In fishing this stretch you must take the current into account. When the water level changes in the lagoon Turnbull Creek has current and the fish will often be upstream or downstream of the deep spots, in those shallower sections of the creek where food is transported by the current.

From the railroad bridge[37] to upstream of the "Ghost Chair" you may find fish just about everywhere. The spots shown on the map are those deeper areas where the fish will congregate in large numbers in low and cold water. The first spot shown on the map (from the railroad going upstream) is facing a dock. It is a little tricky to fish. The large flat in front of the dock is very shallow and almost dry in low water level. The interest of this spot is the drop off at the edge of the flat into the main channel. You can fish this drop off from the flat (you can cross the creek upstream) or from the island on the other side. The drop off along the channel continues downstream along the cut bank. The only practical way to fish this cut bank is to cast from the island.

The second spot shown on the map is the "Deep Spot". On the outer bank of this sharp bend you will stumble upon old pilings in low water. There is a very deep hole in front of these old pilings (deep enough that you may have to swim if you fall in it). Old maps show a significant freshwater tributary at this location. The drainage of the land in this area has been substantially modified. Aside from the deep spot, this area provides good habitat in all water levels and I have seen Black Drum there. The locals have adopted it for still bait fishing, as evidenced by the rod holders lining the shore. You can fish it from either banks crossing upstream or downstream away from the deep spot.

The last spot shown on the map is at the freshwater ditch and "Ghost Chair". The freshwater ditch is relatively new and does not appear on old maps. Again, the locals have obviously adopted

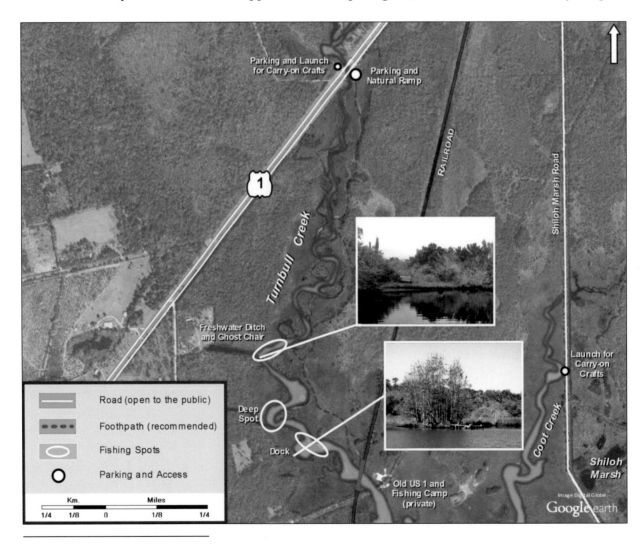

[37] Homeland Security regulations have in the past prohibited fishing on foot within fifty feet of any railroad bridge.

this spot. While every fish of the lagoon is present in this area it is particularly good for Snook and Tarpon when the water is warm enough. This area is best fished on foot from the flat on the east bank just upstream of the freshwater canal and you can cross the creek upstream of the area. From the second bend upstream of the "Ghost Chair" the creek becomes very shallow in several stretches and navigation with even a light boat can be challenging when the water is low. This is a passage for manatee between the deep ditch of the headwaters and the open water of the lagoon and you should be very careful not to hurt them in the narrow sections. Gas motors, if they are not already banned from this area when you read this book, are definitely out of place here. Fishing will be more seasonal, mostly for Snook, and will be much better when the water is high.

Headwaters

At the bridge on US 1 there is an unimproved ramp with limited parking where you can launch a light boat. The access can be a little rough. At times, you may need a four-wheel-drive vehicle. When the water is high, you may have to go through more than one foot of water to get to the parking and ramp. You may even find the parking area under water. There is an alternative parking and launch for carry-on crafts on the northwest side of the bridge. The creek is small this far inland and it can be waded right at the ramp and downstream of it. However, it is rarely good in low water. If you wade it check your back all the time for alligators.

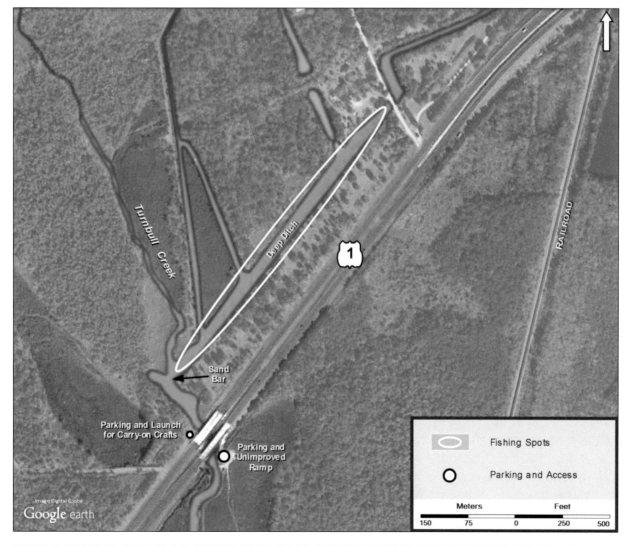

Turnbull Creek upstream of US 1. The deep ditch harbors Tarpon and Snook. The sand bar allows for a wading access and room for a back cast.

Upstream of US 1 Turnbull Creek turns ninety degrees to the northeast and becomes a wide and deep ditch. Nature alone would have done a fair job for the fish in Turnbull Creek. Man meddled with its headwaters and, this time, it seems that it turned out to be an improvement. Construction of the *new* US 1 Highway—the *old* highway is at the fishing camp—required a considerable fill and in all likelihood this is when a wide ditch was dug approximately 1,500 feet along the highway where previously there was one small feeder creek. This wide and deep ditch (10 feet deep in places) is the deepest water around, has variable salinity, and has become a natural habitat for a significant population of juvenile Tarpon (including some quite big). Add a population of Snook, which can also grow quite big in this rich environment. On top of which you will find all the usual suspects of the lagoon, including trout in all sizes all the times. Finally, this deep ditch is the winter home of a growing colony of manatees and their babies and you should be very careful not to disturb them.

The land between the ditch and US 1 is fenced and posted along the highway. However, you can gain access to the creek at the northeast side of the bridge, which is public land, and keep to the shoreline up to the bend. This is marginal and for low water level. At the bend, the sand bar (see picture) provides a hard bottom and room for a back cast. You can work the deep water on either sides of the bar. The bar also faces the natural channel and there is some fish traffic between the deep ditch along US 1 and the original streambed. This fish traffic is at the foot of the sand bar and you would be well advised to lay low and quiet. At times of falling water level current from the stream sometimes attract Snook at the mouth. Wading on this sand bar allows you to see what is coming at you. Indeed, this is *Gator Country*, big time, really. I cannot warn you enough.

On the southeast side of the ditch there are several spots where there is enough clearing in the vegetation and room for a back cast. However, wading is not practical in most places since the banks are steep. And you may not see the alligators coming if you wade in deep water. If you stand on the bank you are now clearly trespassing on a private property. Now is the time to become friends with somebody who owns a light boat.

In this 10-foot-deep ditch you will likely see juvenile Tarpon roll. The hot spot is sometimes at the very end of the ditch, near the culvert. At other times it is midway to the ditch at the mouth of the second canal, or closer to the sandbar, near the first canal. Catching these Tarpon is a tall order, but trying is a ton of fun. Snook, on the other hand, will likely be more cooperative. Again, this is for a canoe, kayak or light boat that you can very conveniently launch from the unimproved ramp off US 1 in low and normal water level when the access is not too rough. Otherwise use the carry-on access on the west side of US 1.

This is the end of this book. A book is linear: it must begin and it must end. But this is not the end of the journey. More than a decade of exploring the lagoons and hunting the fish has taught me that it does not end. Every day spent wading brings another twist: a new fly; a new fishing spot; fish in certain areas in certain conditions and at certain times of the year. The journey does not end and you will not die. You are already in paradise.

INDEX

Disclaimer

Fishing is a sport that carries inherent dangers and wade fishing has its own dangers. Wading unknown waters, such as Mosquito Lagoon and North Indian River Lagoon, Florida can be dangerous and one should take all the usual precautions related to fishing, wading and being on, in, and near water. Among such precautions, it is strongly recommended to carry a cell phone, wade with a fishing partner and notify people of your itinerary and fishing plans. The author has covered this territory and is (reasonably) whole, but offers no warranty as to the reader's experience and makes no representations or warrants of the conditions that one might experience. The reader assumes his or her own risks in wading the territory covered in this book.

Credits

Pictures of birds and animals are from my friend and fishing partner John C. Gamble.
Mike Chambers, former North District Park Ranger, was instrumental in finding old maps with names long forgotten. I cannot dedicate this book twice; if I could, it would be to all field personnel at Canaveral National Seashore and Merritt Island National Wildlife Refuge. Thank you for preserving a gem while at the same time letting us enjoy it.
Thanks to Brevard County Historical Commission for the permission to use historical pictures.
Thanks to Philip Ewanicki, a founding member of the Mid-Coast Flyfishers, for his review and English language editing. Anything less-than-perfect-English left is mine.
Thanks to Claude Fennema's Madsen's Photo Service for the tuning of the digital photos.
I am deeply indebted to Augustin Sebastian at Indian River Field Lab of Florida Fish and Wildlife Conservation Commission for his timely review, comments, and additions.

The Author

Also called *Wading Luc*, Luc Desjarlais is a Canadian spending summers in Sutton in the Province of Québec, a stone-throw from the Vermont U.S. border. Over the last fifteen years he has spent most winters in New Smyrna Beach, Florida. An early retiree and dedicated wade fly-fisher, Wading Luc will likely be found roaming the streams of Northern Vermont and the Canadian Eastern Townships. When wintering in Florida you will likely find him in Mosquito Lagoon terrorizing Red Drum and Spotted Seatrout, unless he is pursuing Shad in the St. Johns River.

Work under way:

Wade Fly Fishing Northern Vermont; and

Wade Fly Fishing the Appalachian Corridor and Western Piedmont in the Eastern Townships of Quebec, Canada.

Work published:

Wade Fly Fishing the Upper St. Johns River Basin (Florida) for American Shad; and

Fishing the North Missisquoi River (Quebec).

Web Site: www.wadeflyfishing.com

The author wading Mosquito Lagoon. Photo credit John C. Gamble.

Made in the USA
Columbia, SC
24 November 2024